THE PSYCHOLOGICALLY
HEALTHY WORKPLACE

THE PSYCHOLOGICALLY HEALTHY WORKPLACE

Building a Win–Win Environment for Organizations and Employees

EDITED BY

MATTHEW J. GRAWITCH and DAVID W. BALLARD

AMERICAN PSYCHOLOGICAL ASSOCIATION

WASHINGTON, DC

Published by
American Psychological Association
750 First Street, NE
Washington, DC 20002
www.apa.org

To order
APA Order Department
P.O. Box 92984
Washington, DC 20090-2984
Tel: (800) 374-2721; Direct: (202) 336-5510
Fax: (202) 336-5502; TDD/TTY: (202) 336-6123
Online: www.apa.org/pubs/books
E-mail: order@apa.org

In the U.K., Europe, Africa, and the Middle East, copies may be ordered from
American Psychological Association
3 Henrietta Street
Covent Garden, London
WC2E 8LU England

**HD
7261
.P793
2016**

Typeset in Goudy by Circle Graphics, Inc., Columbia, MD

Printer: Sheridan Books, Ann Arbor, MI
Cover Designer: Berg Design, Albany, NY

The opinions and statements published are the responsibility of the authors, and such opinions and statements do not necessarily represent the policies of the American Psychological Association.

Library of Congress Cataloging-in-Publication Data

The psychologically healthy workplace : building a win-win environment for organizations and employees / edited by Matthew J. Grawitch and David W. Ballard.
    pages cm
  Includes bibliographical references and index.
  ISBN 978-1-4338-2052-6 — ISBN 1-4338-2052-8 1. Work environment—Psychological aspects. I. Grawitch, Matthew J., editor. II. Ballard, David W., editor.
  HD7261.P793 2015
  658.3'14—dc23
                                    2015011086

British Library Cataloguing-in-Publication Data
A CIP record is available from the British Library.

Printed in the United States of America
First Edition

http://dx.doi.org/10.1037/14731-000

CONTENTS

CONTRIBUTORS

David W. Ballard, PsyD, MBA, Center for Organizational Excellence, American Psychological Association, Washington, DC

Larissa K. Barber, PhD, Department of Psychology, Northern Illinois University, DeKalb

George S. Benson, PhD, Department of Management, University of Texas at Arlington

Melondie Carter, RN, PhD, Capstone College of Nursing, The University of Alabama, Tuscaloosa

Steve Gravenkemper, PhD, Plante Moran, Southfield, MI

Matthew J. Grawitch, PhD, School for Professional Studies, Saint Louis University, St. Louis, MO

Rebecca K. Kelly, PhD, RD, The University of Alabama, Tuscaloosa

Edward E. Lawler III, PhD, Center for Effective Organizations, University of Southern California, Los Angeles

Patrick W. Maloney, PhD, Human Resources, Saint Louis University, St. Louis, MO

Donna Miller, BA, JD, DMTD Consulting, Inc., Summit, NJ

Bob Nelson, Nelson Motivation, Inc., San Diego, CA

José M. Peiró, PhD, Departamento de Psicologia Social, Facultad de Psicologia, Universitat de Valencia, Valencia, Spain

Eduardo Salas, PhD, Department of Psychology, Rice University, Houston, TX

Roy Saunderson, MA, CRP, Rideau's Recognition Management Institute, Montréal, Québec, Canada

Joanne Spigner, BA, MBA, VisionFirst, Madison, NJ

Ron Drew Stone, BBA, Center for Performance and ROI, Inc., Birmingham, AL

Lois E. Tetrick, PhD, Department of Psychology, George Mason University, Fairfax, VA

Sallie J. Weaver, PhD, Armstrong Institute for Patient Safety and Quality, and Department of Anesthesiology & Critical Care Medicine, Johns Hopkins University School of Medicine & Carey School of Business, Baltimore, MD

Cali Williams Yost, BA, MBA, Flex+Strategy Group/Work+Life Fit, Inc., Madison, NJ

THE PSYCHOLOGICALLY
HEALTHY WORKPLACE

INTRODUCTION: BUILDING A PSYCHOLOGICALLY HEALTHY WORKPLACE

MATTHEW J. GRAWITCH AND DAVID W. BALLARD

Management gurus and employee relations advocates have long recognized that employees are the essential building blocks of any organization, although each group tends to take a slightly different approach to leveraging those key resources. The traditional management perspective has emphasized the need to develop effective organizational processes and structures to ensure results. The goal is to create mechanisms (e.g., performance management systems, production processes) that maximize important organizational outcomes.

On the other hand, the employee relations perspective focuses on the people side of the organization. The general premise is that if employees are satisfied with their jobs, they will be more productive workers. The goal from this perspective is often to develop mechanisms (e.g., benefits, vacation time, positive work environment) that maximize employee attitudes toward work (e.g., job satisfaction).

http://dx.doi.org/10.1037/14731-001
The Psychologically Healthy Workplace: Building a Win–Win Environment for Organizations and Employees,
M. J. Grawitch and D. W. Ballard (Editors)

3

Both approaches provide important guiding principles that must be integrated if one is to take a collection of individuals (the employees) and somehow motivate those individuals to (a) engage in activities that are aligned with organizational goals and (b) put forth the necessary effort in pursuing those activities so that expected outcomes are realized. Faced with often-competing life demands, employees have a limited amount of time and energy to respond to these demands; thus, the organization's goal should be to optimize the amount of resources that employees choose to invest in their work role. Notice that we choose the term *optimize* over *maximize* when discussing the interplay between employees and the organization. This is an intentional choice of words. Although an employer could maximize production in the short term by requiring employees to work 80 hours per week, if there is a lack of fit between work demands and employee preferences, employees may suffer fatigue and burnout (Grawitch, Barber, & Justice, 2010; Van den Broeck, Vansteenkiste, De Witte, & Lens, 2008). In addition, these increased job demands can lead to negative health consequences (Hakanen, Schaufeli, & Ahola, 2008) as well as increased absenteeism (Somers, 2009) and turnover intentions (Podsakoff, LePine, & LePine, 2007).

The phenomenon just described exemplifies the symbiotic nature of employee well-being and organizational effectiveness. Focusing on maximizing organizational outcomes at the expense of employee well-being may result in short-term gains for the organization, but it will likely have long-term negative consequences. For example, it has been widely documented that Enron focused almost exclusively on maximizing short-term profits, which led to the development of a culture that was psychologically unhealthy, to say the least (Cruver, 2002). On the other hand, attempting to maximize employee outcomes at the expense of organizational effectiveness is likely to result in long-term negative consequences for the organization. Companies like General Motors have provided employees with lucrative benefits—such as lifetime pensions—that have resulted in long-term negative consequences for the organization's bottom line (Elliott, 2009). Neither approach is viable in the long run.

The true path to sustainability for contemporary organizations rests in a business philosophy that focuses on optimizing the interplay between employee and organizational outcomes (Griffin, Hart, & Wilson-Evered, 2000). This approach allows employees to achieve high levels of both performance and well-being (Quick, 1999). Though many organizations view health through a narrow lens and rely on measures such as health care claims, biometric data from health screenings, and the number of health risks identified in the company's Health Risk Assessment, the World Health

Organization (1948) defined *health* as the alignment of physical, mental, and social well-being. This broader definition of health suggests numerous strategies that can benefit organizations and employees.

This more comprehensive approach to health is heavily emphasized in the psychologically healthy workplace perspective, a concept introduced and promoted by the American Psychological Association (APA; 2015). At its core, this perspective promotes the idea that an effective organization is one that possesses a culture that (a) establishes trust and respect among members of the organization, (b) views employees as assets and values their contributions, (c) communicates regularly with employees, and (d) takes employee needs into consideration when designing new initiatives (Grawitch, Ledford, Ballard, & Barber, 2009). Hence, a psychologically healthy workplace is one in which an organization's culture emphasizes the development of long-term win–win scenarios (optimizing stakeholder value), not one in which the culture emphasizes the maximization of short-term profit (maximizing shareholder value).

KEY COMPONENTS OF A PSYCHOLOGICALLY HEALTHY WORKPLACE

Grawitch, Gottschalk, and Munz (2006), working as research consultants for the APA, provided a multidisciplinary review of research related to the psychologically healthy workplace. Their conclusion was that five types of practices emerge within a psychologically healthy workplace (see Figure 1):

- Employee involvement, which focuses on providing employees with a greater level of autonomy in their work as well as opportunities to be involved in organizational decision making. Examples include participative decision making, self-managed work groups, continuous improvement teams, and multirater performance evaluation systems.
- Work–life balance, which focuses on providing employees with greater flexibility in when, where, or how often they work, as well as benefits to assist them in managing nonwork demands. Examples include telecommuting, flexible shifts, compressed work weeks, job sharing, adequate time off, child care and elder care resources, flexible leave options beyond the minimum required by law, and life management resources such as onsite banking, concierge services, and dry cleaning.

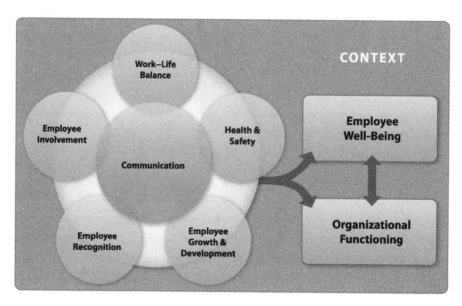

Figure 1. The psychologically healthy workplace.

- Employee growth and development, which focuses on issues related to improving employee competencies and career development. Examples include continuing education courses, skills training provided in house and/or through external training centers, tuition reimbursement, coaching and mentoring, job enlargement and enrichment efforts, and career counseling.
- Employee recognition, which focuses on demonstrating appreciation for employee contributions and includes both monetary and nonmonetary rewards. Examples include fair monetary compensation, performance-based bonuses, employee awards for exceptional performance, recognition events, verbal acknowledgment from managers and supervisors, celebration of accomplishments and major life events, and formalized peer recognition programs.
- Health and safety, which focuses on prevention, assessment, and treatment of potential health risks and problems and encouraging and supporting healthy lifestyle and behavior choices. Examples of health and safety practices include the provision of high-quality health insurance that includes adequate mental health coverage, smoking cessation resources, healthy food options in vending machines and cafeterias, exercise classes, safety and ergonomic assessments, and onsite fitness facilities.

In their review of the literature, Grawitch et al. (2006) provided supporting evidence that when implemented effectively, these five types of psychologically healthy workplace practices could result in improvements in employee well-being (e.g., stress, health, engagement, satisfaction) and in organizational performance (e.g., productivity, turnover, absenteeism, health care costs). In addition, organizations that have been recognized for their efforts to create a psychologically healthy workplace have demonstrated benefits for employees and the organization (APA, 2014). For example, the four organizations that received the APA's 2014 Psychologically Healthy Workplace Award for their comprehensive efforts to promote well-being and performance reported an average turnover rate of just 7% in 2013—significantly less than the national average of 38%, as estimated by the U.S. Department of Labor, Bureau of Labor Statistics (2014). In addition, only 15% of their employees said they intended to seek employment elsewhere within the next year, compared with almost double that number (27%) nationally in the United States. In these winning organizations, an average of 83% of employees said they are motivated to do their very best on the job, compared with just 70% nationally in the United States, and almost three quarters (74%) said they would recommend their organization to others as a good place to work compared with just 57% in the U.S. workforce.

The five workplace practice areas do not exist in isolation from each other. Rather, elements of the five areas can be combined (e.g., recognizing employees who participate in health and safety initiatives) to create more robust and holistic programs within organizations. In addition, numerous authors (e.g., Batt & Valcour, 2003; Gibson, Porath, Benson, & Lawler, 2007; Gravenkemper, 2007; Grawitch et al., 2009; Grawitch, Trares, & Kohler, 2007; Shadur, Kienzle, & Rodwell, 1999; Vandenberg, Richardson, & Eastman, 1999) have argued that employee involvement may be a critical practice that influences the success of various other initiatives. This effect likely stems from its ability to be integrated into each of the other four practice areas, which allows an organization to use employee involvement in identifying, designing, implementing, and evaluating initiatives that meet the needs of the organization and its workforce.

Of course, because each organization is unique, creating a psychologically healthy workplace is not a prescriptive process (Grawitch et al., 2006). There is no one-size-fits-all approach, and the success of any workplace effort is based, in part, on (a) addressing the challenges unique to the particular organization, (b) tailoring programs and policies to meet the specific needs of the organization's workforce, and (c) using effective communication to ensure support and coordination up and down the hierarchy. In addition, building a psychologically healthy workplace is not an end-state that is achieved. Rather, it is a dynamic process whereby the organization assesses its needs, develops and implements evidence-based practices that meet those needs, and evaluates its efforts in an ongoing manner, which provides feedback that is used for continuous improvement. Embedding psychologically healthy workplace principles in the culture of an organization requires far more than simply offering a wellness program, conducting an annual employee survey, allowing telecommuting, facilitating the occasional team-building exercise, or giving employees awards for years of service. Each workplace practice functions in relation to other programs and policies the organization has in place as well as to a variety of internal and external environmental factors. The complex nature of these relationships highlights the importance of taking a comprehensive approach to creating a work environment where both employees and the organization can thrive.

ORGANIZATION OF THIS BOOK

This book is organized around the five types of practices included in APA's Psychologically Healthy Workplace model. To that end, we have brought together experts, both scientists and practitioners, to share their insights on each of the five practice areas. For each practice area, there are two chapters. The first chapter provides a scholarly review of previous research on that practice, and the second chapter provides a perspective from the field, in which the practical implications of each type of practice are discussed.

Chapters 1 and 2 focus on the first of the five categories of psychologically healthy workplace practices: employee involvement. Because employee involvement practices are often linked to the success of other workplace practices (e.g., Grawitch et al., 2009), this provides a starting point from which to consider each of the other four categories of practices. In Chapter 1, Benson and Lawler review the research foundation for involvement practices, provide a context for current application of involvement practices, and discuss the future of involvement research. In Chapter 2, Gravenkemper brings a practitioner perspective to involvement practices, providing specific examples from organizations that have embraced the use of employee involvement as a way to develop a positive workplace culture and improve organizational effectiveness. Exploring a variety of involvement initiatives and participative management approaches, he explores key factors that can facilitate or inhibit involvement and discusses practical considerations for increasing employee involvement.

Chapters 3 and 4 shift the focus to employee growth and development initiatives. In Chapter 3, Salas and Weaver discuss the importance of training and development in contemporary organizations, including the theoretical and empirical underpinnings as well as a list of factors that contribute to the effectiveness of growth and development initiatives. In Chapter 4, Stone provides a framework for considering several categories of growth and development approaches and the practical issues that must be addressed with each. He also reviews the roles and responsibilities of trainer, trainee, supervisor, and senior management and discusses transfer of learning and a long-term strategy for talent development.

Chapters 5 and 6 highlight the role of work–life balance, an issue that has begun to take on much more prominence in contemporary research and practice. In Chapter 5, Barber, Grawitch, and Maloney provide an overview of important empirical research on the topic and explore key barriers that can influence the effectiveness of work–life balance initiatives for employees and the organization. With a broad view of the work–life interface that includes both flexibility and nonwork support, the authors address assessment, development, implementation, utilization, feedback, and refinement of work–life initiatives. In Chapter 6, Yost, Miller, and Spigner focus on how to make work–life balance initiatives achievable and effective for employees and the organization, suggesting a strategic framework that can move organizations toward a more flexible approach to work.

Chapters 7 and 8 emphasize the importance of employee recognition within the context of a psychologically healthy workplace. In Chapter 7, Nelson reviews some of the previous recognition research, the practice category that has received the least amount of directed empirical attention in the past. He reviews some fundamentals of motivation and key aspects of effective recognition practices and discusses individual versus group recognition and implications for managers, human resources professionals, and consultants. In Chapter 8, Saunderson focuses on practical issues related to employee recognition, emphasizing the best practices specified by the Recognition Management Institute. He discusses the reward–recognition continuum, offers tips for getting leadership commitment, and provides case examples of effective recognition practices.

Chapters 9 and 10 highlight the broadest of the five categories of workplace practices: health and safety. In Chapter 9, Tetrick and Peiró provide an overview of contemporary psychology theory and research in the areas of health and safety, emphasizing the importance of climate and leadership. They explore key variables that facilitate or inhibit the effectiveness of health and safety interventions and highlight both the positive and negative effects the work environment can have on employee well-being. In Chapter 10, Kelly and Carter discuss ways in which health and safety practices can be implemented within contemporary organizations, providing practical examples from the University of Alabama and a discussion of some of the challenges that are likely to be encountered when attempting to design, implement, and evaluate health and safety initiatives. The authors include tips for organizations and managers as well as sample tools for planning, delivering, and evaluating health and safety programs.

Finally, in the Concluding Remarks, we integrate key points made in the previous chapters. We briefly discuss the ways in which various types of practices can work together before identifying future research issues that must be addressed within the study of the psychologically healthy workplace. We also suggest a framework for considering the different practices within a psychologically healthy workplace through the lens of the specific functions they serve for employees and organizations. Our hope is that this book will broaden the healthy workplace discussion for researchers, practitioners, and employers alike, provide them with an overarching framework that expands the concept of organizational health, and stimulate new innovations in research and practice.

REFERENCES

American Psychological Association. (2014). *Psychologically Healthy Workplace Awards and Best Practices Honors 2014*. Retrieved from http://www.apaexcellence.org/assets/general/2014-phwa-magazine.pdf

American Psychological Association. (2015). Creating a psychologically healthy workplace. Retrieved from http://www.apaexcellence.org/resources/creatingahealthyworkplace

Batt, R., & Valcour, M. (2003). Human resource practices as predictors of work-family outcomes and employee turnover. *Industrial Relations: A Journal of Economy and Society, 42*, 189–220. http://dx.doi.org/10.1111/1468-232X.00287

Cruver, B. (2002). *Anatomy of greed: The unshredded truth from an Enron insider*. New York, NY: Carroll & Graf.

Elliott, D. J. (2009, May 29). *What happens to the GM pensions in bankruptcy?* Retrieved from http://www.brookings.edu/papers/2009/0529_gm_pensions_elliott.aspx

Gibson, C. B., Porath, C. L., Benson, G. S., & Lawler, E. E., III. (2007). What results when firms implement practices: The differential relationship between specific practices, firm financial performance, customer service, and quality. *Journal of Applied Psychology, 92*, 1467–1480. http://dx.doi.org/10.1037/0021-9010.92.6.1467

Gravenkemper, S. (2007). Building community in organizations: Principles of engagement. *Consulting Psychology Journal: Practice and Research, 59*, 203–208. http://dx.doi.org/10.1037/1065-9293.59.3.203

Grawitch, M. J., Barber, L. K., & Justice, L. (2010). Re-thinking the work-life interface: It's not about balance, it's about resource allocation. *Applied Psychology: Health and Well-Being, 2*, 127–159.

Grawitch, M. J., Gottschalk, M., & Munz, D. C. (2006). The path to a healthy workplace: A critical review linking healthy workplace practices, employee well-being, and organizational improvements. *Consulting Psychology Journal: Practice and Research, 58,* 129–147. http://dx.doi.org/10.1037/1065-9293.58.3.129

Grawitch, M. J., Ledford, G. E., Ballard, D. W., & Barber, L. K. (2009). Leading the healthy workforce: The integral role of employee involvement. *Consulting Psychology Journal: Practice and Research, 61,* 122–135. http://dx.doi.org/10.1037/a0015288

Grawitch, M. J., Trares, S., & Kohler, J. M. (2007). Healthy workplace practices and employee outcomes. *International Journal of Stress Management, 14,* 275–293. http://dx.doi.org/10.1037/1072-5245.14.3.275

Griffin, M. A., Hart, P. M., & Wilson-Evered, E. (2000). Using employee opinion surveys to improve organizational health. In L. R. Murphy & C. L. Cooper (Eds.), *Healthy and productive work: An international perspective* (pp. 15–36). New York, NY: Taylor & Francis.

Hakanen, J. J., Schaufeli, W. B., & Ahola, K. (2008). The Job Demands-Resources model: A three-year cross-lagged study of burnout, depression, commitment, and work engagement. *Work & Stress, 22,* 224–241. http://dx.doi.org/10.1080/02678370802379432

Podsakoff, N. P., LePine, J. A., & LePine, M. A. (2007). Differential challenge stressor-hindrance stressor relationships with job attitudes, turnover intentions, turnover, and withdrawal behavior: A meta-analysis. *Journal of Applied Psychology, 92,* 438–454. http://dx.doi.org/10.1037/0021-9010.92.2.438

Quick, J. C. (1999). Occupational health psychology: Historical roots and future directions. *Health Psychology, 18,* 82–88. http://dx.doi.org/10.1037/0278-6133.18.1.82

Shadur, M. A., Kienzle, R., & Rodwell, J. J. (1999). The relationship between organizational climate and employee perceptions of involvement. *Group & Organization Management, 24,* 479–503. http://dx.doi.org/10.1177/1059601199244005

Somers, M. J. (2009). The combined influence of affective, continuance and normative commitment on employee withdrawal. *Journal of Vocational Behavior, 74,* 75–81. http://dx.doi.org/10.1016/j.jvb.2008.10.006

U.S. Department of Labor, Bureau of Labor Statistics. (2014). *Job Openings and Labor Turnover Survey, January 2013–December 2013 (preliminary)* [Database]. Retrieved from http://www.bls.gov/jlt/data.htm

Vandenberg, R. J., Richardson, H. E., & Eastman, L. J. (1999). The impact of high involvement work processes on organizational effectiveness: A second-order latent variable approach. *Group & Organization Management, 24,* 300–339. http://dx.doi.org/10.1177/1059601199243004

Van den Broeck, A., Vansteenkiste, M., De Witte, H., & Lens, W. (2008). Explaining the relationships between job characteristics, burnout, and engagement: The role of basic psychological need satisfaction. *Work & Stress, 22,* 277–294. http://dx.doi.org/10.1080/02678370802393672

World Health Organization. (1948). Preamble to the Constitution of the World Health Organization as adopted by the International Health Conference, New York, 19–22 June, 1946. Retrieved from http://who.int/about/definition/en/print.html

1

EMPLOYEE INVOLVEMENT: RESEARCH FOUNDATIONS

GEORGE S. BENSON AND EDWARD E. LAWLER III

Employee involvement (EI) is an approach to work-system design that emphasizes high levels of employee decision-making authority. An extensive body of research literature going back decades supports the principles of EI systems as well as the effectiveness of specific practices such as self-managing teams, cross-training, quality circles, gain sharing, employee ownership, and participative decision making in the workplace. High-involvement management practices (defined as an integrated set of human resource and work design practices that are designed to give all employees the skills, information, power, and rewards to make decisions in the workplace) have generated enormous interest among researchers in many different disciplines and geographies. Taken together, this work clearly indicates the multiple benefits of EI in terms of productivity, profitability, and employee well-being. This chapter reviews the research foundation of these practices and puts the current use of these practices in context.

http://dx.doi.org/10.1037/14731-002
The Psychologically Healthy Workplace: Building a Win–Win Environment for Organizations and Employees,
M. J. Grawitch and D. W. Ballard (Editors)

The basic principles of EI were first tested in the 1960s and 1970s with important experiments in Europe and the United States in large manufacturing plants. One of the most visible was in a Volvo plant in Sweden that used semi-autonomous teams to assemble cars. However, EI did not gain wide acceptance by industry until the 1980s (Boxall & Macky, 2009; Cappelli & Neumark, 2001). This was the beginning of the quality movement in manufacturing and new high-involvement startup or "greenfield" manufacturing plants. Broad adoption of such high-involvement practices as work teams, flat organization structures, cross-training, skill-based pay, and cooperative union management relationships followed (Lawler, 1986).

By the middle of the 1990s there was significant growth in *high-involvement* work practices (also labeled *participative*, *flexible*, or *high-performance* practices) in the United States and Europe. At that time there was also significant interest in the popular business press, and academic research demonstrated their effectiveness through case studies and larger surveys of organizational performance (Adler, Goldoftas, & Levine, 1997; Appelbaum, Bailey, Berg, & Kallenberg, 2000; Appelbaum & Batt, 1995; Bailey, 1993; Lawler, Mohrman, & Ledford, 1998; Macduffie, 1995).

Increasing competition and the transformation of manufacturing industries appear to have driven the widespread adoption of EI (Locke, Kochan, & Piore, 1995). By 2000, studies showed that some form of EI practices were in place in a large proportion of workplaces in industrialized countries, including half of all U.S. firms and two thirds of the Fortune 1000 (Cooke, 1994; Freeman, Kleiner, & Ostroff, 2000; Gittleman, Horrigan, & Joyce, 1998; Kling, 1995; Osterman, 1994; O'Toole, Lawler, & Meisinger, 2007).

Current implementation of high-involvement practices is more difficult to gauge. Over the past 10 years there have been no new notable large-scale surveys of EI work practices in the United States. The Workplace Employment Relations Survey (WERS) in the United Kingdom was last conducted in 2011. A comparison of the adoption of various involvement practices with 2004 surveys indicates that EI has remained stable or decreased slightly (Van Wanrooy et al., 2013). In the United States the last available surveys indicate that the rates of adoption of EI have leveled off or begun to decline slightly (O'Toole et al., 2007). It is unclear whether this trend represents companies pulling back from the use of EI practices or that the acceptance of these practices has become so widespread that EI has reached a saturation point, with few organizations and industries left as good candidates to transform.

So much research on high-involvement and high-performance work practices has accumulated over the past 25 years that the basic foundations of EI are now largely unquestioned. To some degree they have simply become the way work is organized and are no longer seen as transformative practices.

In the following pages we review these foundations and the current state of research on EI, organizational performance, and employee well-being.

THEORETICAL FOUNDATIONS OF EMPLOYEE INVOLVEMENT

EI at its core is based on theories of human motivation that grew out of the cognitive revolution in psychology in the 1950s. Maslow's work on high-order needs and self-actualization was particularly important because it indicated that individuals could be motivated by intrinsic rewards, not just by tangible rewards and punishments. Also influential was the work on expectancy theory and job satisfaction that showed relationships between attitudes and behavior. The work on motivation influenced subsequent research on job enrichment and job design (Oldham & Hackman, 1980; Oldham, Hackman, & Pearce, 1976), which took several forms, though all included a strong emphasis on information, decision-making power, incentives, and feedback as factors that influenced job performance.

In a series of books, Lawler (1986, 1992, 1996) built on this work and detailed an integrated set of principles for organizational design. He included practices that distribute information and decision-making power to employees, give them incentives for success, and give them the skills and knowledge they need to be effective. Table 1.1 shows how Lawler saw the relationship between management practices and employees having the knowledge, foundation, power, and rewards they must have to make EI effective. He stressed that effectiveness requires employees to have all four: power, information, knowledge, and reward.

Based on classic motivation theory, EI suggests that employees will exert effort and work efficiently when they feel they are in control of their

TABLE 1.1
Employee Involvement Practices

Employee involvement principles	Employee involvement practices
Knowledge	Skill-based pay Commitment to training
Information	Gain sharing Open books
Power	Job enrichment Work teams
Rewards	Gain sharing Employee ownership Profit sharing

work, are given meaningful work, receive feedback on their performance, and are rewarded for the success of the business. Lawler and others persuasively argued that employees will work harder and smarter in organizations where they are incented to make decisions concerning the conduct of their jobs and participate in the business as a whole (e.g., Cotton, 1993; Lawler, 1986).

Though there are different theories of EI, they all call for decision-making power, incentives for employees to take responsibility for their performance, skill development, the provision of information to make decisions, and job security. The motivation theory that underlies EI suggests that these practices are complementary and generally need to be implemented together to create an effective work system. Though research has shown that EI is an integrated set of practices, researchers have seldom agreed on what the exact combination of practices should be. As a result, most studies have used measurement scales representing multiple practices determined by factor or cluster analysis to address the natural variation in the practices used by firms (Fernie & Metcalf, 1995; Huselid, 1995; Koch & McGrath, 1996; Lawler, Mohrman, & Benson, 2001; Scholarios, Ramsay, & Harley, 2000; Wood & de Menezes, 1998). A 2013 review of the high-performance work literature identified 61 unique practices, but decentralized participative decision making was a core practice and the most commonly investigated practice across 193 studies (Posthuma, Campion, Masimova, & Campion, 2013).

RESEARCH ON EMPLOYEE INVOLVEMENT AND ORGANIZATIONAL PERFORMANCE

Research generally shows that EI increases individual, team, and unit productivity in industries as diverse as professional services, steel manufacturing, apparel, medical imaging, and semiconductor fabrication. Hodson and Roscigno (2004) coded organizational practices and work-life experience from 204 English-language ethnographies published in books and sociology journals and concluded that EI showed positive relationships with both organizational success and employee well-being. The consistency of positive results from EI across a number of studies in so many sectors of the economy suggests that the benefits of EI are real and robust across most sectors.

Studies examining EI practices as part of a larger set of high-involvement or high-performance practices have generally indicated positive relationships with organizational performance. In one of the first studies on HR and performance, Ichniowski (1990) found that firms that used HR practices (including training and flexible job design) had higher sales per employee and higher overall firm performance. He concluded that a complementary set of HR practices, which includes elements of EI, was positively related to firm performance if they were implemented together. Numerous studies of gain sharing, profit sharing, and employee ownership plans show that they increase organizational performance (Lawler, 2003; Rosen, Case, & Staubus, 2005). Many of these studies show that giving employees a piece of the action is most effective when it is combined with other EI practices such as problem-solving groups, participative decision making, and the provision of business information.

The most widely cited paper on HR practices and performance (Huselid, 1995) reported significant relationships between HR practices and two performance indices: sales per employee and gross return on assets. The two HR indices were labeled *skills and work structures* (which included employee participation programs) and *motivation* (which included incentive rewards). For large organizations, studies conducted by the Center for Effective Organizations at the University of Southern California have found consistent relationships between the adoption of EI by the Fortune 1000 companies and several measures of financial and market performance (Lawler et al., 2001). Finally, Combs, Liu, Hall, and Ketchen (2006) examined 92 studies of high-performance work practices and estimated a low, but significant, overall correlation of .20 with organizational performance. They concluded that EI practices, including incentive compensation, training, information sharing, and team working, were all positively and significantly correlated with performance. A more recent meta-analysis using data from 29 countries yielded similar estimates of this relationship worldwide (Rabl, Jayasinghe, Gerhart, & Kühlmann, 2014).

While the positive correlations between EI and high-performance work systems (HPWS) with unit and organizational performance have been consistent across various settings, research over the past 20 years has also shown these practices to have greater impacts on some organizations than others. Research has moved away from a one-size-fits-all universalistic theory of the effects of practices on performance to a contingency or fit-based theory of effectiveness (Boxall & Macky, 2009; Delery & Doty, 1996; Kaufman, 2010). Specifically, studies have identified industry conditions, company strategy, organizational climate, and the nature of the tasks performed by workers as moderators of EI and HPWS effectiveness (Michie & Sheehan, 2005).

HPWS appear to be more common and more effective in high-growth industries and industries with competitive rivalry to incentivize innovation in management practices (Batt, 2002; Datta, Guthrie, & Wright, 2005). Research has also demonstrated that strategy also plays a role in the effectiveness of EI and HPWS (Camps & Luna-Arocas, 2009; Guthrie, Spell, & Nyamori, 2002; Lepak & Snell, 2002; Michie & Sheehan, 2005; Youndt & Snell, 2004; Youndt, Snell, Dean, & Lepak, 1996). Specifically, HPWS are more common and effective in firms pursuing differentiation or innovation strategies (Batt, 2002; Guthrie, 2001; Lepak, Taylor, Tekleab, Marrone, &

Cohen, 2007). Finally, EI is more effective in firms with low capital intensity where human capital is more central to operations (Batt, 2002; McClean & Collins, 2011).

In addition to research on the moderating conditions of the EI and performance relationship there has also been some debate over the relationship of EI to firm financial performance for two main reasons. First, there is some evidence that EI practices are often accompanied by wage increases that are needed to attract higher skilled employees, and they may offset some or all of the gains in productivity. Unfortunately, only a small number of studies have actually examined the effect of EI on wage costs and profitability. Cooke (1994) concluded, on the basis of a sample of manufacturing firms in Michigan, that the use of self-managed teams and quality circles was associated with both higher wages and productivity. In that study, the productivity gains outweighed the higher labor costs incurred by the firms. EI was associated with 21% better net performance as measured by value added per employee less wage costs, even though those firms had 6% to 7% higher wages. On the other hand, Cappelli and Neumark (2001) found that the productivity gains from high-performance work practices are largely offset by increased labor costs. With two waves of data from the 1992 and 1997 National Employer Survey (NES), they concluded that firms did not see an increase in labor productivity as measured by output per dollar spent on labor.

The second major point of debate is the question of causality. Although many studies find a positive correlation between the adoption of high-involvement practices and organizational performance, the question arises as to whether high involvement leads to increased business performance, or whether firms with above-average performance are more likely to adopt involvement practices. There is the possibility that firms with high performance have the resources needed to make investments in employees and adopt high-involvement practices. It may also be the case that firms with higher quality managers and employees are more likely to perform better and also to adopt high-involvement practices.

Reverse causality, self-selection, and heterogeneity bias have been specifically addressed in several studies. In response to questions about reverse causality, Huselid and Becker (1996) conducted a longitudinal study with a second wave of data from Huselid's (1995) earlier work. They did not find statistically significant results and argued that the differences were largely due to measurement error and range restriction that occurred because the research design focused only on firms that adopted the high-performance practices during the 2-year study period. Using statistical methods to correct this bias, Huselid and Becker estimated results similar to Huselid's (1995) estimates, but these findings have been widely debated (Gerhart, Wright, McMahan, & Snell, 2000).

The direction of causality was also addressed by Wright, Gardner, Moynihan, and Allen (2005), who examined 68 empirical studies that reported significant correlations between HR practices and performance and found that only five used a research design in which HR practices were used to predict future organizational performance. They found significant correlations between involvement practices and performance, but the results were inconclusive as to the direction of causality. Their results were similar to those of Guest, Michie, Conway, and Sheehan (2003), who found that HR practices were related to higher profits among a sample of firms in the United Kingdom, but that the correlation disappeared when prior performance was controlled. Overall, the research on EI suggests that the positive relationship between EI and organizational performance is reciprocal and evolves over time. Except in cases of new facilities or greenfield projects, organizations are not likely to see large changes in EI practices from year to year. Further, the effects of EI on profits may also take time to materialize. More recently, high-involvement practices have been examined in two long-term longitudinal studies in the United Kingdom (Birdi et al., 2008; Tregaskis, Daniels, Glover, Butler, & Meyer, 2013) and on balance the research evidence is clear that EI is positively correlated with individual productivity, operational performance, and financial results.

RESEARCH ON EMPLOYEE INVOLVEMENT
AND GROWTH, DEVELOPMENT, AND WAGES

Advocates of EI have made strong theoretical arguments that EI practices should also lead to higher skills and wages for employees. The primary reason is that EI requires higher levels of responsibility and subsequently requires higher wages to attract and retain qualified employees. Increased participation in decision making creates additional value for the organization but also demands more training and skills.

There is evidence that EI reduces demand for unskilled labor (Caroli & Van Reenen, 2001) and increases investment in employee development (Black & Lynch, 1996; Frazis, Gittleman, & Joyce, 2000). Cappelli and Neumark (2001) found that high-involvement practices were associated with increased labor costs per employee, which suggests that it increased investment in employee training and wages. Organizations that adopt EI practices are also likely to invest in technology, particularly information technology, which requires additional education and training to operate (Black & Lynch, 1996; Black, Lynch, & Krivelyova, 2004; Bresnahan, Brynjolfsson, & Hitt, 2002; Hunter & Lafkas, 2003). Using data from four representative surveys from 1992 to 2006, Green (2012) concluded that EI has promoted the use of higher order cognitive and interactive skills in workplaces across the United Kingdom.

Along with increased skills, EI should lead to increased wages (Bartling, Fehr, & Schmidt, 2012; Osterman, 2006; Steigenberger, 2013). One reason is that EI increases productivity, which should increase an employer's ability to pay workers. Another reason is that EI can increase the power of employees to demand higher wages either formally through union representation or indirectly as a byproduct of their expanded contributions and new roles within organizations.

However, research results regarding the relationship between EI and wages are mixed. Several studies have concluded that organizations with EI and related practices generally pay higher wages (Chadwick & Fister, 2001; Cooke, 1994; Freeman & Lazear, 1994). More recently Bockerman, Bryson, and Ilmakunnas (2013) examined a nationally representative survey from Finland and found that workers in high-involvement jobs enjoyed a 15% to 36% wage premium. Other researchers have concluded that wages rise in some cases and not in others. For instance, Batt (2004) found that employee discretion at work was positively related to wages, whereas the use of specific practices (e.g., problem-solving teams) was not.

Finally, there are studies that conclude that wages do not rise with the adoption of high-involvement practices. Osterman (2000, 2006) found no relationship between the adoption of high-performance work practices and subsequent wage increases. Similarly, Handel and Gittleman (2004) concluded that there is little evidence that high-performance work is associated with higher wages.

Osterman (2006) attributed the lack of consistency in the findings concerning pay changes to differences in the data and the measurement of high involvement and employee wages across studies. In a reanalysis of data from the 1997 NES, he also raised the possibility that the wage benefits of EI are not spread evenly across different types of organizations, or even within organizations to different types of employees. Osterman concluded that core blue-collar employees enjoy higher wages in HPWS, while managerial and clerical employees do not. He argued that this situation may account for the nonfindings in some studies, given that they fail to differentiate between core and managerial employees; they also do not account for the fact that frontline employees in high-involvement workplaces likely reduce the need for higher paid managerial employees. This argument regarding the adoption of EI in traditional low-wage manufacturing was supported by Appelbaum, Bailey, Berg, and Kallenberg (2000). They found significant wage increases from high involvement in steel and apparel manufacturing industries, but not in medical imaging.

RESEARCH ON EMPLOYEE INVOLVEMENT
AND EMPLOYEE ATTITUDES AND MOTIVATION

EI practices are theorized to positively affect organizational performance through some combination of creating more efficient work processes and increasing the motivation of workers (Bodah, McHugh, & Yim, 2008; Huselid, 1995; Ichniowski, Kochan, Levine, Olson, & Strauss, 1996; Lawler, 1986; Wood & Wall, 2007). That is, the positive effects of EI on organizational performance come from the increased utilization of the knowledge and skills of employees. This increased efficacy of workers then motivates them to give extra effort, resulting in higher productivity coupled with lower absenteeism, grievances, and turnover, all of which ultimately have a positive effect on the bottom line.

A major critique of the early research on high-performance practices was that most studies of the performance effects of EI tended to assume a positive effect on employee attitudes, abilities, and effort when examining organizational performance. They focused on the relationship between practices and organizational outcomes, such as sales per employee, return on assets, and market returns, leaving the effect of the work practices on employees as a "black box." Research over the past 10 to 20 years has shifted toward employee attitudes and motivation as the source of the productivity and profitability gains that arise from EI. This work has consistently shown positive effects of involvement practices on employee attitudes and work climate (Vandenberg, Richardson, & Eastman, 1999). EI practices are associated with increased job satisfaction and greater trust in management (Freeman, Kleiner, & Ostroff, 2000; Guest, 1999). More recent studies found similar relationships between employee autonomy and empowerment with employee well-being and happiness (Cheng, 2014; Fan et al., 2014; Van der Meer & Wielers, 2013; Yanadori & van Jaarsveld, 2014). Current work in positive organizational psychology also draws heavily on employee involvement as a source of employee thriving and energy at work (Spreitzer, Sutcliffe, Dutton, Sonenshein, & Grant, 2005).

Research also shows that EI practices promote positive attitudes toward the organization, which in turn lead to extra effort (Cappelli & Rogovsky, 1998), prosocial behavior (O'Reilly & Chatman, 1986), innovation (Fernandez & Moldogaziev, 2013), safety (Probst & Brubaker, 2001), and employee retention (Koys, 2001). Several studies have shown that high involvement contributes to HR climates that are associated with greater employee commitment and discretionary effort. Many studies find that EI, as part of a larger set of high-commitment work practices, positively influences employee attitudes, absenteeism, turnover, and subsequent firm performance (Arthur, 1994; Lam & White, 1998; Scholarios et al., 2000; Takeuchi, Chen, & Lepak, 2009; Tsui, Pearce, Porter, & Tripoli, 1997). Overall, research suggests that employees respond positively to high-involvement practices under most conditions, and this leads to greater job satisfaction and organizational commitment. These attitudes then have benefits for employee performance, safety, and the service climate in organizations.

This research shows that employee attitudes and well-being provide one of the critical pathways through which EI leads to organizational performance. The common link between these studies appears to be the process of social exchange in which employees see EI practices as an effort to promote worker interests and well-being and reciprocate with positive attitudes and discretionary effort toward company goals (Evans & Davis, 2005; Kehoe & Wright, 2013; Kizilos, Cummings, & Cummings, 2013; Takeuchi et al., 2009). This means that for EI programs to thrive, the employees need to interpret the involvement practices as a genuine reflection of value that the organization places in the frontline worker (Chuang & Liao, 2010; Messersmith, Patel, Lepak, & Gould-Williams, 2011; Takeuchi et al., 2009). Though most studies show that employees are likely to perceive involvement practices in a positive manner, this may not always be the case (Kuvaas, 2008; Nishii, Lepak, & Schneider, 2008; Nishii & Wright, 2008; Searle et al., 2011).

Recent work on how employees react to HPWS suggests that the ways in which the motivation for implementing the practices is perceived by employees is a key determinant in whether they embrace the practices. If employees perceive that the practices are implemented only to increase productivity or get more out of employees, they tend to resist and undermine the changes. For example, using data from a large supermarket chain, Nishii and colleagues studied the attributions that employees make for the *why* of high-involvement practices and found that employees who view the practices as a win–win situation have different behavioral and attitudinal reactions to the practices than do those who feel the practices were implemented simply to get the most out of employees (Nishii et al., 2008; Nishii & Wright, 2008).

RESEARCH ON EMPLOYEE INVOLVEMENT AND WORKLOAD, STRESS, AND INJURIES

Although there is significant research demonstrating the benefits of EI, an alternate perspective argues that EI practices are implemented as a means to subvert unionism and increase workloads rather than to benefit employees (Bodah et al., 2008; Godard, 2004, 2010; Godard & Delaney, 2000). There is the possibility of employers using expanded responsibility of frontline employees to increase job demands, raise production targets, and decrease headcounts without supporting employees, developing skills, and increasing wages. If increased performance demands are accompanied by the threat of layoff or the replacement of workers who are not able to adapt to an environment of higher expectations, then EI will ultimately be labeled as the next chapter in the continuing efforts of management to exploit workers.

Using data on British employees, Ramsay, Scholarios, and Harley (2000) argued that new work practices in general have had the effect of increasing stress and workload on employees. Increased stress from EI is thought to arise from several sources. First, though employees are given discretion in their jobs, the pace of the work usually increases (Berggren, 1994). Second, the nature of the work itself can become more stressful for frontline employees as responsibility and uncertainty increase. Third, Barker (1993) argued that self-managed teams encourage workers to monitor each other, which can be an even more coercive and stressful form of control than traditional supervision. Some research has found workplace transformation increases workloads, work hours, and stress (Danford, Richardson, Stewart, Tailby, & Upchurch, 2008; Frick, Goetzen, & Simmons, 2013; Harley, Allen, & Sargent, 2007; Mackie, Holahan, & Gottlieb, 2001; White, Hill, McGovern, Mills, & Smeaton, 2003). There is also some evidence that EI leads to greater stress and insecurity for supervisors who are included in involvement practices (Mahony, 2007). In a study of telephone operating companies, Batt (2004) found that while workers in participative teams had higher job satisfaction related to their increased discretion, their supervisors reported lower perceived job security and lower job satisfaction relative to supervisors in work groups without participation.

In addition, there have also been studies that conclude that work transformation may be associated with injury (Brenner, Fairris, & Ruser, 2004; Fairris & Brenner, 2001). Though the empirical evidence for increased stress, injuries, and hours is mixed, the negative findings are balanced by the larger number of studies showing positive effects of EI on stress and safety. Though there are certainly examples where EI practices are associated with negative worker outcomes in terms of stress and workload, these appear to represent extreme versions of involvement practices. Employees are also likely to have more negative experiences with involvement practices if they are not fully implemented. Being held responsible for production and given variable pay but not control over work processes leads to anxiety and role overload (Jensen, Patel, & Messersmith, 2013).

Advocates of EI acknowledge that the nature of work performed by frontline employees often involves greater risk, higher level skills, and more difficult decisions. However, when high-involvement practices are implemented, these new stresses are thought to be outweighed by the motivational and psychological benefits of greater autonomy, responsibility, and the opportunity to develop and use new skills and knowledge. Appelbaum et al. (2000) argued that additional discretionary effort from employees does not necessarily mean that their workload has increased, only that employees are performing higher order work. In a representative sample of U.K. employees, Wood and de Menezes (2011) found enriched jobs and high-involvement management practices both negatively related to anxiety on the job. A 2011 meta-analysis found that lack of control or autonomy on the job is related to a wide range of negative psychical symptoms including fatigue, sleep disturbances, and loss of appetite independent of work hours and workload (Nixon, Mazzola, Bauer, Krueger, & Spector, 2011).

As for the relationship between EI and workplace safety, a significant body of work shows that individual involvement practices including information sharing, participation, and team working promote a climate of safety and reduce accidents on the job. Studies done in industrial settings including chemical plants and manufacturing demonstrate that teams with more decision-making authority and control over the different aspects of their work have fewer work-related injuries (Hechanova-Alampay & Beehr, 2001; Kaminski, 2001). In a study of Canadian companies, Zacharatos, Barling, and Iverson (2005) found that HPWS promote both trust in management and a safety climate which in turn increased employees' safety awareness and reduced the number of accidents on the job.

CONCLUSION

EI is a core aspect of the healthy workplace (Grawitch, Gottschalk, & Munz, 2006; Grawitch, Ledford, Ballard, & Barber, 2009), and this review of the research foundations of EI suggests clear benefits for firms and workers. At the same time, it also seems clear that EI has not met the promise suggested by the strongest advocates as a means to truly transform all workplaces into healthy workplaces or "mutual gains enterprises." Many questions remain concerning the future of specific EI practices, but given the evidence that many involvement work practices yield a consistent competitive advantage along with benefits for workers, there is good reason to believe that EI practices will continue to be utilized. However, talk is likely lessening about the transformation of workplaces and how EI is a progressive approach to management. Many practices that are associated with EI are simply assumed best practice in companies and will continue to be adopted and utilized as such. Thus, rather than being seen as part of a new approach to management, EI management practices will simply be adopted because they are seen as the right way to manage an effective organization.

REFERENCES

Adler, P., Goldoftas, B., & Levine, D. (1997). Ergonomics, employee involvement, and the Toyota production system: A case study of NUMMI's 1993 model introduction. *Industrial & Labor Relations Review, 50*, 416–438. http://dx.doi.org/10.2307/2525183

Appelbaum, E., Bailey, T., Berg, P., & Kallenberg, A. (2000). *Manufacturing advantage: Why high-performance work systems pay off.* Ithaca, NY: ILR Press.

Appelbaum, E., & Batt, R. (1995). *The new American workplace: Transforming work systems in the United States.* Ithaca, NY: ILR Press.

Arthur, J. B. (1994). Effects of human resource systems on manufacturing performance and turnover. *Academy of Management Journal, 37*, 670–687. http://dx.doi.org/10.2307/256705

Bailey, T. (1993). Organizational innovation in the apparel industry. *Industrial Relations: A Journal of Economy and Society, 32*, 30–48.

Barker, J. R. (1993). Tightening the iron cage: Concertive control in self-managing teams. *Administrative Science Quarterly, 38*, 408–437. http://dx.doi.org/10.2307/2393374

Bartling, B., Fehr, E., & Schmidt, K. (2012). Screening, competition, and job design: Economic origins of good jobs. *The American Economic Review, 102*, 834–864. http://dx.doi.org/10.1257/aer.102.2.834

Batt, R. (2002). Managing customer services: Human resource practices, quit rates, and sales growth. *Academy of Management Journal, 45*, 587–597. http://dx.doi.org/10.2307/3069383

Batt, R. (2004). Who benefits from teams? Comparing workers, supervisors, and managers. *Industrial Relations: A Journal of Economy and Society, 43*, 183–212. http://dx.doi.org/10.1111/j.0019-8676.2004.00323.x

Berggren, C. (1994, Winter). Point/counterpoint: NUMMI vs. Uddevalla. *MIT Sloan Management Review, 35*(2), 37–45.

Birdi, K., Clegg, C., Patterson, M., Robinson, A., Stride, C. B., Wall, T. D., & Wood, S. J. (2008). The impact of human resource and operational management practices on company productivity: A longitudinal study. *Personnel Psychology, 61*, 467–501. http://dx.doi.org/10.1111/j.1744-6570.2008.00136.x

Black, S. E., & Lynch, L. M. (1996). Human-capital investments and productivity. *The American Economic Review, 86*, 263–267.

Black, S. E., Lynch, L. M., & Krivelyova, A. (2004). How workers fare when employers innovate. *Industrial Relations: A Journal of Economy and Society, 43*, 44–66. http://dx.doi.org/10.1111/j.0019-8676.2004.00318.x

Bockerman, P., Bryson, A., & Ilmakunnas, P. (2013). Does high involvement management lead to higher pay? *Journal of the Royal Statistical Society, 176*, 861–885.

Bodah, M. M., McHugh, P. P., & Yim, S. J. (2008). Employee involvement programs and collective bargaining: The role of labor relations climate. *Journal of Collective Negotiations, 32*, 245–260. http://dx.doi.org/10.2190/CN.32.3.f

Boxall, P., & Macky, K. (2009). Research and theory on high-performance work systems: Progressing the high-involvement stream. *Human Resource Management Journal, 19*, 3–23.

Brenner, M., Fairris, D., & Ruser, J. (2004). "Flexible" work practice and occupational safety and health: Exploring the relationship between cumulative trauma disorders and workplace transformation. *Journal of Industrial Relations, 43*, 242–266.

Bresnahan, T., Brynjolfsson, E., & Hitt, L. (2002). Information technology, workplace organization, and the demand for skilled labor: Firm-level evidence. *The Quarterly Journal of Economics, 117*, 339–376. http://dx.doi.org/10.1162/003355302753399526

Camps, J., & Luna-Arocas, R. (2009). High involvement work practices and firm performance. *International Journal of Human Resource Management, 20*, 1056–1077.

Cappelli, P., & Neumark, D. (2001). Do "high-performance" work practices improve establishment-level outcome? *Industrial & Labor Relations Review, 54*, 737–775.

Cappelli, P., & Rogovsky, N. (1998). Employee involvement and organizational citizenship: Implications for labor law reform and "lean production." *Industrial & Labor Relations Review, 51*, 633–653. http://dx.doi.org/10.2307/2525012

Caroli, E., & Van Reenen, J. (2001). Skill-based organizational change? Evidence from a panel of British and French establishments. *The Quarterly Journal of Economics, 116*, 1449–1492. http://dx.doi.org/10.1162/003355301753265624

Chadwick, C., & Fister, T. (2001). *Innovative human resource practices and outcomes for workers.* Unpublished manuscript, University of Illinois at Urbana-Champaign, Department of Management.

Cheng, Z. (2014). The effects of employee involvement and participation on subjective well-being: Evidence from urban China. *Social Indicators Research, 118*, 457–483. http://dx.doi.org/10.1007/s11205-013-0430-8

Chuang, C. H., & Liao, H. U. I. (2010). Strategic human resource management in service context: Taking care of business by taking care of employees and customers. *Personnel Psychology, 63*, 153–196. http://dx.doi.org/10.1111/j.1744-6570.2009.01165.x

Combs, J., Liu, Y., Hall, A., & Ketchen, D. (2006). How much do high performance practices matter? A meta-analysis of their effects on organizational performance. *Personnel Psychology, 59*, 501–528. http://dx.doi.org/10.1111/j.1744-6570.2006.00045.x

Cooke, W. N. (1994). Employee participation programs, group-based incentives, and company performance: A union-non-union comparison. *Industrial & Labor Relations Review, 47*, 594–609. http://dx.doi.org/10.2307/2524660

Cotton, J. (1993). *Employee involvement.* Newbury Park, CA: Sage.

Danford, A., Richardson, M., Stewart, P., Tailby, S., & Upchurch, M. (2008). Partnership, high performance work systems and quality of working life. *New Technology, Work and Employment, 23,* 151–166. http://dx.doi.org/10.1111/j.1468-005X.2008.00210.x

Datta, D., Guthrie, J., & Wright, P. (2005). Human resource management and labor productivity: Does industry matter? *Academy of Management Journal, 48,* 135–145. http://dx.doi.org/10.5465/AMJ.2005.15993158

Delery, J., & Doty, D. H. (1996). Modes of theorizing in strategic human resource management: Tests of universalistic, contingency, and configurational performance predictions. *Academy of Management Journal, 39,* 802–835. http://dx.doi.org/10.2307/256713

Evans, W. R., & Davis, W. D. (2005). High-performance work systems and organizational performance: The mediating role of internal social structure. *Journal of Management, 31,* 758–775. http://dx.doi.org/10.1177/0149206305279370

Fairris, D., & Brenner, M. (2001). Workplace transformation and the rise in cumulative trauma disorders: Is there a connection? *Journal of Labor Research, 22,* 15–28. http://dx.doi.org/10.1007/s12122-001-1001-3

Fan, D., Cui, L., Zhang, M., Zhu, C., Hartel, C., & Nyland, C. (2014). Influence of high performance work systems on employee subjective well-being and job burnout: Empirical evidence from the Chinese healthcare sector. *The International Journal of Human Resource Management, 25,* 931–950. http://dx.doi.org/10.1080/09585192.2014.876740

Fernandez, S., & Moldogaziev, T. (2013). Employee empowerment, employee attitudes and performance: Testing a causal model. *Public Administration Review, 73,* 490–506. http://dx.doi.org/10.1111/puar.12049

Fernie, S., & Metcalf, D. (1995). Participation, contingent pay, representation and workplace performance: Evidence from Great Britain. *British Journal of Industrial Relations, 33,* 379–415. http://dx.doi.org/10.1111/j.1467-8543.1995.tb00445.x

Frazis, H., Gittleman, M., & Joyce, M. (2000). Correlates of training: An analysis using both employer and employee characteristics. *Industrial & Labor Relations Review, 53,* 443–462. http://dx.doi.org/10.2307/2695968

Freeman, R. B., Kleiner, M. M., & Ostroff, C. (2000). *The anatomy of employee involvement and its effects on firms and workers* (Working Paper No. 8050). Cambridge, MA: National Bureau of Economic Research. http://dx.doi.org/10.3386/w8050

Freeman, R., & Lazear, E. (1994). *An economic analysis of works councils* (Working Paper No. 4918). Cambridge, MA: National Bureau of Economic Research.

Frick, B., Goetzen, U., & Simmons, R. (2013). The hidden costs of high-performance work practices: Evidence from a large German steel company. *Industrial & Labor Relations Review, 66,* 198–226.

Gerhart, B., Wright, P., McMahan, G., & Snell, S. (2000). Measurement error in research on human resources and firm performance: How much error is there and how does it influence effect size estimates? *Personnel Psychology, 53*, 803–834. http://dx.doi.org/10.1111/j.1744-6570.2000.tb02418.x

Gittleman, M., Horrigan, M., & Joyce, M. (1998). "Flexible" workplace practices: Evidence of a nationally representative survey. *Industrial & Labor Relations Review, 52*, 99–115. http://dx.doi.org/10.2307/2525245

Godard, J. (2004). A critical assessment of the high-performance paradigm. *British Journal of Industrial Relations, 42*, 349–378. http://dx.doi.org/10.1111/j.1467-8543.2004.00318.x

Godard, J. (2010). What is best for workers? The implications of workplace and human resource practices revisited. *Industrial Relations: A Journal of Economy and Society, 49*, 466–488. http://dx.doi.org/10.1111/j.1468-232X.2010.00610.x

Godard, J., & Delaney, J. T. (2000). Reflections on the "high performance" paradigm's implications for industrial relations as a field. *Industrial & Labor Relations Review, 53*, 482–502.

Grawitch, M., Gottschalk, M., & Munz, D. (2006). The path to a healthy workplace: A critical review linking healthy practices, employee well-being and organizational improvements. *Consulting Psychology Journal: Practice and Research, 58*, 129–147. http://dx.doi.org/10.1037/1065-9293.58.3.129

Grawitch, M. J., Ledford, J. E., Ballard, D. W., & Barber, L. K. (2009). Leading the healthy workforce: The integral role of employee involvement. *Consulting Psychology Journal: Practice and Research, 61*, 122–135. http://dx.doi.org/10.1037/a0015288

Green, F. (2012). Employee involvement, technology and evolution in job skills: A task-based analysis. *Industrial & Labor Relations Review, 65*, 36–66.

Guest, D. E. (1999). Human resource management—the workers' verdict. *Human Resource Management Journal, 9*, 5–25. http://dx.doi.org/10.1111/j.1748-8583.1999.tb00200.x

Guest, D. E., Michie, J., Conway, N., & Sheehan, M. (2003). A UK study of the relationship between human resource management and corporate performance. *British Journal of Industrial Relations, 41*, 291–314.

Guthrie, J. (2001). High-involvement work practices, turnover, and productivity: Evidence from New Zealand. *Academy of Management Journal, 44*, 180–190.

Guthrie, J., Spell, C., & Nyamori, R. O. (2002). Correlates and consequences of high involvement work practices: The role of competitive strategy. *International Journal of Human Resource Management, 13*, 183–197. http://dx.doi.org/10.1080/09585190110085071

Handel, M. J., & Gittleman, M. (2004). Is there a wage payoff to innovative work practices? *Industrial Relations: A Journal of Economy and Society, 43*, 67–97. http://dx.doi.org/10.1111/j.0019-8676.2004.00319.x

Harley, B., Allen, B. C., & Sargent, L. D. (2007). High performance work systems and employee experience of work in the service sector: The case of aged care. *British Journal of Industrial Relations, 45*, 607–633. http://dx.doi.org/10.1111/j.1467-8543.2007.00630.x

Hechanova-Alampay, R., & Beehr, T. A. (2001). Empowerment, span of control, and safety performance in work teams after workforce reduction. *Journal of Occupational Health Psychology, 6,* 275–282. http://dx.doi.org/10.1037/1076-8998.6.4.275

Hodson, R., & Roscigno, V. (2004). Organizational success and worker dignity: Complementary or contradictory? *American Journal of Sociology, 110,* 672–708. http://dx.doi.org/10.1086/422626

Hunter, L., & Lafkas, J. (2003). Opening the box: Information technology, work practices and wages. *Industrial & Labor Relations Review, 56,* 224–243. http://dx.doi.org/10.2307/3590936

Huselid, M. (1995). The impact of human resource management practices on turnover, productivity, and corporate performance. *Academy of Management Journal, 38,* 635–672. http://dx.doi.org/10.2307/256741

Huselid, M., & Becker, B. (1996). Methodological issues in cross-sectional and panel estimates of the human resource-firm performance link. *Industrial Relations: A Journal of Economy and Society, 35,* 400–422. http://dx.doi.org/10.1111/j.1468-232X.1996.tb00413.x

Ichniowski, C. (1990). *Human resource management systems and the performance of U.S. manufacturing businesses* (Working Paper No. 3449). Cambridge, MA: National Bureau of Economic Research.

Ichniowski, C., Kochan, T., Levine, D., Olson, C., & Strauss, G. (1996). What works at work: Overview and assessment. *Industrial Relations: A Journal of Economy and Society, 35,* 299–333. http://dx.doi.org/10.1111/j.1468-232X.1996.tb00409.x

Jensen, J. M., Patel, P. C., & Messersmith, J. G. (2013). High-performance work systems and job control: Consequences for anxiety, role overload, and turnover intentions. *Journal of Management, 39,* 1699–1724.

Kaminski, M. (2001). Unintended consequences: Organizational practices and their impact on workplace safety and productivity. *Journal of Occupational Health Psychology, 6,* 127–138. http://dx.doi.org/10.1037/1076-8998.6.2.127

Kaufman, B. E. (2010). SHRM theory in the post-Huselid era: Why it is fundamentally misspecified. *Industrial Relations: A Journal of Economy and Society, 49,* 286–313. http://dx.doi.org/10.1111/j.1468-232X.2009.00600.x

Kehoe, R. R., & Wright, P. M. (2013). The impact of high-performance human resource practices on employees' attitudes and behaviors. *Journal of Management, 39,* 366–391. http://dx.doi.org/10.1177/0149206310365901

Kizilos, M., Cummings, C., & Cummings, T. (2013). How high-involvement work processes increase organizational performance: The role of organizational citizenship behavior. *Journal of Applied Behavioral Science, 49,* 413–436. http://dx.doi.org/10.1177/0021886313479998

Kling, J. (1995, May). High performance work systems and firm performance. *Monthly Labor Review, 118,* 29–36.

Koch, M., & McGrath, R. (1996). Improving labor productivity: Human resource management policies do matter. *Strategic Management Journal, 17,* 335–354. http://dx.doi.org/10.1002/(SICI)1097-0266(199605)17:5<335::AID-SMJ814> 3.0.CO;2-R

Koys, D. (2001). The effects of employee satisfaction, organizational citizenship behavior, and turnover on organizational effectiveness: A unit-level longitudinal study. *Personnel Psychology, 54,* 101–114. http://dx.doi.org/10.1111/ j.1744-6570.2001.tb00087.x

Kuvaas, B. (2008). An exploration of how the employee–organization relationship affects the linkage between perception of developmental human resource practices and employee outcomes. *Journal of Management Studies, 45,* 1–25.

Lam, L. W., & White, L. P. (1998). Human resource orientation and corporate performance. *Human Resource Development Quarterly, 9,* 351–364. http://dx.doi. org/10.1002/hrdq.3920090406

Lawler, E. E., III. (1986). *High involvement management: Participative strategies for improving organizational performance.* San Francisco, CA: Jossey-Bass.

Lawler, E. E., III. (1992). *The ultimate advantage: Creating the high involvement organization.* San Francisco, CA: Jossey-Bass.

Lawler, E. E., III. (1996). *From the ground up: Six principles for building the new logic corporation.* San Francisco, CA: Jossey-Bass.

Lawler, E. E., III. (2003). *Treat people right! How organizations and individuals can propel each other into a virtuous spiral of success.* San Francisco, CA: Jossey-Bass.

Lawler, E. E., III, Mohrman, S. A., & Benson, G. (2001). *Organizing for high performance: Employee involvement, TQM, reengineering, and knowledge management in the Fortune 1000.* San Francisco, CA: Jossey-Bass.

Lawler, E. E., III, Mohrman, S. A., & Ledford, G. E., Jr. (1998). *Strategies for high performance organizations: Employee involvement, TQM, and reengineering programs in Fortune 1000 corporations.* San Francisco, CA: Jossey-Bass.

Lepak, D. P., & Snell, S. A. (2002). Examining the human resource architecture: The relationships among human capital, employment, and human resource configurations. *Journal of Management, 28,* 517–543. http://dx.doi.org/10.1016/ S0149-2063(02)00142-3

Lepak, D. P., Taylor, M. S., Tekleab, A. G., Marrone, J. A., & Cohen, D. J. (2007). An examination of the use of high investment human resource systems for core and support employees. *Human Resource Management, 46,* 223–246. http:// dx.doi.org/10.1002/hrm.20158

Locke, R., Kochan, T., & Piore, M. (1995). Reconceptualizing comparative industrial relations: Lessons from international research. *International Labour Review, 134,* 139–162.

Macduffie, J. P. (1995). Human resource bundles and manufacturing performance: Organizational logic and flexible production systems in the world auto industry. *Industrial & Labor Relations Review, 48,* 197–221. http://dx.doi.org/10.2307/ 2524483

Mackie, K. S., Holahan, C. K., & Gottlieb, N. H. (2001). Employee involvement management practices, work stress, and depression in employees of a human services residential care facility. *Human Relations, 54,* 1065–1092. http://dx.doi.org/10.1177/0018726701548004

Mahony, D. (2007). How participatory work practices affect front-line supervisors. *Journal of Labor Research, 28,* 147–168.

McClean, E., & Collins, C. J. (2011). High-commitment HR practices, employee effort, and firm performance: Investigating the effects of HR practices across employee groups within professional services firms. *Human Resource Management, 50,* 341–363. http://dx.doi.org/10.1002/hrm.20429

Messersmith, J. G., Patel, P. C., Lepak, D. P., & Gould-Williams, J. (2011). Unlocking the black box: Exploring the link between high-performance work systems and performance. *Journal of Applied Psychology, 96,* 1105–1118. http://dx.doi.org/10.1037/a0024710

Michie, J., & Sheehan, M. (2005). Business strategy, human resources, labor market flexibility and competitive advantage. *The International Journal of Human Resource Management, 16,* 445–464. http://dx.doi.org/10.1080/095851904 2000339598

Nishii, L. H., Lepak, D. P., & Schneider, B. (2008). Employee attributions of the "why" of HR practices: Their effects on employee attitudes and behaviors, and customer satisfaction. *Personnel Psychology, 61,* 503–545. http://dx.doi.org/10.1111/j.1744-6570.2008.00121.x

Nishii, L. H., & Wright, P. M. (2008). Variability within organizations: Implications for strategic human resource management. In D. B. Smith (Ed.), *The people make the place: Dynamic linkages between individuals and organizations* (pp. 225–248). Mahwah, NJ: Erlbaum.

Nixon, A., Mazzola, J., Bauer, J., Krueger, J., & Spector, P. (2011). Can work make you sick? A meta-analysis of the relationships between job stressors and physical symptoms. *Work & Stress, 25,* 1–22. http://dx.doi.org/10.1080/02678373.2011.569175

Oldham, G. R., & Hackman, J. (1980). Work design in the organizational context. In B. Staw & L. L. Cummings (Eds.), *Research in organizational behavior* (Vol. 2, pp. 247–278). Greenwich, CT: JAI.

Oldham, G. R., Hackman, J., & Pearce, J. L. (1976). Conditions under which employees respond positively to enriched work. *Journal of Applied Psychology, 61,* 395–403. http://dx.doi.org/10.1037/0021-9010.61.4.395

O'Reilly, C., & Chatman, J. (1986). Organizational commitment and psychological attachment: The effects of compliance, identification, and internalization on prosocial behavior. *Journal of Applied Psychology, 71,* 492–499. http://dx.doi.org/10.1037/0021-9010.71.3.492

Osterman, P. (1994). How common is workplace transformation and who adopts it? *Industrial & Labor Relations Review, 47,* 173–188. http://dx.doi.org/10.2307/2524415

Osterman, P. (2000). Work reorganization in an era of restructuring: Trends in diffusion and effects on employee welfare. *Industrial & Labor Relations Review, 53*, 179–196. http://dx.doi.org/10.2307/2696072

Osterman, P. (2006). The wage effects of high performance work organization in manufacturing. *Industrial & Labor Relations Review, 59*, 187–204.

O'Toole, J., Lawler, E. E., III, & Meisinger, S. R. (2007). *The new American workplace.* New York, NY: Palgrave Macmillan.

Posthuma, R. A., Campion, M. C., Masimova, M., & Campion, M. A. (2013). A high performance work practices taxonomy: Integrating the literature and directing future research. *Journal of Management, 39*, 1184–1220. http://dx.doi.org/10.1177/0149206313478184

Probst, T. M., & Brubaker, T. L. (2001). The effects of job insecurity on employee safety outcomes: Cross-sectional and longitudinal explorations. *Journal of Occupational Health Psychology, 6*, 139–159. http://dx.doi.org/10.1037/1076-8998.6.2.139

Rabl, T., Jayasinghe, M., Gerhart, B., & Kühlmann, T. M. (2014). A meta-analysis of country differences in the high-performance work system-business performance relationship: The roles of national culture and managerial discretion. *Journal of Applied Psychology, 99*, 1011–1041. http://dx.doi.org/10.1037/a0037712

Ramsay, H., Scholarios, D., & Harley, B. (2000). Employees and high-performance work systems: Testing inside the black box. *British Journal of Industrial Relations, 38*, 501–531. http://dx.doi.org/10.1111/1467-8543.00178

Rosen, C., Case, J., & Staubus, M. (2005). Every employee an owner. Really. *Harvard Business Review, 83*, 122–130, 150.

Scholarios, D., Ramsay, D., & Harley, B. (2000). *'High commitment' management practices and employee outcomes: Evidence from Britain and Australia* (Working paper in human resource management, ER, and OS, Number 9). Melbourne, Australia: University of Melbourne.

Searle, R., Den Hartog, D. N., Weibel, A., Gillespie, N., Six, F., Hatzakis, T., & Skinner, D. (2011). Trust in the employer: The role of high-involvement work practices and procedural justice in European organizations. *The International Journal of Human Resource Management, 22*, 1069–1092. http://dx.doi.org/10.1080/09585192.2011.556782

Spreitzer, G. M., Sutcliffe, K. M., Dutton, J. E., Sonenshein, S., & Grant, A. M. (2005). A socially-embedded model of thriving at work. *Organization Science, 16*, 537–549. http://dx.doi.org/10.1287/orsc.1050.0153

Steigenberger, N. (2013). Power shifts in organizations: The role of high-performance work systems. *The International Journal of Human Resource Management, 24*, 1165–1185. http://dx.doi.org/10.1080/09585192.2012.706817

Takeuchi, R., Chen, G., & Lepak, D. P. (2009). Through the looking glass of a social system: Cross-level effects of high-performance work systems of employees' attitudes. *Personnel Psychology, 62*, 1–29. http://dx.doi.org/10.1111/j.1744-6570.2008.01127.x

Tregaskis, O., Daniels, K., Glover, L., Butler, P., & Meyer, M. (2013). High performance work practices and firm performance: A longitudinal case study. *British Journal of Management, 24,* 225–244. http://dx.doi.org/10.1111/j.1467-8551.2011.00800.x

Tsui, A. S., Pearce, J. L., Porter, L. W., & Tripoli, A. M. (1997). Alternative approaches to the employee-organization relationship: Does investment in employees pay off? *Academy of Management Journal, 40,* 1089–1121. http://dx.doi.org/10.2307/256928

Vandenberg, R. J., Richardson, H. A., & Eastman, L. J. (1999). The impact of high involvement work processes on organizational effectiveness: A second-order latent variable approach. *Group & Organization Management, 24,* 300–339. http://dx.doi.org/10.1177/1059601199243004

Van der Meer, P., & Wielers, R. (2013). What makes workers happy? *Applied Economics, 45,* 357–368. http://dx.doi.org/10.1080/00036846.2011.602011

Van Wanrooy, B., Bewley, H., Bryson, A., Forth, J., Freeth, S., Stokes, L, & Wood, S. (2013). *The 2011 Workplace Employment Relations Study: First findings.* U.K. Department for Business Innovation & Skills. Retrieved from https://www.gov.uk/government/organisations/department-for-business-innovation-skills

White, M., Hill, S., McGovern, P., Mills, C., & Smeaton, D. (2003). 'High performance' management practices, working hours and work-life balance. *British Journal of Industrial Relations, 41,* 175–195.

Wood, S., & de Menezes, L. (1998). High commitment management in the UK: Evidence from the Workplace Industrial Relations Survey, and Employers' Manpower and Skills Practices Survey. *Human Relations, 51,* 485–515.

Wood, S., & de Menezes, L. (2011). High-involvement management, high performance work systems and well-being. *International Journal of Human Resource Management, 22,* 1586–1610.

Wood, S. J., & Wall, T. D. (2007). Work enrichment and employee voice in human resource management-performance studies. *International Journal of Human Resource Management, 18,* 1335–1372.

Wright, P. M., Gardner, T. M., Moynihan, L. M., & Allen, M. R. (2005). The relationship between HR practices and firm performance: Examining the causal order. *Personnel Psychology, 58,* 409–446.

Yanadori, Y., & van Jaarsveld, D. D. (2014). The relationships of informal high performance work practices to job satisfaction and workplace profitability. *Industrial Relations: A Journal of Economy and Society, 53,* 501–534. http://dx.doi.org/10.1111/irel.12066

Youndt, M. A., & Snell, S. A. (2004). Human resource configurations, intellectual capital, and organizational performance. *Journal of Managerial Issues, 16,* 337–360.

Youndt, M. A., Snell, S. A., Dean, J. W., Jr., & Lepak, D. P. (1996). Human resource management, manufacturing strategy, and firm performance. *Academy of Management Journal, 39,* 836–866. http://dx.doi.org/10.2307/256714

Zacharatos, A., Barling, J., & Iverson, R. (2005). High performance work systems and occupational safety. *Journal of Applied Psychology, 90,* 77–93.

2

EMPLOYEE INVOLVEMENT: PRACTITIONER PERSPECTIVES

STEVE GRAVENKEMPER

Organizations are increasingly interested in implementing employee involvement (EI) initiatives that link directly to their key business objectives. This chapter supplements the literature review from Chapter 1 with practical examples from organizations that embrace EI as a way to build healthy organizational cultures that drive desired business results. I highlight key themes that cut across these organizations and identify several barriers that block or limit success. Using examples drawn from interviews with organizational leaders, I provide insight into the manner in which their organizations leverage EI initiatives to achieve desired organizational outcomes. Such initiatives have been used to influence organizational goals such as innovation, talent development, and return-on-investment. These practical examples provide tips and tools for other organizations that could benefit from increased EI.

http://dx.doi.org/10.1037/14731-003
The Psychologically Healthy Workplace: Building a Win–Win Environment for Organizations and Employees,
M. J. Grawitch and D. W. Ballard (Editors)

This chapter takes a broad-based look at EI from a practitioner's perspective. Rather than limiting my exploration to EI as a defined set of human resources and management practice initiatives, I explore the many ways in which EI initiatives and participative management approaches can benefit organizations in a wide range of industries and situations. Hence this chapter covers such issues as key factors supporting EI, barriers to EI, communication considerations, change management challenges, and employee engagement (which has gained attention in organizations and in research circles). The chapter presents examples of companies from a variety of industries that use a wide range of initiatives and approaches that increase EI. An underlying premise is that increasing EI improves employee well-being and organizational functioning, provided that such initiatives are aligned with an organization's senior leadership practices, organizational culture, mission, vision, and values. I conclude with some suggestions for increasing EI and engagement in the workplace. In addition, I explore workplace practices of best-in-class organizations that embrace EI and participation.

KEY FACTORS THAT FACILITATE EMPLOYEE INVOLVEMENT

This section explores key factors that facilitate EI in the workplace. These factors are based on common themes identified by organizational leaders as well as my observations from my consulting experience. These factors are viewed as important elements that are positively aligned with the nature of EI initiatives and participative decision making.

Senior Leadership and the Organizational Culture Support Employee Involvement

Perhaps the most important factor that facilitates EI is the degree to which the organization's leadership philosophy and culture are aligned with the underlying principles that serve as a foundation for EI. Lawler (1986) asserted that "high involvement management starts with beliefs about people that support their being involved.... A high involvement organization's core values and principles must be congruent with the idea of EI and responsibility for decision making" (p. 192). Lawler (1986; see Exhibit 2.1) also outlined core assumptions that even today serve as good rules of thumb in assessing the congruence of EI initiatives with organizational culture and leadership.

"People are our most important asset" is the type of phrase that senior leaders will verbalize if their organizational culture embraces EI activities. The litmus test for leaders comes in supporting this phrase via behaviors and decisions. Those leaders and organizations that are best suited for involvement

EXHIBIT 2.1
Core Values and Principles Congruent With Employee Involvement

Human Relations
- People should be treated fairly and with respect.
- People want to participate.
- When people participate, they accept change.
- When people participate, they are more satisfied and committed to the organization.

Human Resources
- People are a valuable resource because they have ideas and knowledge.
- When people have input in decisions, better solutions are developed.
- Organizations should make a long-term commitment to the development of people because it makes them more valuable to the organization.

High Involvement
- People can be trusted to make important decisions about their work activities.
- People can develop the knowledge to make important decisions about the management of their work activities.
- When people make decisions about the management of their work, the result is greater organizational effectiveness.

Note. From *High-Involvement Management* (pp. 192–193), by E. E. Lawler III, 1986, San Francisco, CA: Jossey Bass. Copyright 1986 by John Wiley & Sons. Reprinted with permission.

practices are those whose philosophy and approach are congruent with the statements in Exhibit 2.1. "Walking the talk" becomes the critical differentiator between organizations that embrace the activities versus those that simply go through the motions.

Organizations that embrace EI demonstrate confidence in employee problem solving. They encourage calculated risk taking with the belief that professional growth accelerates if employees are provided with opportunities to experiment with new approaches in addressing organizational challenges. Senior leaders are willing to take some risk because they see leadership development as an important outcome of such programs. Gordon Krater, the managing partner of Plante Moran, emphasized that it is "important to let them make a difference" (G. Krater, personal communication, 2009). He added that "brilliance comes when they try something different." Bob Riney, executive vice president and chief operating officer of Henry Ford Health System, related that senior leaders encourage innovation and continuous learning as key components of employee development (B. Riney, personal communication, 2009). From this perspective, when employees are passionate about trying new approaches, they will either succeed or learn, which in turn contributes to their development. Jill Morin, former executive officer for Kahler Slater, cited a strong business case supporting EI within the organizational culture: "The more diverse the group, the more creative and innovative the design will be" (J. Morin, personal communication, 2009). Dick Heath, former headmaster of Sandia Preparatory School in Albuquerque, described the importance of patience and being willing to "stand by and let people try some things" (D. Heath, personal communication, 2009).

Chris Paterson is the CEO of Sunshine State Health Plan, a Florida organization that provides health plans to governmental clients. Shortly after being named the CEO, Paterson had the couches removed from his office and brought in a table that quickly became a daily gathering place for the management team and other employees. One wall is a whiteboard, which serves to stimulate dialogue. He is pleased that the table has created an environment that is conducive to discussion and problem solving. According to Paterson, his team spends a large percentage of the day seated at the table working both independently and collaboratively. Depending on the issues addressed, other employees will join the discussion at the table. He did acknowledge one drawback, however: "When I have to take a private phone call, I have to leave my office" (C. Paterson, personal communication, 2012).

A Clear Vision for How Involvement Relates to the Achievement of Key Organizational Objectives

John Kotter (1996) advocated for the importance of establishing a clear and compelling vision to provide a launching pad for organizational change efforts. Similarly, EI initiatives are most successful when organizational objectives are translated into specific requests and suggestions related to how individuals can support the achievement of organizational goals in their specific role within the organization. Organizational objectives may span a diverse set of issues: improving quality, safety, and productivity in manufacturing organizations; enhancing patient care and satisfaction in health-care settings; or surpassing client expectations in professional service firms, among others. Dr. Herman Gray from the Children's Hospital of Michigan outlined a vision in which each hospital employee would make a positive difference regarding customer service improvement and embedded this message in the core mission, vision, and values of the organization (H. Gray, personal communication, 2009). Jill Morin of Kahler Slater discussed the importance of tapping into the passions of employees. Connecting with individual passions was instrumental to achieving the organization's goal of transforming Kahler Slater from an architecture firm that constructs buildings to an interdisciplinary design firm that creates experiences aligned with client vision (J. Morin, personal communication, 2009). Gerard van Grinsven, former president and CEO of the Henry Ford West Bloomfield Hospital, emphasized the importance of creating "memorable experiences" for hospital guests so that positive interactions and experiences become associated with their stay at the hospital (G. van Grinsven, personal communication, 2009).

Defining Employee Involvement Initiatives at the Front End

Identifying specific "real work" problems to address provides an important sense of purpose. Ground rules for participation are helpful in enabling work teams in the launch stage, especially for employees who may be participating for the first time in such initiatives. These ground rules include listing parameters such as the time commitment required, degree of autonomy provided to the work group, training that may be needed (e.g., process improvement or problem-solving tools), and how the work output will be evaluated or used. One key decision is whether time for participation in such initiatives will be provided as part of the normal work day. In addition, it becomes important to initially define the scope of the task at hand with the understanding that the project may expand or narrow as it evolves. Regardless of whether the issue to be addressed was proposed by management or employees, providing a clear definition of the problem is helpful in guiding the work of the team.

Examples of projects that might become the focus of EI initiatives can be found throughout contemporary organizations. A cross-disciplinary health-care team may be assigned the task of reducing emergency room waiting times by 20 minutes. A manufacturing team may be assigned the task of reducing defects by 95% on a problematic automotive part. A hotel property may ask a group of employees to provide suggestions for improving guest satisfaction by 30%. A cross-functional customer service team might be tasked with creating specific action plans to raise the level of employee engagement by 20% during the next six months. A credit union might assign an employee team to explore the results of its employee survey and provide specific suggestions for how to best address key themes identified in the results.

Training in Specific Problem-Solving Methodologies

Many organizations provide training to help employees tackle the projects they are assigned. While specific methodologies vary, EI-related training focuses on some common elements. First, these problem-solving approaches identify specific problems to address and create a shared language and approach to improve communication and standardize processes across the organization. Second, teams typically participate in idea generation or brainstorming activities that can be used to identify both the cause of problems and various approaches for tackling them. Third, suggestions that seem to have the most promise are prioritized. Fourth, deciding on a course of action leads to implementation. Fifth, a period of observation allows evaluation of how effective the suggestions or action plans have been. This final step may lead to a second round of problem-solving activities. Though the specific techniques may vary, these common elements provide a structure that employs a collaborative problem-solving approach to addressing organizational challenges.

Examples of these approaches are listed in the remainder of this chapter. Many forms of creative problem-solving methodologies can be applied to organizational problem solving (deBono, 1999; Higgins, 2006). Kaizen and quality circles have often been used to address challenges in manufacturing and other industries. *Kaizen* is a philosophy of continuous improvement and can employ a variety of lean management tools to address objectives such as increasing productivity, performance, and quality. Kaizen events engage multiple participants in an organization and focus on highlighting problems while simultaneously training and empowering participants to solve them. Quality circles typically engage small work groups of six to 12 participants to address problems within each group's areas of responsibilities. Both kaizen and quality circles provide training by facilitators skilled in these participatory processes. Root cause analysis is often employed in the aerospace and nuclear power industries to address and prevent reoccurrences of human, process, and equipment errors. Honda of America, Mfg., trains teams in its Now, New, and Next Honda approach, which is a proprietary multistep problem-solving process applied to problems across the globe. Kahler Slater used a proprietary iterative design problem-solving methodology to shift its focus from buildings to customer experiences and solutions. Action learning teams add a reflection and facilitator questioning component that can accelerate team learning (Marquardt, 1999). Each approach solicits employee participation in an effort to better understand and solve problems.

Provision of the Resources Needed to Successfully Complete Initiatives

Positioning EI initiatives for success includes providing the resources required to complete assignments and projects. Examples of relevant resources include people, time, training, and tools. Honda of America, Mfg., puts the associate who provides a suggestion at the center of problem-solving and implementation efforts. If associates working in manufacturing provide a suggestion that is accepted, they receive engineering support if such support can be helpful in addressing technical aspects of the solution. In this way, associates remain active participants in all phases of implementation. This creates a stronger sense of ownership and empowerment.

Feedback Is Provided, and Decisions Are Made

For organizations embracing EI initiatives, providing feedback to the team becomes a key component of success. Timely and specific feedback is especially important in maintaining momentum as well as increasing motivation, as employees feel they are making a significant contribution to the organization. Both positive and constructive criticism become important in accelerating employee learning and in making important course corrections in a timely manner. Timely feedback and decision making increase the feeling by employees that their efforts are worthwhile, subsequently increasing the likelihood that they or others will eagerly engage in future EI initiatives.

Successes and Victories Are Celebrated

It is important to celebrate victories that emerge from EI initiatives. Catching people "doing things right" accelerates momentum in the organization. These celebrations serve as prime motivators and rewards. They also convey the high value that the organization places on employee participation. This message enhances the perception that employees can make a significant difference in organizations.

KEY FACTORS THAT INHIBIT EMPLOYEE INVOLVEMENT

Several factors contribute to the failure of EI initiatives or, at a minimum, lead to less-than-desirable outcomes. Frequently, these factors serve as demotivators that can decrease organizational effectiveness. Consequently, I encourage leaders and organizations to consider what their objectives are and whether EI initiatives are valued and viewed as helpful in addressing key organizational challenges. I would discourage using EI initiatives in situations in which organizations have already made decisions and where senior leaders are not genuinely open to considering suggestions offered by employees.

Lack of Alignment With Organizational Culture and Senior Leadership Philosophy and Actions

For some organizational cultures and senior management teams, EI is a poor fit. Examples of these include organizations that are heavily top-down in both their culture and their leadership approach and those with a strong command-and-control structure. Grawitch, Gottschalk, and Munz (2006) warned that "employee problem solving teams (an employee involvement activity) cannot be successfully implemented in an organization if the leadership of that organization has cultivated a culture in which employee suggestions are ignored" (p. 145). In these situations, I suggest that the safest option is to not rock the boat. Individuals who knowingly self-select into very top-down organizations may be comfortable and satisfied in following this chain of command and knowing that highly specific rules and regulations guide decision making and behavior.

On the other hand, some organizational cultures discourage experimentation and innovation. In these organizations, it is not safe to fail. It is thus safest to follow the status quo or build incrementally on processes and procedures that have been proven to be successful. For example, in some organizations, specific departments (e.g., research and development) may have the freedom and autonomy to pursue new ideas, whereas other departments do not have the same charge or sponsorship.

I suggest that organizations whose culture and leadership teams are not aligned with EI initiatives be true to who they are. Acknowledging that EI is not a core organizational value likely will save time and significant frustration within the organization. It also reduces the possibility of EI being relegated to the "flavor of the month" initiative. Organizations are better served by not going through the motions if it is predetermined that suggestions will be ignored and feedback will not be provided.

Several approaches may be beneficial in the event that an organization proceeds with EI initiatives in spite of misalignment. The first approach is to select the interventions that are least threatening to the organization. For example, an organization might implement an employee suggestion program focusing on issues that might be important to employees but that would be low threat to senior leadership. As another example, an organization might involve employees in providing input that can be used to establish a process for requesting time off.

Alternatively, organizations could explore the potential of EI by designing a pilot project in an area of high interest to the senior management team. This would give the organization an opportunity to test out the benefits of EI. Any action items could then be presented as suggestions for further exploration rather than recommendations requiring action. Sometimes, these types of pilot programs can be positioned outside of the formal chain of command (i.e., parallel teams). This approach is most appropriate as a "culture buster" initiative when a significant executive sponsor wants to take a fresh look at an important strategic initiative outside the bounds of the formal organizational structure. Such an initiative likely has a greater chance of success at a location that is remote or separate from core operations.

Searching for the Quick Fix or Magic Bullet

The leaders interviewed for this chapter would agree that creating a culture that embraces EI takes time and commitment. In some situations organizations are in search of the quick fix or magic bullet to solve a multitude of organizational problems. Frequently, leaders within the organization may have read about the benefits of EI activities in a business book or magazine or in the popular press. Consequently, though the concept of EI sounds appealing on the surface, leaders can become quickly disenchanted when they learn that comprehensive EI initiatives may take time to implement and require more of their personal time and support than they initially budgeted.

My suggestion is to set very modest expectations. Work toward establishing a phased-in approach that first emphasizes activities that are relatively easy to implement. In a best-case scenario, an organization can look toward building a pattern of successes that supports this approach. In a worst-case scenario, in which the organization has invested little, if any, resources and leadership is not prepared to stay the course, interest in the concept of EI can prove to be fleeting.

Fear or Lack of Trust

Lawler (1986) advised that EI initiatives are most likely to fail if employees worry that increased efficiencies will result in job loss. It is difficult for people to actively engage in these initiatives if they envision that their participation will have only negative consequences. Similarly, our experience in consulting suggests that EI initiatives are likely to fail if there is significant distrust between employees and the senior leadership team. This lack of trust may be founded in actual or perceived actions by senior management. Without a change in the leadership team or a demonstrated visible commitment on behalf of the organization to build trust, efforts here are likely to fail.

Apathy or Disengagement

Over time, apathy or active disengagement can become the norm within an organization. Though at one time employees, managers, and leaders may have been engaged and involved, that time may have long passed. Often there are visible signs illustrating a lack of EI. Two examples follow.

The Forklift Test

A plant manager once told me that his favorite method for assessing the amount of pride that employees had in their workplace was the "forklift test." He related that the exterior physical condition of the forklift was a measure of employees' pride and the care they took in the plants that he managed. He explained that if there are multiple dents and chipped paint on plant forklifts, then another dent or chip does not make much difference. At one plant that he inherited, he provided forklift drivers with the free paint of their choice to apply a fresh coat to their machines. This manager recalled the pride that each forklift driver had when he photographed them standing next to their forklifts. He noted that the drivers were much more careful with their forklifts once they personally applied the fresh coat of paint. I recalled this story much later when I walked into a plant and observed the forklifts. Numerous dents and scratches made it difficult to determine what the original paint color had been. As I completed my plant tour, I came to appreciate the value of the forklift test as an indicator of other problems.

"Who Cares?" Employee Survey

In another instance, I was consulting with an organization that was rolling out the annual employee survey. The response from employees was very subdued during this event. I learned from a participant later that day that the unofficial nickname for the employee survey was "Who Cares?" This employee explained that it was the third year for the survey and the employees felt that nothing had been done in the previous 2 years that demonstrated that the organization had taken action based on the survey results or that leaders had even heard what employees were saying.

Intervention efforts in these situations can be quite challenging. In this case, significant targeted effort over a sustained period is required to break through existing apathy. This process may be akin to the amount of fuel expended by a rocket lifting off and breaking through the gravitational pull of the earth versus the amount of energy required to remain on the guided course after breaking through. Similar to the forklift metaphor, often an accumulation of events and incidents contributes to the current state.

COMMUNICATION AND EI

Communication plays a central role in EI initiatives. Grawitch et al. (2006) emphasized the importance of communication in tying together the five types of psychologically healthy workplace practices outlined in their framework. Three types of communication are important in effective EI initiatives.

- *Top-down communication* informs, updates, clarifies, and translates the meaning of key messages to employees. Keeping employees in the information loop is a key component of such initiatives.
- *Bottom-up communication* identifies challenges or problems, provides suggestions, and creates buy-in from employees. This is especially helpful as employees often have the closest line of sight to the challenges being addressed.

- *Two-way dialogue* encourages exchange of information between different levels in the organization and across various functions. Such exchanges are helpful in generating increased buy-in, promoting a collaborative mind-set, and increasing transparency in communication.

Ideally, all three of these types of communication occur simultaneously. However, some may be more prominent at different stages of an EI initiative. Using all three forms of communication closes the communication gaps that can emerge, particularly when more complex problems are addressed.

This story illustrates potential communication breakdowns in a traditional top-down change initiative. Early in my career, I was asked to conduct a series of focus groups with employees at a large utility company to better understand why a new change initiative was not achieving desired results. The senior leader suspected that somehow a breakdown in the organization was adversely affecting implementation. In the groups, I asked three questions: Do you know that change is coming? Do you know what the change will be? And do you understand what *you* are expected to do differently to support this change?

In conveying the results to senior management, I included my observation of how informed each of the three hierarchical levels (i.e., senior leaders, middle managers, and frontline supervisors) felt. As seen in Figure 2.1, the largest breakdown occurred at the frontline supervisory level. Since that initial assignment, I have repeatedly observed this pattern in organizational change initiatives.

At Westminster Savings Credit Union, Barry Forbes challenges himself and others in the organization with a simple question: "Are you clear?" (B. Forbes, personal communication, 2009). The organization places emphasis on understanding the target audience for various communications, including anticipating and addressing questions as part of the creation of the messaging. Bob Riney of the Henry Ford Health System described the importance of creating context for messages. He emphasized the importance of spending time creating messages that have personal meaning for people and translating larger concepts into specific examples to which employees can relate. Henry Ford then uses employee advisory groups to test future organization messages and solicit feedback on their reception systemwide (R. Riney, personal communication, 2009). This pattern of translating messages into specific examples and then soliciting input related to how messages are being received provides an open feedback loop related to organizational communication and reduces the likelihood of communication breakdowns or gaps.

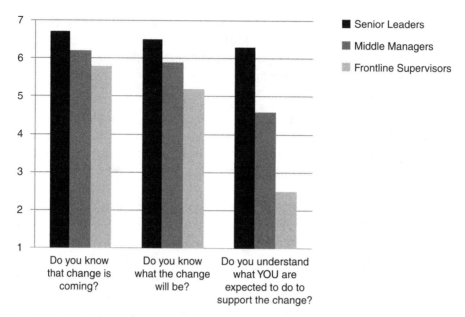

Figure 2.1. Communication breakdown. Scale: 7 = *strongly agree*; 6 = *agree*; 5 = *somewhat agree*; 4 = *neutral*; 3 = *somewhat disagree*; 2 = *disagree*; 1 = *strongly disagree.*

CHANGE AND EMPLOYEE INVOLVEMENT

By their nature, EI initiatives imply that change is coming. The change may result, for example, from suggestions for improving a manufacturing process, suggestions to increase inpatient satisfaction during hospitalizations, or suggestions on how to better explain the features and benefits of a new product or service. The change may result from senior leaders' request that a cross-functional team collaborate to tackle big issues facing the organization. A rapidly changing marketplace may require collaborative brainstorming efforts to effectively respond to these changes in a way that positions organizations to thrive in a constantly changing competitive environment.

Such initiatives have significant implications for the mind-set with which organizations address change. According to Lawler (1986),

> a crucial part of the change process should be the adoption of a learning stance. Organizations need to try things, see how they work, learn from this and improve them. It is unrealistic to expect to 'get it right' the first time. (p. 231)

EI initiatives can therefore be a helpful mechanism to assist organizations in adjusting, evolving, and succeeding in a changing environment.

One focus of this chapter is to provide practitioners with tools and models that have practical relevance for EI initiatives. John Kotter (1996) presented one well-known change model in his book, *Leading Change*. Another change model, presented by Elizabeth Gibson and Andrew Billings (2003), is based on a compelling multiyear change initiative at Best Buy, the electronics retailer. Though the following paragraphs provide a high-level description of these two models, readers are encouraged to explore the Kotter and the Gibson and Billings volumes for additional details.

Kotter's (1996) model proposed that effective leading of change efforts progresses through eight stages: (a) establishing a sense of urgency, (b) creating the guiding coalition, (c) developing a vision and a strategy, (d) communicating the change vision, (e) empowering broad-based action, (f) generating short-term wins, (g) consolidating gains and producing more change, and (h) anchoring new approaches in the culture.

Many of the stages proposed by Kotter (1996) can be easily adapted to EI initiatives. He described Phases 1 through 4 as "defrosting" activities that set the stage for change. Empowering broad-based action speaks directly to the spirit of EI initiatives. Ultimately, anchoring new approaches within the culture addresses the importance of alignment with that culture, which is an important element for long-term change.

At the risk of oversimplifying Gibson and Billings's (2003) work, I would like to pull out two key elements of the intervention that are relevant to EI initiatives. The first is a conceptual model embedded in learning theory that describes how people respond individually to change. Learning theory suggests that people process change on three levels: cognitive, motivational, and behavioral. Gibson and Billings translated this into more user-friendly language that focuses the attention of the organization on better understanding each area:

- Head: Are the changes and the rationale for them well understood? Have the things that must change been well communicated? Have people's mind-sets changed?
- Heart: How do people feel about the changes? What is their level of motivation regarding the changes, and are they adequately prepared for change?
- Hands: Are people using the new behaviors and practices? How well? What results are being obtained?

Gibson and Billings (2003) described this approach when working with Best Buy. Leveraging EI, the position of change implementation team (CIT) leader was created. CIT leaders were recruited directly from Best Buy retail stores. They were trained in change management methodology and asked to leverage their knowledge of Best Buy culture to successfully implement a new standard operating procedure for each store across the country. This change effort was put in place after the first attempt to implement the new standard operating procedure failed (Gibson & Billings, 2003). This approach using CIT leaders mirrored principles of action learning (Marquardt, 1999) as their new positions provided significant professional and personal growth while they tackled a key organizational strategic imperative. Change management interventions outlined by Gibson and Billings targeted each of the three levers (i.e., head, heart, hands) that have a significant impact on how individuals respond to change.

EMPLOYEE ENGAGEMENT: AN EMERGING CONSTRUCT

Employee engagement is an emerging construct that is heard frequently in consulting work. Although the concept is very popular among human resource consulting firms and an accelerating number of organizations, research has trailed that popularity. Schaufeli, Salanova, Gonzáles-Romá, and Bakker (2002) defined *employee engagement* as "a positive, fulfilling, work-related state of mind that is characterized by vigor, dedication and absorption" (p. 74). Macey and Schneider (2008) proposed three key components of engagement: trait (positive view of life and work), state (feelings of energy and absorption), and behavioral (extra-mile behavior). Macey and Schneider also suggested that much of the appeal of employee engagement to organizations has been the multiple efforts at linking this construct to organizational performance, including bottom-line results. They acknowledged that an increasing number of available survey instruments (both commercial and proprietary) focus on employee engagement. Tim Garrett, the former chief administrative officer of Honda of America, Mfg., added that "engagement adds a line of sight related to overarching organizational goals that EI does not" (T. Garrett, personal communication, 2009).

Gerard van Grinsven related that employee engagement was the number one outcome measure for him as president and CEO at the Henry Ford West Bloomfield Hospital. He challenged his team to create "memorable experiences" for hospital guests. He cited data that indicated high employee engagement scores were linked to lower employee turnover, higher patient satisfaction survey results, and lower patient readmissions (G. van Grinsven, personal communication, 2009).

The focus on employee engagement will likely increase in research related to employee well-being and organizational performance. Therefore, it is important to make brief mention of this construct from a practitioner's perspective. Gravenkemper (2007) described six principles of engagement that blend well with EI initiatives and are consistent with some of the key themes outlined by various change management models: communicate a compelling message, build a guiding coalition, create principle-based versus compliance-based guidelines for decisions and behaviors, identify early engagement indicators, generate continuous opportunities for dialogue at all levels, and plan assimilation strategies for new members and new leaders.

Creating principle-based versus compliance-based guidelines for decisions and behaviors is consistent with the underlying assumption that employees are highly capable of making decisions that are consistent with core cultural values. Stubblefield (2005) echoed this sentiment:

> I don't believe in micromanaging employees. When people have a shared sense of mission, vision and values, they can effectively work toward common goals and manage themselves and their responsibilities. In effect, this is the true test of culture: Will people live the values and vision even when no one is there to enforce them? Will they voluntarily exhibit behavior consistent with cultural standards? In our case, will they care about the customer or patient, even when they are off duty (and not being paid to care)? (p. 19)

Generating continuous opportunities for dialogue at all levels aligns with the importance of two-way communication that supports EI initiatives. "You cannot have an execution culture without robust dialogue—one that brings reality to the surface through openness, candor and informality" (Bossidy & Charan, 2002, p. 102). Such a point of view would be consistent with Collins's (2001) research that found that great organizations learn to "confront the brutal facts" (p. 65). Creating dialogue effectively leverages the information provided by employees who are located closest to the shop floor, customer, and end user. This additional information can be helpful in problem identification and problem solving.

EMPLOYEE INVOLVEMENT: PRACTICAL CONSIDERATIONS

Any organization considering EI initiatives must take some practical steps. First, create a shared understanding regarding why the organization is interested in increasing EI. Is there a strong business case for this type of measure? Is the organization looking to better align EI with the organization's mission, vision, and values? Is the organization looking for alternative perspectives on a specific challenge?

Next, recognize that EI initiatives cover a broad spectrum of activities (e.g., setting up an employee suggestions box versus establishing a high-involvement work-team program). Organizations should select those activities that make the most sense at the present time, given the issues the intervention will be designed to address and the culture within which the activities will be implemented.

Finally, EI initiatives adopt an exploratory and learning mind-set. Many solutions and suggestions may best follow a continuous improvement model. Rarely are suggestions perfect the first time out of the box; many may require tweaking or modification. Capturing lessons learned along the way, helping team members internalize this learning, and transporting the knowledge throughout the organization can accelerate the improvement process and enhance outcomes for employees and the organization alike.

INNOVATION, TALENT DEVELOPMENT, AND RETURN-ON-INVESTMENT

Three areas in which EI initiatives are increasingly used by organizations are talent development, innovation, and return-on-investment.

Talent Development

Working together in teams provides employees the opportunity to develop important leadership skills such as influencing, collaboration, consensus building, critical thinking, and problem solving. Examples in this chapter included Everyday Excellence at Children's Hospital of Michigan, Henry Ford Health System's employee advisory groups, and Plante Moran's Participation Committee. Each of these teams enables staff members throughout these organizations to both contribute in a meaningful way to the organization and develop important leadership skills. Chris Paterson of Sunshine Health also noted the importance of selection for organizations embracing EI initiatives: "You have to hire people who believe more gets accomplished by working together rather than working apart" (C. Paterson, personal communication, 2009).

Innovation

Organizations are increasingly seeing the value of diverse perspectives in developing new products, services, and process improvements. Soliciting ideas from employees who are closest to the customer, products, services, and processes is often an excellent mechanism that contributes to both incremental and breakthrough innovations. Kahler Slater's Fun @ 4 program, Sandia Prep's students' performance dance team, and Honda of America's Now, New, and Next Honda and Voluntary Involvement Program (VIP) initiatives provide practical evidence of the benefit of this approach.

Return-on-Investment

The Denison Culture Survey (see Denison et al., 2012) has been collecting data that demonstrate a positive correlation between healthy organizational cultures and important organizational outcome measures for more than 20 years. Involvement, which includes subscales on empowerment, team orientation, and capability development, is one of the four basic traits defining culture. Anecdotal evidence—such as Westminster Savings Credit Union customers saying that they drive past other financial institutions to patronize Westminster—provides supporting evidence that EI also contributes to positive financial results.

CASE EXAMPLES

Honda of America, Mfg.

Tim Garrett, former chief administrative officer of Honda of America, Mfg., described an early challenge he faced involved convincing associates that the company was genuinely interested in encouraging EI. He recalled meeting with new associates and explaining that they had two jobs: (a) "Whatever you do, do it to the best of your ability" (Today's Job) and (b) "constantly look for opportunities to make us a better, stronger and competitive company" (Tomorrow's Job). Garrett related that Honda of America wanted their best efforts—but also their minds in offering suggestions that they felt might improve the company. In essence, the organization was looking to create associates who were proactive and active participants in helping Honda of America become a better, stronger, and more competitive company by improving quality, safety, and productivity (T. Garrett, personal communication, 2009).

Key to Honda's success in these efforts was the creation of the VIP initiative for associates. From the beginning, associate participation in this program was voluntary, not mandatory. Among the important aspects of the VIP initiative was the use of associate suggestions. Those associates who offered up suggestions automatically became actively engaged in implementing the suggestion. For example, if associates on the production line suggested an idea that might improve quality or efficiency, they would then be provided with the resources required to see the suggestion through from start to finish. Such resources might include technical support from the engineering department or tools and equipment necessary to implement the suggestions. Associates were involved during every step of the process rather than the idea simply being shipped off for engineering to tackle independently.

Consequently, the program promoted a sense of ownership, achievement, and pride in the solution.

Another key element of the VIP initiative was the Now, New, and Next Honda process for tackling other identified challenges. In this proprietary, multistep problem-solving process, teams collaboratively addressed challenges they identified. It provided a structured problem-solving approach to address identified challenges, encouraged a collaborative problem-solving process that increased EI, and could be helpful in solving future challenges. Teams would then present their work to senior Honda executives and fellow associates at all levels. Teams highly valued the opportunity and recognition associated with presenting the work completed by their teams.

Kahler Slater

Jill Morin, former executive officer of Kahler Slater in Milwaukee, Wisconsin, described how the firm transformed itself into an interdisciplinary design firm in the mid-1900s. Key to this transformation was the emphasis on designing experiences consistent with the client's vision. A critical factor in hiring for Kahler Slater was that clients valued the expertise and passion of the staff. In the process of reorganizing the firm, the executive team asked each member of the organization, "What are you passionate about?" This question opened the door for new ideas and suggestions from staff members (J. Morin, personal communication, 2009).

The iterative process of creating a new strategic plan for Kahler Slater mirrored the iterative process of design. Teams were provided autonomy in developing their business plans. Morin's belief was that "those people who own the idea are better able and willing to execute on this. To own it, you have to create it." Another key driver of this approach was the belief that "the more diverse the group, the more creative and innovative the design would be" (J. Morin, personal communication, 2009). Kahler Slater teams are now involved in creating their annual business plans. Staff members are also encouraged to create plans for implementing new ideas that they have. John Horky, who carries the title of "The HR Guy," related that one of the consistently highest-rated categories for the firm on the Best Places to Work Survey is in providing staff members the autonomy and resources to achieve their objectives (J. Horky, personal communication, 2009). To help staff members feel involved in their work, Kahler Slater ensures that all members of the team who will have significant roles on a project attend initial team meetings.

One specific suggestion from staff members was to formalize a process for generating activities or programs that increased the creativity of the firm and the staff. Fun @ 4 is another initiative, in which staff members walk around the office spontaneously asking other staff about the projects they are working on. Individuals are encouraged to present projects so that they can receive input or engage in brainstorming with coworkers. Lunchtime learning sessions were then also initiated to increase creativity. And last, staff members would watch movies together to spur creativity.

Children's Hospital of Michigan

Founded in 1886, the Children's Hospital of Michigan received the designation of 2009–2010 Best Children's Hospitals from *US News & World Report* and 25 Best Children's Hospitals from *Parents* magazine. Upon being named president in 2005, Dr. Herman Gray recognized the need to create a clear vision for the organization. This vision centered on becoming the best children's hospital in the country. At a town hall meeting of 300 to 350 employees, he emphasized the theme of customer service to patients, families, and visitors to the hospital that was grounded in the mission, vision, and values of the organization. He outlined what employees could expect from him as well as his expectations for employees. He visited the environmental services team with the message that every employee is important to achieving the vision. Gray emphasized the continued message that each staff member either directly impacted patient care or enabled others to provide good patient care. He concluded meetings with hospital staff with "Go out and make a difference!" (H. Gray, personal communication, 2009).

Everyday Excellence was created as a cross-functional team of hospital managers and staff. The focus of this team was to develop strategies, tools, and suggestions to ensure hospital employees focused on the theme of delivering outstanding care every day. Gray publicly celebrated victories by sharing positive letters that he received from patients and their families. He also publicly recognized outstanding staff members. Along with executive team members, Gray hosted "Monday meetings" with middle managers, in which he emphasized one key theme each week. These meetings were based on a huddle approach to summarize highlights and respond to any questions or suggestions that managers might have. Upon receiving a suggestion that these meetings should be more fun, Dr. Gray introduced music and dancing at these events as celebration and team-building tools.

Frontline hospital employees created the behavioral standards that now guide the behavior of all hospital employees. The ambulatory staff created a customer program that solicits input from outpatients. The emergency room staff is currently working to reduce time in the waiting room. There has been a significant increase in patient ratings of hospital care in the past 4 years.

Plante Moran

Plante Moran is an accounting and business advisory firm headquartered in Southfield, Michigan. For 16 consecutive years, Plante Moran has been named by *Fortune* magazine as one of the 100 Best Companies to Work For. Gordon Krater, managing partner of Plante Moran, attributes much of the firm's success to the strong organizational culture that has been created. He described the phrase "We care" as a core guiding principle that influences firm decision making and how staff members treat one another and their clients. He described people as the firm's most important asset and emphasized the importance of enabling staff members to feel that they make a difference (G. Krater, personal communication, 2009).

During the past year, Krater conducted approximately 30 group meetings with associates in each of the Plante Moran offices. The meetings were designed to help management address associates' concerns and to solicit suggestions for improving the firm. This resulted in a wide-ranging dialogue around financial information, pay, current topics, and future firm directions. This process helped reinforce the message that associates "are part of the solution" with regard to future opportunities and challenges. These meetings helped Krater take the pulse of the firm and understand what was most important to staff members while soliciting staff member suggestions to improve the firm.

Plante Moran's annual firm conference, which brings together the entire staffs from each office, received high marks across the board from staff members. It provides senior leadership with a forum to celebrate the firm's culture, communicate key messages, and provide important information and updates. Many staff members described the conference as a re-recruiting tool. Others said this is a day when they feel the full power of the organization's culture on display. Speeches by new partners on this day serve as inspiration to others who aspire to become partners in the firm. The conference enables staff members to reestablish and build new relationships with individuals from other offices.

Chris McCoy, the partner who leads the human resources department, described the importance of consensus in Plante Moran's decision making. Though decisions may take longer, dialogue increases buy-in among key stakeholders. Unlike other professional services firms in which partner compensation is decided by senior management, the firm uses an independent committee of nonmanaging partners to make decisions on partner pay. The idea is to create greater transparency and fairness and to increase the collaborative decision-making skills of the committee members (C. McCoy, personal communication, 2009).

McCoy described the Personal Tightrope Action committee, which focuses on work–life balance issues within the firm, as one example of EI. The committee established Saturday day care during the accounting busy season to relieve some of the burden on parents during this busy period. This program provides structured daycare activities and entertainment and provides lunch for children (C. McCoy, personal communication, 2009).

Sandia Preparatory

Sandia Preparatory School is an independent coeducational school in Albuquerque, New Mexico, with a college program for Grades 6 through 12 on one campus. Sandia Prep received a 2009 Psychologically Healthy Workplace Award from the American Psychological Association.

Dick Heath (headmaster at Sandia Prep for 25 years) said that "collaboration is better than competition," and this key piece of their culture drove decision making and activities. A second key idea was that "things that bubble up from the bottom are better than things handed down from the top." The culture provides the autonomy for students to "be themselves," and prepares graduates to be well-rounded citizens (D. Heath, personal communication, 2009).

After much deliberation, the Sandia Prep faculty decided to scrap the traditional schedule in favor of a rotating schedule in which classes would be offered at different times each day. This enabled students to match their peak learning times of the day with their classes as well as was more accommodating to those students who might have to miss some class time because of extracurricular activities.

The school provides money to fund special projects in the technology support group. Other faculty members can present their ideas to this group. Headmaster Heath explained, "We wanted to fund the pioneers." These projects are then shared among the faculty so that others will also benefit.

Headmaster Heath emphasized the importance of being able to "stand by and let people try some things." Students and faculty are consistently encouraged to provide suggestions to improve the school. Sandia's dance team was one idea that came from students. This competitive dance team now performs at multiple school functions each year. Headmaster Heath commented that although "it's easier to think about why you can't do something," he works toward emphasizing how things can be done.

Westminster Savings Credit Union

Westminster Savings Credit Union was the recipient of the 2009 Psychologically Healthy Workplace Award from the American Psychological Association in the medium-sized not-for-profit category. President and CEO Barry Forbes emphasized that EI and participation are key components of the organization's culture. The organization is careful to keep employees informed about how the business is doing and to explain why decisions are made. Forbes also asks for employees' opinions on the process of information sharing itself (B. Forbes, personal communication, 2009).

The employee opinion survey was revamped in a comprehensive effort to improve the organization. Employees helped develop the survey and assisted with its rollout. They had key roles in both analyzing the results and developing subsequent action plans. Communications are sent out during the year to update employees on the status of action plans and progress that has been made. "We made [the survey] theirs," said Forbes.

As committees are formed, employees are provided the opportunity to serve on those in which they have the greatest interest. The intent is to provide all employees with opportunities to make additional contributions to the organization. Forbes estimated that approximately 70% of the employees at Westminster Savings Credit Union are actively involved in various employees committees, including community involvement, corporate citizenship, and technology.

In a recent credit union national survey, Westminster Savings Credit Union was rated best-in-class when compared with peers across Canada. He attributed this honor to employees' embracing the organization's three core values: service, quality, and caring. Customer and member focus groups suggest that the organizational culture is good for business. Customers often describe service as a key differentiator, relating that they "are treated as people, not numbers." Several customers noted on the survey that they drive past several other financial institutions to do business with Westminster.

Henry Ford Health System

The Henry Ford Health System in Southeast Michigan was awarded the Malcolm Baldrige National Quality Award in 2011. Bob Riney, executive vice president and chief operating officer, said that EI and participation helps "refuel" staff members whose daily responsibilities can leave them psychologically and physically exhausted. Riney added that employee participation is crucial, as there are "few other industries where employees have to deal with customers at their most vulnerable place in life" (R. Riney, personal communication, 2009).

Management is careful to establish two-way dialogue with employees, creating transparency and informing employees of key initiatives. The organization keeps employees informed about what is happening in the hospital through tools that include podcasts, employee newsletters, and rounds conducted locally by leadership at each of the Henry Ford facilities. A communication council staffed by employees provides feedback on messages directed to the organization. This emphasis on transparency is based on trust in "employees' abilities to put things in context."

Employee advisory groups representing a cross-section of positions and levels are appointed to facilitate a two-way dialogue between leaders and employees. These meetings are helpful in allowing leaders to respond directly to concerns while also helping to increase employees' awareness of economic issues impacting the health care system. They also provide a vehicle to explore how new hospital initiatives, communications, and programs are being received by employees.

Henry Ford Health System employees organize community service activities as part of what Riney calls a "culture of giving." He described participation in the American Heart Walk as a particular source of pride among employees. Henry Ford has consistently placed in the top three in the country for funds raised by this event.

Ritz Carlton: Dearborn

When Gerard van Grinsven took the top leadership role at the Ritz Carlton in Dearborn, Michigan, he embraced the challenge of restoring the glory of a property that had a shining past. At the time van Grinsven stepped in, the property ranked at the bottom of employee satisfaction surveys and in the bottom half of customer satisfaction ratings when compared with Ritz Carlton properties around the world. In tackling this challenge, van Grinsven initiated Re-Born, a 1-week training program in which former Dearborn Ritz Carlton employees who had developed successful careers within the chain recounted stories of better and prouder times at the property and offered encouragement to the current team. Van Grinsven's goal was to actively engage employees in the turnaround process, saying that "if I focus on employees, they'll take care of the customers" (van Grinsven, personal communication, 2009).

Soon afterward, the Dearborn Ritz Carlton opened a service excellence program, for which the CEO of Ritz Carlton established a "pride and joy" campaign, with the goal of making Dearborn the best Ritz Carlton facility in the system. He frequently went on walkabouts where he would greet and engage in individual conversations with employees. Even early in the process, he noticed employees standing straighter and greeting each other more frequently. During the first year, the Grille Restaurant at the Dearborn Ritz Carlton received the Restaurant of the Year rating in Metro Detroit. Many of the programs have been replicated by other Ritz Carlton properties. In just over a year, the Dearborn Ritz Carlton's employee satisfaction ranking improved from 50th in the Ritz Carlton system to fifth, and guest satisfaction ratings improved from 31st to ninth in the system.

REFERENCES

Bossidy, L., & Charan, R. (2002). *Execution: The discipline of getting things done.* New York, NY: Crown Business.

Collins, J. (2001). *Good to great.* New York, NY: Harper-Collins.

deBono, E. (1999). *Six thinking hats.* New York, NY: Back Bay Books/Little, Brown and Company.

Denison, D., Hooijberg, R., Lane, N., & Lief, C. (2012). *Leading culture change in global organizations: Aligning culture and strategy.* San Francisco, CA: Jossey-Bass.

Gibson, E., & Billings, A. (2003). *Big change at Best Buy: Working through hypergrowth to sustained excellence.* Palo Alto, CA: Davies-Black.

Gravenkemper, S. (2007). Building community in organizations: Principles of engagement. *Consulting Psychology Journal: Practice and Research, 59,* 203–208. http://dx.doi.org/10.1037/1065-9293.59.3.203

Grawitch, M. J., Gottschalk, M., & Munz, D. C. (2006). The path to a healthy workplace: A critical review linking healthy workplace practices, employee well-being, and organizational improvements. *Consulting Psychology Journal: Practice and Research, 58,* 129–147. http://dx.doi.org/10.1037/1065-9293.58.3.129

Higgins, J. M. (2006). *101 creative problem solving techniques: The handbook of new ideas for business.* Winter Park, FL: New Management.

Kotter, J. (1996). *Leading change.* Boston, MA: Harvard Business School Press.

Lawler, E. E., III. (1986). *High-involvement management.* San Francisco, CA: Jossey Bass.

Macey, W. H., & Schneider, B. (2008). The meaning of employee engagement. *Industrial and Organizational Psychology: Perspectives on Science and Practice, 1,* 3–30. http://dx.doi.org/10.1111/j.1754-9434.2007.0002.x

Marquardt, M. J. (1999). *Action learning in action: Transforming problems and people for world-class organizational learning.* Palo Alto, CA: Davies-Black.

Schaufeli, W. B., Salanova, M., Gonzáles-Romá, V., & Bakker, A. B. (2002). The measurement of engagement and burnout: A two sample confirmatory analytic approach. *Journal of Happiness Studies, 3,* 71–92. http://dx.doi.org/10.1023/A:1015630930326

Stubblefield, A. (2005). *The Baptist health care journey to excellence: Creating a culture of WOWs!* Hoboken, NJ: Wiley.

3

EMPLOYEE GROWTH AND DEVELOPMENT: CULTIVATING HUMAN CAPITAL

EDUARDO SALAS AND SALLIE J. WEAVER

We open this chapter with the example of a company that was once one of only two organizations to top *Fortune*'s Best Companies to Work For list for 2 consecutive years. This company reported more than $29 billion in revenue during 2010 and has achieved near market dominance since 2009 (Fortune, 2012). That is almost a five-fold increase in revenue over 2005 despite a nearly unprecedented bottoming out of the global economy. Employees of this organization are encouraged to work on projects in non-hierarchical teams, are expected to dedicate 1 full day per week to projects that inspire them, and have access to an employee education program that more closely mirrors a major university—offering opportunities to develop skills ranging from highly advanced technical skills to interpersonal skills,

This work was completed while Dr. Weaver was completing doctoral work at the University of Central Florida.

http://dx.doi.org/10.1037/14731-004
The Psychologically Healthy Workplace: Building a Win–Win Environment for Organizations and Employees,
M. J. Grawitch and D. W. Ballard (Editors)

even opportunities for personal growth (Boyce, 2009). For example, in a program of courses offered as part of the School for Personal Development, a department of the organization's employee development program, employees learn how to develop their emotional intelligence through the practice of nonjudgmental self-awareness, mindful listening and e-mailing, and meditation. Reactions to this course have been positive, with employees reporting that it has fostered creativity by enhancing their ability to remain relaxed and open to new ideas, and others describing the course as "life changing" (Boyce, 2009; Tan, 2012).

And, yes, we are talking about Google, the company chosen for more than 67% of U.S. Internet searches (comScore, 2014).

Direct and indirect personnel costs are often an organization's largest line item, accounting for 50% or more of operating costs (U.S. Bureau of Labor Statistics, 2009). In light of recent global economic events, human capital policies, management, and resources are under intense scrutiny. Under contracting economic conditions, as during the recent recession, personnel-related line items are traditionally viewed as costs to be managed and minimized. However, one commonality among high-performing organizations is their enculturation and dedication to the development of human capital—these organizations embrace employees as assets whose value can be increased via investment when growth and development opportunities align with the organizational mission, overarching values, goals, and strategies (U.S. Government Accountability Office, 2000). Shifts in the global labor pool have left employees who demonstrate a combination of technical, cultural, and interpersonal skills, as well as adaptability and flexibility, as a major organizational commodity (Manpower Inc., 2010). Labor shortages at all skill levels and large numbers of retirees exiting the labor pool simultaneously were identified as two of the top 10 trends in the U.S. workforce, prompting levels of investment in training and development per employee to rise 13.5% in 2010 and remain at just over $1,200 through 2013 despite generally gloomy economic indicators (American Society for Training and Development [ASTD], 2014; Society for Human Resource Management, 2013). In addition, a survey of executives working in organizations that foresee no additional layoffs in the near future found that 60% plan to increase programs dedicated to developing high-potential employees (Deloitte Consulting, LLC, 2010). This continued investment in employee training and development underscores that organizations recognize the role that continuous growth and development play in achieving a psychologically healthy workforce and the competitive advantage this offers in today's globalized economy.

Healthy organizations strive to simultaneously maximize employee "goals for well-being with company objectives for profitability and productivity" (Sauter, Lim, & Murphy, 1996, p. 250). Furthermore, these organizations see productivity and employee well-being not as separate yet parallel aims, but rather as deeply intertwined interdependent goals. For example, a survey of over 28,000 employees working in 15 different countries found that in companies that actively promoted employee health and well-being, employees were 8 times more likely to be highly engaged, 3 times more likely to view their organization as productive, and almost 4 times more likely to view their organization as encouraging creativity and innovation (Dornan & Jane-Llopis, 2010).

As detailed by Grawitch and Ballard in the introduction to this volume, *organizational health* is defined as a process of continual evolution, not a final end-state. Continuous learning, growth, and development are inherent in this notion of continual evolution. Opportunities to build, expand, and hone one's knowledge, skills, and attitudes (KSAs) introduce opportunities for change and challenge, with valued proximal and immediate outcomes for individual employees (e.g., advanced skill acquisition, stress reduction, promotion eligibility) and organizations (e.g., increased value of human capital, advanced skills necessary for competitive advantage in employees already assimilated into organizational culture). For example, Kaye and Jordan-Evans (2008) reported that opportunities for career growth, learning, and development, as well as opportunities for exciting and challenging work, were cited among the top five reasons employees stay with a particular company. Strategic approaches to developmental practices offer opportunities for employees to advance personally while simultaneously increasing productivity and generating greater overall organizational value.

This chapter summarizes the conceptual and empirical foundations for initiatives designed to facilitate a psychologically healthy workplace through employee growth and development. We begin by first defining key terms and concepts. Next, we review the theoretical underpinnings of growth and development initiatives as well as relevant empirical evidence drawn from the existing organizational psychology, occupational health, education and training, and communication literatures. On the basis of this review of existing evidence, we present a list of factors contributing to the effectiveness of growth and development initiatives is presented.

DEFINING GROWTH AND DEVELOPMENT

Employee growth and development have generally been conceptualized as relatively broad terms referring to learning processes, the outcomes of learning processes, or a somewhat muddled combination. Although the opportunities for development vary widely, they share several commonalities as summarized by D'Abate, Eddy, and Tannenbaum (2003) in their definition of *developmental interactions*—interactions between two or more people with the goal of personal or professional development, which can take a variety of forms and may occur as brief interactions or throughout a long-term relationship. The specific scope, purpose, and content of such initiatives can vary greatly (e.g., leadership development, teamwork development, innovation, decision making, stress management), but they share a common goal as opportunities for employees to expand their job-relevant KSAs and apply the competencies they have gained to new situations (Grawitch, Gottschalk, & Munz, 2006). Training, mentoring, coaching, opportunities for promotion and career advancement, and tuition reimbursement are all examples of opportunities for employees to gain new skills and enhance their experience. Table 3.1 lists several such opportunities and summarizes key findings from a recent ASTD (2009) report regarding their prevalence. Such initiatives have been theorized to function via one or more of several mechanisms: expanding an employee's knowledge, skill, affective, or physiological resource pool; expanding or optimizing an employee's coping strategies; and increasing employee motivation.

Empirically, access to training and other development opportunities has been linked with employee motivation, job satisfaction, and stress. For

TABLE 3.1
Average Percentage of Employees With Access to and Usage of
Different Learning Opportunities

Type of learning opportunity	Percent of employees with access	Percent of employee usage
Formal training activities (e.g., classes, workshops, online courses)	98.8	89
On-the-job learning	98.7	88
Job aids	92.6	79.5
Knowledge bases (e.g., searchable reference materials)	87.8	74.8
Mentoring and coaching	77.4	68.9
Knowledge sharing (e.g., communities of practice, on-call experts)	83.4	67.3
Employer-supported conference support	44.9	46.9
Financial support for membership in professional associations	43.9	44.7
Tuition reimbursement	82	13

Note. From *2009 State of the Industry Report*, by the American Society for Training and Development (ASTD), 2009. Copyright 2009 by ASTD. Adapted with permission.

example, Grawitch, Trares, and Kohler (2007) found that employees who were offered more opportunities for growth and development reported higher work–life balance satisfaction ($r = .65$), greater organizational commitment ($r = .57$), less emotional exhaustion ($r = -.50$), lower turnover intentions ($r = -.44$), and greater overall well-being ($r = .26$). These results can translate into positive gains for the organization by enhancing organizational effectiveness and improving work quality, as well as by helping the organization attract and retain top-quality employees.

GROWTH AND DEVELOPMENT INITIATIVES: THEORY AND RESEARCH

Each of the development categories represents deep and broad bodies of literature. In addition, development initiatives can occur across multiple levels of analysis including the individual (e.g., individual training, mentoring, coaching), team (e.g., team training), and organizational (e.g., strategies for linking learning opportunities to strategic organizational objectives) levels (Birdi, Patterson, & Wood, 2007). Therefore, it is beyond the scope of this chapter to attempt to provide a truly comprehensive review of each type of development opportunity. Our goal is to summarize critical theoretical underpinnings and results in order to extract key components of initiative effectiveness. Conceptualizing developmental interactions at all of these levels, however, begins with a foundation in theories of adult learning and instructional design. Therefore, we provide a brief overview of adult learning theory before describing specific categories of development activities. More comprehensive treatments of these theories and a myriad of others can be found in Aguinis and Kraiger (2009) and Winne and Nesbit (2010).

Developing Adult Learners

Knowles and colleagues' (Knowles, 1973; Knowles, Holton, & Swanson, 2005) foundational theory of adult learning recognized five significant factors impacting learning that differentiated adult learning styles from those of children. Knowles's theory asserted that adults are autonomous and self-directed, and that they come into the learning environment with a pre-existing reservoir of knowledge and experience. An adult's readiness to learn is related to the developmental tasks of his or her social roles, and an adult orientation to learning is problem focused versus subject focused. Finally, an adult motivation to learn is mainly internally driven. These assertions suggest several practical approaches to structuring adult growth and development experiences. First, adults want a sense of control over the learning process; thus, the role of trainers and teachers becomes that of learning facilitators who help learners connect new material to previous experience and focus on the relevancy and immediacy with which learners can apply targeted KSAs to their own goals. For example, Smith-Jentsch, Jentsch, Payne, and Salas (1996) found that pilots who had negative pretraining experiences (e.g., a near crash) related to training content (assertiveness) performed higher in a posttraining simulation session.

Similarly, Anderson's adaptive character of thought (ACT-R) theory conceptualizes human cognition as the interaction of declarative knowledge, represented as schema-like chunks of information, and procedural knowledge, represented by production rules (e.g., if–then statements; Anderson 1993, 1996). In contrast to learning theories that suggest that learning and growth appears in an aha moment of insight, ACT-R underscores that active diagnosis, practice, and feedback are critical components for mastery (Anderson & Schunn, 2000). Similarly, Mezirow (1981) framed adult learning as a process dedicated to transforming the learners' frames of references, including their mind-sets, associated meaning, and perspectives.

Specifically, Mezirow (2000) outlined four specific ways in which learning occurs: first, through the expansion of existing meaning (i.e., current mental models and schemas are further refined, differentiated, and elaborated); second, through the creation of new meanings that complement existing frames of reference (i.e., new schemas are created that complement but do not change existing frames of reference); next, through the transformation of point of view (i.e., upon reflection a point of view is deemed dysfunctional and replaced); and finally, through transformation of point of reference (i.e., upon reflection, a distorted or incomplete frame of reference is reorganized; Sherlock & Nathan, 2008; Taylor, 2007).

Whereas transformations of one's point of reference means changing other-related perspectives, *point-of-view transformation* refers to changes in deeper, more self-focused perspectives. Reflection, critique, and analysis of one's cognitive and affective assumptions are critical to Mezirow's theory, which has led some to criticize the theory as having an overly individualized focus (e.g., Clark & Wilson, 1991).

Overall, these theories (and many others) form the foundation for models of employee growth and development. They have also helped to formulate practical instructional strategies and mechanisms for facilitating the transfer of newly developed or refined KSAs into daily work. We now move on to provide brief overviews of several broad categories of opportunities for employee development.

Training

Training is the classic exemplar of employee development. Specifically, *training* is defined as

> the systematic acquisition of knowledge (i.e., what we need to know), skills (i.e., what we need to do), and attitudes (i.e., what we need to feel) (KSAs) that together lead to improved performance in a particular environment. (Salas, Wilson, Priest, & Guthrie, 2006, p. 473)

The aim of training is to achieve cognitive, behavioral, or attitudinal development through concrete understanding and practical application of job-relevant competencies. This definition underscores that effective training is much more than a place, a single program, or a lecture (Salas & Cannon-Bowers, 2001). Organizational training today goes far beyond the traditional classroom. To make opportunities for learning and development more directly accessible to employees and to more efficiently use training time, simulation-based training, virtual training, social networks, dynamic knowledge bases, and on-the-job training have all gained significant market share in the library of employee learning opportunities. For example, in 2001 only 11.5% of formal learning hours were dedicated to technology-based learning opportunities compared with 29.1% in 2011 (ASTD, 2011).

The integration of such technologies has presented an interesting issue for training and development researchers. The science of training and adult learning has developed greatly over the past 3 decades (Salas & Cannon-Bowers, 2001), with multiple theoretical models examining the antecedents and processes underlying organizational training effectiveness (e.g., Baldwin & Ford, 1988; Cannon-Bowers, Salas, Tannenbaum, & Mathieu, 1995; Goldstein, 1986; 1993; Kozlowski, Brown, Weissbein, Salas, & Cannon-Bowers, 2000). However, these models share two commonalities: They are most often designed in a traditional input-process-output framework, and they usually focus at the individual level (e.g., individual-level inputs and outputs). For example, Colquitt, LePine, and Noe's (2000) model of training effectiveness and training motivation describes individual-level antecedents of training in terms of individual ability (e.g., cognitive ability, basic skills), job attitudes (e.g., job involvement, organizational commitment), individual self-efficacy, and individual training motivation. Learning outcomes identified in the model include cognitive, behavioral, and affective outcomes, with transfer of training leading to job performance. This model also incorporates work environment (e.g., climate, opportunities to perform trained skills, justice), personality, and age as factors affecting inputs, mediators, and final outcomes.

The key to effective training, regardless of modality or strategy, is transfer-appropriate processing. *Transfer-appropriate processing* refers to the degree to which the cognitive processes learners engage in during training mirror those required for actual performance in novel situations on the job (Morris, Bransford, & Franks, 1977). Three specific training strategies that have demonstrated superiority due to their engagement of transfer-appropriate processing are scaffolding feedback, variable practice, and simulation (Baldwin & Ford, 1988; Hesketh & Ivancic, 2002).

The literature clearly indicates that effective training must include opportunities for practice, but the type of practice may encourage (or hinder) transfer-appropriate processing. For example, Schmidt and Bjork (1992) demonstrated in their review of the learning and training literature that variable practice promotes transfer-appropriate processing by encouraging trainees to learn and attend to a wider range of cues relevant to effective demonstration of trained KSAs. Variable practice means practicing new KSAs in a range of situations over time, whereas massed practice focuses on practice in a single context or setting. For example, cramming the night before an exam using only the exact materials presented in class (massed practice) will result in less effective transfer (i.e., to the test) compared with studying the material throughout the course of the semester and augmenting it with outside information and a variety of practice questions (variable practice). Another example is the classic beanbag study conducted by Kerr and Booth (1978), which found that participants who practiced throwing a beanbag from multiple distances outperformed those who practiced throwing the beanbag only at the exact distance they were to be tested on. The participants who practiced at multiple distances formed a more complex understanding of the relationships between the strength of their throw and bag distance, the effects of increasing or decreasing the strength of their throw, and other key relationships necessary for applying these newly learned skills across a range of situations.

Feedback is a vital component of KSA development. However, different approaches to feedback have differential effectiveness. Evidence to date suggests that scaffolding feedback (i.e., reducing the amount of feedback over time during training) is more effective than providing explicit feedback after every trial (Schmidt & Bjork, 1992; Shute, 2008). Specifically, scaffolding feedback prompts transfer-appropriate processing because it requires the learner to attend to and learn the subtle cues associated with effective performance. When feedback is provided after every trial, learners are less likely to engage in deep-level problem solving to determine how to improve performance, to think about cues they may have missed, or to integrate newly learned material with existing KSAs in order to formulate new task strategies. Explicit feedback provided after every in-training performance episode can actually become a crutch that learners come to rely on too heavily, thereby hindering their transfer of trained KSAs into the actual work environment.

Finally, simulation-based training has been found superior to traditional didactic-based training designs in promoting transfer-appropriate processing (Bell & Kozlowski, 2008; Fowlkes, Dwyer, Oser, & Salas, 1998). Simulation-based training allows for richer practice scenarios that more closely mirror the broad range of cues trainees will encounter when trying to apply newly learned KSAs on the job. In addition, this training offers a mechanism for trainees to try out a broader range of task strategies, as well as examine and compare the outcomes of these different strategies across a range of contexts.

On-the-Job Training

Despite being one of the oldest opportunities for development, with roots in apprenticeship models of learning, *on-the-job training* (OJT) is a relatively ill-defined term applied to a diffuse range of both informal and formal processes promoting knowledge and skill acquisition (Levine, 1997). OJT commonly refers to one-on-one developmental processes occurring in the actual work setting while the trainee carries out actual work tasks and observes and learns new job-relevant knowledge or skills from a more experienced employee (Baldwin, 2005; Rothwell, 1999). OJT is perceived as a relatively cost-effective, customizable, and efficient means to enhance transfer of training, so it is unsurprising that over 98% of organizations offered access to OJT between 2008 and 2009—making it the second most commonly provided opportunity for employee development (ASTD, 2009). However, few theoretical models explicating the functional mechanisms of OJT have been developed, and relatively few empirical or comparative effectiveness studies of OJT have been reported.

Attempting to redress this gap, DiazGranados, Lyons, Sims, Salas, and DeRouin-Jessen (2008) developed a theoretical model of OJT outlining key inputs, mediators, and outcomes. Specifically, the model incorporates three broad dimensions of OJT design characteristics: degree of structure (i.e., degree that training is formalized in both content and presentation), content (i.e., targeted KSAs, training strategies, organizational context), and practice and feedback (i.e., degree to which practice and feedback are guided, immediate, and specific). The effect of these inputs on critical learning and performance outcomes is hypothesized to be moderated by both trainee-related variables (e.g., motivation, self-efficacy, personality, goal orientation) and trainer-related variables (e.g., knowledge or skill, authority, accountability, personality). Given that OJT occurs in the live work environment, transfer should be high compared with other forms of training. However, the effectiveness of OJT is highly contingent upon the effectiveness of the trainer—if the trainer being shadowed or observed engages in undesirable work habits or takes inappropriate shortcuts, then learning will be hindered and trainees may develop habits that are difficult to unlearn. Therefore, OJT programs must include a well-developed and structured train-the-trainer component that teaches future OJT trainers how to effectively develop and mentor their students.

More formalized structures designed to capture and compile job-relevant knowledge, which employees can access efficiently in the midst of task completion, have also been subsumed under the broad umbrella of OJT (Kozlowski, Chao, & Jensen, 2009). Job aids, knowledge bases, and information management systems are physical resources accessible to employees during their normal workday, support effective performance, and can be used to develop additional knowledge (Rossett & Schafer, 2007). These tangible and often technology-based performance support tools were offered on average by over 85% of organizations rated "BEST" by ASTD between 2008 and 2009, second only to formal training and more traditional conceptualizations of on-the-job learning opportunities (ASTD, 2009).

Although the notion of expertise underscores that individuals who have developed extensive knowledge regarding certain tasks through deliberate practice and feedback should be able to perform these tasks more effectively and efficiently than novices, expertise alone cannot completely mitigate the relative limitations of human attention, memory, and concentration. Job aids such as checklists, cheat sheets, and quick reference cards supplement existing expertise and training by providing just-in-time information as well as a mechanism for ensuring that all steps in a particular task strategy are completed, even under conditions where employee attention may be divided (e.g., multitasking). Although such simple reminders may seem mundane, they have been associated with enhanced training transfer, generalization, and sustainment; improved effectiveness and consistency in both individual and team performance; and decreased errors (e.g., Duncan, 1985; Hales & Pronovost, 2006; Haynes et al., 2009; Weick & Roberts, 1993). Job aids reduce the cognitive workload required when performing a task and have been found to help focus attentional resources (Van Merrienboer, Kirschner, & Kester, 2003; Van Merrienboer & Sweller, 2005). In addition, they can be used to supplement and support training.

Mentoring

Mentoring is arguably the oldest form of employee development. Apprentice models of learning and professional growth have been documented since nearly the beginning of recorded history. *Mentors* are defined as individuals with more advanced organizational knowledge and experience who advise, guide, and support more junior individuals known as *protégés* (Allen, Eby, Poteet, Lentz, & Lima, 2004; Kram, 1985). Specifically, mentors help protégés learn technical knowledge and organizational protocols and procedures as well as norms, values, and behavioral standards. They also help protégés develop self-efficacy, self-esteem, and feelings of competence (Kram, 1983; Ragins, Cotton, & Miller, 2000).

The mentoring process has thus been conceptualized by Kram (1985) in terms of two broad categories of support: career support (e.g., sponsorship, coaching) and psychosocial support (e.g., enhancing the protégé's sense of personal identity and competence). The psychosocial support provided by mentors plays a key role in the personal growth and psychological health of their protégés, influencing the development of protégé work identity and self-esteem (Allen & Eby, 2003).

Today, however, *mentoring* is a term used broadly to describe a myriad of interpersonal processes and organizational practices varying in their degree of formality and standardization. Much of the theoretical and empirical literature surrounding the mentoring construct has focused specifically on differentiating formal mentoring relationships from informal mentoring relationships. Formal mentoring relationships are defined in terms of a relationship between (traditionally) a more senior mentor and (traditionally) a more junior protégé. As opposed to informal mentoring relationships that form spontaneously, formal mentoring programs engage in a formal matching process (though the actual process of matching is usually ill defined or ill standardized), into which the mentor and protégé may or may not have input. In addition, formal mentoring relationships are often rather standardized in terms of regularity of meetings between mentor and protégé and often exist with a set duration (e.g., 6 months, 1 year). Recent developments in the mentoring literature underscore that mentoring is no longer restricted to hierarchical relationships. For example, researchers have begun to examine peer mentorships (Huizing, 2012; Parker, Hall, & Kram, 2008). In addition, more recent conceptualizations underscore that the effects of mentoring are reciprocal, not simply unidirectional—there is growing evidence of the influence and effects that protégés also have on their mentors (Allen, Poteet, & Burroughs, 1997; Eby, 2011).

Formal and informal mentoring differ in terms of both processes and outcomes. Ragins and Cotton (1999) compared and contrasted formal and informal mentoring relationships. In addition to superficially differing in terms of how the relationship is initiated (spontaneous vs. formal matching), how long the relationship lasts (long term vs. short term), and when or how the relationship is structured, they also highlighted several differences in deep-level relationship processes. For example, motivational theory and social exchange theory suggest that the motivation of informal mentors may differ significantly from the motivation of formal mentors. According to social exchange theory, individuals are motivated to enter into and maintain relationships in which the benefits of the relationship outweigh the costs. Therefore, mentors in formal programs may perceive greater costs associated with the relationship compared with informal mentors. Allen, Eby, and Lentz (2006) argued in favor of this notion by noting that individuals in formal relationships may feel forced into participation or into working with a particular protégé whom they might not have chosen in an informal setting. In support of this argument, they found that mentors who perceived having more input into the matching process reported greater mentorship quality and that they provided greater career support.

Formal mentoring programs have also historically attempted to match dyads from different departments to avoid potential perceptions of favoritism. However, being in different departments, by default, limits the ability of formal mentors to engage in certain mentoring functions such as exposure (i.e., creating opportunities for the protégé and his or her work to be visible to other organizational members, providing access to assignments the protégé may not have access to on his or her own), protection (i.e., serving as a line of defense for potential professional threats to the protégé), sponsorship (i.e., advocating for the protégé), and challenging assignments (i.e., creating assignments that specifically challenge the protégé to enhance his or her competency in a given area). This approach also limits the potential that mentors and protégés share similar interests, job functions, and career paths. In support of this notion, Allen et al. (2006) noted that identification and attraction are key interpersonal processes related to the development and maintenance of mentoring relationships according to mentoring theory (Kram, 1983; Levinson, Darrow, Klein, Levinson, & McKee, 1978). Their results also indicated that mentor–protégé dyads from the same department gave higher protégé ratings of mentorship quality and career support. From the mentor's perspective, being in the same department was associated with greater psychosocial support. In addition, Noe (1988) found that time spent with the mentor in formal relationships did not differ between people in the same department versus outside the same department. Noe's results suggest that mentorship quality does not necessarily depend on quantity (i.e., time spent with one's mentor).

In terms of outcomes, Ragins and Cotton (1999) found that protégés participating in informal mentoring reported that they received higher levels of both career and psychosocial support compared with protégés in formal programs. In addition, they found that formal mentoring was especially associated with less career and psychosocial support for female protégés. This work supports several previous studies indicating that formal mentoring programs are generally less effective compared with informal programs (Chao, Walz, & Gardner, 1992; Wanberg, Welsh, & Hezlett, 2003). In addition, protégés with a history of mainly informal mentors were found to receive significantly greater compensation compared with formally mentored protégés (Ragins & Cotton, 1999).

In light of such evidence, Allen and colleagues (2006) offered several theoretically based recommendations for organizations hoping to avoid the pitfalls of poorly designed and executed formal mentoring programs. Specifically, they noted that organizations should strive to integrate protégé and mentor input into the matching process; provide high-quality training for mentors (and protégés) regarding what behaviors comprise effective mentoring relationships; match protégés and mentors within the same department so that dyads have more time together and so that mentors have the opportunity to offer the full range of support, including sponsorship, exposure, and challenge; and consider fostering peer mentoring relationships because peers are closer in rank to protégés. Furthermore, recent investigations of virtual mentoring have supported their effectiveness (Ensher, Heun, & Blanchard, 2003; Smith-Jentsch, Scielzo, Yarbrough, & Rosopa, 2008).

Coaching

Like mentoring, executive coaching (EC) is a formalized process involving a coach and a coachee. Executive coaches, however, tend to be external to the organization—usually consultants with a background in industrial-organizational psychology, counseling, or clinical psychology. As summarized by Gregory, Levy, and Jeffers (2008), *coaching* is a one-on-one, collaborative relationship focused on optimizing performance through the collection of data, goal setting, and feedback.

Unlike mentors, coaches are hired by the organization to develop optimal employee performance related to organizational goals. Furthermore, coaches often do not have the industry-specific knowledge or experiences that mentors and protégés often share. EC programs also tend to focus on C-suite executives (e.g., CEO, COO), whereas mentoring programs are often found at lower levels of the organization. Some suggest that EC may be somewhat more viable at this high level compared with formal mentoring, considering that few formal mentors may be available at the C-suite level. In addition, there is evidence that mentoring relationships, regardless of their formality, are reciprocal, whereas no evidence to date suggests that EC is a reciprocal process.

The processes that form EC are similar to traditional conceptualizations of counseling psychology and performance feedback. According to D'Abate et al. (2003), coaching usually involves collecting data regarding the behavior of the coachee on the job and the outcomes associated with those behaviors. The coach may make observations of the coachee in real time, gather objective data (e.g., division outputs), and interview the coachee (and, in some cases, even relevant coworkers or others). The coach and coachee then review this data, with the coach providing feedback and facilitating self-reflection and goal setting by the coachee. The pair reviews progress and reassesses goals and performance in subsequent meetings.

The concept of coaching has also been integrated at lower organizational levels in the form of on-the-job coaching for frontline employees. Unlike executive coaches, on-the-job coaches are internal organizational members, usually responsible for observing and providing feedback to members of their own department on specific behaviors or protocols. Such coaching programs have been suggested as mechanisms to support transfer of training and long-term sustainment of organizational change initiatives. For example, TeamSTEPPS, a team-training program developed by the Department of Defense and the Agency for Healthcare Research and Quality (Clancy & Tornberg, 2007) specifically targeting health care providers, incorporates coaching as a critical component of training design and implementation. TeamSTEPPS coaches are responsible for providing specific feedback and guidance for physicians, nurses, and other clinicians regarding the use of teamwork skills and communication protocols such as closed-loop communication. Compared with OJT, which involves acquisition of new skills or knowledge in the work environment, on-the-job coaching focuses more on supporting the use of previously acquired, specific skill sets.

To date, the empirical literature on coaching is sparse and generally lacking from an experimental design standpoint. What literature does exist to date generally suggests that EC has positive outcomes, though much of this evidence is anecdotal or, at best, correlational. Therefore, more rigorous studies of coaching effectiveness are needed. This will most likely require organizational researchers to borrow evaluation methods from their clinical cousins, approaching evaluation from a clinical trial standpoint rather than other, more traditional training evaluation methods.

Leadership Development

Well-developed leaders with the demonstrated capacity and motivation to strategically affect follower behaviors, cognitions, and attitudes have historically been the engines through which organizational goals and strategy are realized. *Leadership* is defined as a multidimensional, social influence process between leaders and followers who intend real changes that reflect mutual purposes (Rost, 1991a). As a process of influence, leadership has been found to impact organizational behavior and outcomes at multiple levels, including follower job satisfaction and motivation, team learning and performance, and overall organizational performance indicators (Judge & Piccolo, 2004). Furthermore, many organizations offer opportunities to develop leadership skills to a broader pool of employees spanning all organizational levels in an effort to more effectively meet present business challenges.

Today, leadership development is rooted in behavioral theories focused on describing the actual behaviors effective leaders engage in and how these behaviors, in turn, influence follower motivation and behavior. For example, the foundational Ohio State–Michigan studies (Katz & Kahn, 1952; Stogdill, 1963) identified consideration (i.e., demonstrating concern for employee well-being) and initiating structure (i.e., setting goals, defining task strategies, removing barriers to goal attainment) as two dimensions of leadership behavior. Later theories, such as transformational leadership (Bass, 1995; Burns, 1978), further identified more fine-grained dimensions of effective leader behavior, such as modeling behavior that followers want to emulate (idealized influence); challenging followers to ask difficult questions and actively challenge the status quo (intellectual stimulation); articulating a clear, driving vision (inspirational motivation); and demonstrating active concern for follower development (individualized consideration). Practically, these theoretical developments laid the necessary foundation for investigation into how to develop and train effective leaders.

Models of leadership development underscore that leadership has generally been conceptualized as an individual-level skill or ability that can be developed via training or other interactions (e.g., Day, 2000; Rost, 1991b). Though over 30 meta-analyses on the topic of leadership have been conducted, until recently, none had focused explicitly on investigating the effects of leadership development interventions. A qualitative and quantitative review of leadership intervention studies (i.e., studies in which leadership was actually manipulated) by Avolio and colleagues (Avolio & Chan, 2008; Avolio & Gardner, 2005) explored six categories of leadership development activities: training, role-playing, scenario or vignette, assignments, expectations, and a broad category named "other" containing interventions not fitting within the previous five categories. Results indicated that all six types of leadership interventions positively affected work outcomes (Reichard & Avolio, 2005). Specifically, findings suggested that participants in leadership development activities had a 66% chance of positive outcomes, whereas individuals in the control comparison groups had only a 34% chance of positive outcomes, on average. Interestingly, the positive relationship held even for those interventions lasting less than 1 day.

The broad umbrella of leadership development has been used to describe activities aimed at preparing individuals to function in formal leadership roles (i.e., leader development) as well as activities aimed at preparing individuals (who may or may not serve in formal leadership roles) to develop social networks and relationships, which create organizational value through enhanced cooperation and resource sharing (Day, 2000). Whereas leader development activities focus on intrapersonal development (e.g., self-regulation, self-awareness, self-motivation), leadership development activities focus on building interpersonal competence (e.g., social skills, social awareness). Therefore, leader development activities can be conceptualized as individual-based differentiation strategies, whereas leadership development activities function more as integration strategies.

This perspective also has been influential in the literature investigating leadership in situations where there is no formal leader. Studies of leadership emergence focus on the traits and other antecedents predictive of who will step in to fill an unofficial leadership role or how the behavioral markers of leadership will be fulfilled by a constellation of group members. For example, in discussing leadership in teams, Day, Gronn, and Salas (2004) suggested that at the team level, leadership capacity is an outcome that can be developed and grown through purpose-driven learning. In this sense, leadership capacity is defined as a pooled resource emerging from the combined collaborative inputs of team members. Theories of shared or distributed leadership underscore that it is an emergent property of a group or team, meaning that it arises as a product of collective interaction—in opposition to the traditionally individual-focused view of leadership—and that expertise and leadership capacity is distributed across multiple team members (Kozlowski, Gully, Salas, & Cannon-Bowers, 1996; Pearce & Conger, 2003; Woods, Bennett, Harvey, & Wise, 2004).

In terms of their contribution to the creation of a psychologically healthy workplace, organizational leadership development efforts also contribute to the psychological health of followers. For example, transformational leaders support followers by enhancing their confidence and self-efficacy to achieve an idealized state. By appealing to followers' deeply held beliefs, transformational leadership has been shown to impact follower core-self evaluations, which, in turn, affect follower motivation and behavior on the job (Judge & Piccolo, 2004). In addition, transformational leadership has been linked with important outcomes such as organizational citizenship behaviors—specifically by influencing follower goal commitment and intrinsic motivation, both key components of organizational productivity and effectiveness (Piccolo & Colquitt, 2006). Overall, such results suggest that opportunities to develop leadership skills not only can impact those individuals participating but also can have a broader positive influence.

Although Riggio (2008) indicated that many opportunities for leadership development take the form of traditional development (e.g., mentoring, training), his review suggested that these programs focus to a much greater extent on self-awareness, self-regulation, introspection, and reflection. However, both Day and Riggio highlighted the need to focus on the evaluation of leadership development techniques, underscoring that the criteria and empirical evidence regarding program effectiveness remain lacking. From a practical perspective related to the need for objective and diagnostic evaluations of leadership development opportunities, Hernez-Broome and Hughes (2004) underscored the need to demonstrate return on investment for leadership development programs.

Continuing Education

Continuing education opportunities generally refer to formal educational activities occurring after the core components of one's professional education are completed (Jarvis, 1995; McIntosh, 1979; Venables, 1976). Continuing education is generally designed to support ongoing learning, and in the current decade has come to be synonymous with updating one's skills as new technologies are developed and integrated into the workplace. For example, health care professionals are often required to spend 50 hours or more per year in continuing education courses designed to bring them up-to-date on recent advances in medical knowledge, procedures, and technology.

One of the most common examples of continuing education support offered by organizations is tuition reimbursement—that is, financial assistance for direct costs associated with advanced educational courses offered with the intent of developing either general job-related competencies (e.g., advanced degree program) or specific skills (e.g., workshop or short course designed to enhance a specific skill set). Though tuition reimbursement typically accounts for the smallest proportion of workplace learning budgets (12.89% in 2011), this finding may point to disuse rather than lack of access. For example, the 2009 ASTD State of the Industry report found that tuition reimbursement was available to 82% of employees, yet only 13% actually used this opportunity. This statistic is supported by earlier work suggesting that lack of organizational marketing and communication for this development opportunity contributes to low participation rates (Corporate Leadership Council, 2003).

Classic theories of human capital (e.g., Becker, 1964) suggest that employees can develop both general and organizational-specific skills. Such perspectives maintain that investing in developing organization-specific skills can lead to decreased turnover, whereas investment in the development of general skills may actually increase turnover of highly skilled employees. Furthermore, tuition reimbursement has been touted as a means to enhance recruitment of motivated high performers (Cappelli, 2004). Flaherty (2007) examined these assumptions and found that though employees with stronger turnover intentions are often most likely to participate in tuition reimbursement, employees who participated had a significantly reduced probability of leaving within 5 years. In addition, results indicated that tuition support for general skills training is beneficial to retention when general and organization-specific skills are complementary.

Opportunities for continuing education can also take several other forms. Employers may offer support for employees to attend conferences or workshops or provide support for membership in job-relevant professional associations. However, much less work to date has explored the relative effectiveness of such opportunities.

GROWTH AND DEVELOPMENT INITIATIVE EFFECTIVENESS: KEY FACTORS

Our review of the theoretical foundations and empirical evaluations of various interventions designed to facilitate a psychologically healthy organization through employee growth and development suggests that several critical factors affect initiative effectiveness.

Align Opportunities for Development With Strategic Organizational Goals

To achieve the dual purpose of fostering a psychologically healthy workplace and optimizing organizational performance, developmental opportunities must focus on enhancing or cultivating those competencies underlying effective performance. This means conducting comprehensive task analyses to determine what competencies are necessary and which KSAs are relevant. This also means conducting comprehensive needs analyses to identify what content should emphasize, who most needs access to developmental opportunities, who is motivated or not motivated to take advantage of such access, when such opportunities should be available, and how they should be designed and configured (Goldstein & Ford, 2002).

Align Opportunities for Development With Work Cycles

Developmental opportunities must be offered in a way that aligns with work cycles so individuals can take advantage of them. For example, a team-training course that is offered only during the busiest part of an organization's work cycle will not be used even if individuals are highly motivated to attend because it will cause too great of a disruption in productivity. This notion also underscores that development must be treated as an organizational goal in parallel with output-oriented goals. Organizations that offer access to development opportunities but implicitly punish employees for actually using them by focusing solely on output-related performance goals will not be successful.

Give Employees Something They Can Use

Related to the alignment issues, there must be opportunities for employees to put new KSAs into practice on the job. The literature on training transfer underscores that for new skills to transfer, the work environment must both afford and support their use. Furthermore, individuals will be more motivated to actually use development opportunities they have access to when they perceive that the opportunity for growth focuses on relevant skill sets.

Strive to Address Both Immediate Learning Needs and Broader Employee Career Goals

Career development and growth involves both proximal and long-term goals. Therefore, individuals need not only the opportunity to enhance immediately relevant skills (e.g., specific training on a new technology) but also access to and support for development opportunities focused on long-term career enhancement. Individuals participating in long-term career planning, for example, have been found to show greater work-role flexibility (Birdi, Allan, & Warr, 1997). Such adaptability is critical for organizational performance today.

Create a Climate That Supports Development in the Context of Team Performance

Teams are ubiquitous in organizations today and individual employees are often members of multiple teams. Opportunities for development must be designed to balance individual growth with the development of team skills. In this sense, individual employees must not only be experts in their given task arena but also be expert team members with the skill and ability to effectively communicate, coordinate, and cooperate. Therefore, developmental opportunities must focus not only on enhancing intrapersonal competence but also on developing interpersonal competence.

Reinforce Individuals Who Recognize They Have Room to Improve

As demonstrated in Table 3.1, access to developmental opportunities is not enough. Individuals must be motivated to take advantage of this access and actually participate in available opportunities. However, in some organizational contexts, attending training or openly recognizing skill deficiencies is considered shameful and looked upon negatively. Effective development strategies openly celebrate continuous learning. This means that administrators, supervisors, and peers recognize growth as a continuous process, especially considering the rate of information and technology generation today. Recognizing gaps in one's own KSAs and taking advantage of opportunities to fill in these gaps should be celebrated and supported. Individuals should be reinforced for using such available opportunities and the remediation stigma must be banished.

CONCLUSION

The science underlying employee growth and development initiatives is deep and broad. However, a need remains to explore the theoretical underpinnings and underlying relationships as the antecedents, methods, processes, and outcomes of such initiatives continue to evolve. For example, although formalized training programs (e.g., in-house courses, continuing education courses) have been the foundation of organizational employee development initiatives, existing research underscores that the majority of employee learning occurs outside of formalized, face-to-face training settings. Employees consistently attribute less than 10% of their personal development to formalized training programs (Flynn, Eddy, & Tannenbaum, 2006; Tannenbaum, 1997).

Opportunities for development in the workplace of today and tomorrow means "helping people learn from their work, rather than taking them away from their work to learn" (Moxley & O'Connor Wilson, 1998; as cited in Day, 2000, p. 6). Future theoretical and empirical work must examine in greater detail the processes of informal learning in order to provide greater insight into how organizations can best support it as an opportunity for development and growth.

In addition, whereas many approaches to development have employed a one-size-fits-all approach, recent literature suggests this approach may not be optimal—that it in fact limits learner outcomes and reduces the efficiency of learning time (Bell & Kozlowski, 2008; Cannon-Bowers & Bowers, 2009). Future approaches to development need to explore how to best adapt and individualize learning opportunities and the outcomes of such efforts.

Also needed is a further understanding of the conceptual underpinnings of blended learning approaches: growth and development approaches incorporating multiple methodologies for learning using both face-to-face and distributed learning technologies, as well as performance support materials such as job aids and knowledge bases (Bonk & Graham, 2005; Rossett, 2002). However, a clearer understanding of how to blend developmental strategies, at what levels to do so, how to measure and evaluate blended learning, and the role of moderators in the effectiveness of blended learning approaches continues to evolve (Graham & Dziuban, 2008). In exploring blended learning to support a psychologically healthy workplace, questions remain regarding which types of developmental opportunities are complementary or supplementary to one another, what is the most valuable combination given a particular mix of employee characteristics, and what types of employees benefit most from such opportunities (Sims, Burke, Metcalf, & Salas, 2008).

In summary, this chapter offered insight into the conceptual background underlying opportunities for growth and development, as well as several key factors contributing to the effectiveness of such opportunities. However, as technology and human innovation continue to expand the realm of possibilities in terms of the design and delivery of such initiatives, the underlying theories and empirical evidence continue to grow. Organizations offering opportunities for their employees to grow and develop are addressing a major component in the creation of a psychologically healthy workplace, simultaneously inspiring, motivating, and growing their human capital.

REFERENCES

Aguinis, H., & Kraiger, K. (2009). Benefits of training and development for individuals and teams, organizations, and society. *Annual Review of Psychology, 60,* 451–474. http://dx.doi.org/10.1146/annurev.psych.60.110707.163505

Allen, T. D., & Eby, L. T. (2003). Relationship effectiveness with mentors: Factors associated with learning and quality. *Journal of Management, 29,* 469–486. http://dx.doi.org/10.1016/S0149-2063(03)00021-7

Allen, T. D., Eby, L. T., & Lentz, E. (2006). Mentorship behaviors and mentorship quality associated with formal mentoring programs: Closing the gap between research and practice. *Journal of Applied Psychology, 91,* 567–578. http://dx.doi.org/10.1037/0021-9010.91.3.567

Allen, T. D., Eby, L. T., Poteet, M. L., Lentz, E., & Lima, L. (2004). Career benefits associated with mentoring for protégés: A meta-analysis. *Journal of Applied Psychology, 89,* 127–136. http://dx.doi.org/10.1037/0021-9010.89.1.127

Allen, T. D., Poteet, M. L., & Burroughs, S. M. (1997). The mentor's perspective: A qualitative inquiry and future research agenda. *Journal of Vocational Behavior, 51,* 70–89. http://dx.doi.org/10.1006/jvbe.1997.1596

American Society for Training and Development. (2009). *2009 State of the Industry report.* Retrieved from http://www.astd.org/content/research/stateOfIndustry.htm

American Society for Training and Development. (2011). *2011 State of the Industry report.* Retrieved from http://www.astd.org/content/research/stateOfIndustry.htm

American Society for Training and Development. (2014). *2014 State of the Industry report.* Retrieved from https://www.td.org/Publications/Research-Reports/2014/2014-State-of-the-Industry?mktcops=c.learning-and-development~c.lt~c.sr-leader

Anderson, J. R. (1993). Problem solving and learning. *American Psychologist, 48,* 35–44. http://dx.doi.org/10.1037/0003-066X.48.1.35

Anderson, J. R. (1996). ACT: A simple theory of complex cognition. *American Psychologist, 51*, 355–365. http://dx.doi.org/10.1037/0003-066X.51.4.355

Anderson, J. R., & Schunn, C. D. (2000). Implications of the ACT-R learning theory: No magic bullets. In R. Glaser (Ed.), *Advances in instructional psychology* (Vol. 5, pp. 1–33). Mahwah, NJ: Erlbaum.

Avolio, B. J., & Chan, A. (2008). The dawning of a new era for genuine leadership development. In G. P. Hodgkinson & J. K. Ford (Eds.), *International review of industrial and organizational psychology* (Vol. 23, pp. 197–238). New York, NY: Wiley. http://dx.doi.org/10.1002/9780470773277.ch6

Avolio, B. J., & Gardner, W. L. (2005). Authentic leadership development: Getting to the root of positive forms of leadership. *The Leadership Quarterly, 16*, 315–338. http://dx.doi.org/10.1016/j.leaqua.2005.03.001

Baldwin, T. T. (2005). On-the-job training. In S. Cartwright (Ed.), *The Blackwell encyclopedic dictionary of human resource management* (2nd ed., p. 263). Malden, MA: Blackwell.

Baldwin, T. T., & Ford, J. K. (1988). Transfer of training: A review and directions for future research. *Personnel Psychology, 41*, 63–105. http://dx.doi.org/10.1111/j.1744-6570.1988.tb00632.x

Bass, B. M. (1995). Theory of transformational leadership redux. *The Leadership Quarterly, 6*, 463–478. http://dx.doi.org/10.1016/1048-9843(95)90021-7

Becker, G. S. (1964). *Human capital.* Chicago, IL: University of Chicago Press.

Bell, B. S., & Kozlowski, S. W. J. (2008). Active learning: Effects of core training design elements on self-regulatory processes, learning, and adaptability. *Journal of Applied Psychology, 93*, 296–316. http://dx.doi.org/10.1037/0021-9010.93.2.296

Birdi, K., Allan, C., & Warr, P. (1997). Correlates and perceived outcomes of 4 types of employee development activity. *Journal of Applied Psychology, 82*, 845–857.

Birdi, K. S., Patterson, M. G., & Wood, S. J. (2007). Learning to perform? A comparison of learning practices and organizational performance in profit- and non-profit-making sectors in the UK. *International Journal of Training and Development, 11*, 265–281. http://dx.doi.org/10.1111/j.1468-2419.2007.00285.x

Bonk, C. J., & Graham, C. R. (2005). *Handbook of blended learning: Global perspectives, local designs.* San Francisco, CA: Pfeiffer.

Boyce, B. (2009, September). Google searches. *Shambhala Sun, 18*(1), 34–41.

Burns, J. M. (1978). *Leadership.* New York, NY: Harper & Row.

Cannon-Bowers, J. A., & Bowers, C. A. (2009). Synthetic learning environments: On developing a science of simulation, games and virtual worlds for training. In S. W. J. Kozlowski & E. Salas (Eds.), *Learning, training and development in organizations* (pp. 229–262). New York, NY: Routledge.

Cannon-Bowers, J. A., Salas, E., Tannenbaum, S. I., & Mathieu, J. E. (1995). Toward theoretically based principles of training effectiveness: A model and initial empirical investigation. *Military Psychology, 7*, 141–164. http://dx.doi.org/10.1207/s15327876mp0703_1

Cappelli, P. (2004). Why do employers pay for college? *Journal of Econometrics, 121*, 213–241. http://dx.doi.org/10.1016/j.jeconom.2003.10.014

Chao, G. T., Walz, P. M., & Gardner, P. D. (1992). Formal and informal mentorships: A comparison on mentoring functions and contrast with nonmentored counterparts. *Personnel Psychology, 45*, 619–636. http://dx.doi.org/10.1111/j.1744-6570.1992.tb00863.x

Clancy, C. M., & Tornberg, D. N. (2007). TeamSTEPPS: Assuring optimal teamwork in clinical settings. *American Journal of Medical Quality, 22*, 214–217. http://dx.doi.org/10.1177/1062860607300616

Clark, M. C., & Wilson, A. L. (1991). Context and rationality in Mezirow's theory of transformational learning. *Adult Education Quarterly, 41*, 75–91.

Colquitt, J. A., LePine, J. A., & Noe, R. A. (2000). Toward an integrative theory of training motivation: A meta-analytic path analysis of 20 years of research. *Journal of Applied Psychology, 85*, 678–707. http://dx.doi.org/10.1037/0021-9010.85.5.678

comScore. (2014). *comScore releases March 2014 U.S. search engine rankings.* Retrieved from http://www.comscore.com/Insights/Press-Releases/2014/4/comScore-Releases-March-2014-U.S.-Search-Engine-Rankings

Corporate Leadership Council. (2003). *Trends in tuition aid programs* (Corporate Executive Board Catalogue No. CLC1-1100OH). Arlington, VA: Author.

D'Abate, C. P., Eddy, E. R., & Tannenbaum, S. I. (2003). What's in a name? A literature-based approach to understanding mentoring, coaching, and other constructs that describe developmental interactions. *Human Resource Development Review, 2*, 360–384. http://dx.doi.org/10.1177/1534484303255033

Day, D. V. (2000). Leadership development: A review in context. *The Leadership Quarterly, 11*, 581–613. http://dx.doi.org/10.1016/S1048-9843(00)00061-8

Day, D. V., Gronn, P., & Salas, E. (2004). Leadership capacity in teams. *The Leadership Quarterly, 15*, 857–880.

Deloitte Consulting, LLC. (2010). *Managing talent in a turbulent economy: Where are you on the recovery curve?* Retrieved from http://images.forbes.com/forbesinsights/StudyPDFs/TalentPulseJan2010.pdf

DiazGranados, D., Lyons, R., Sims, D. E., Salas, E., & DeRouin-Jessen, R. E. (2008, August). *On-the-job training: A review and a theoretical model.* Poster presented at the 116th Annual Conference of the American Psychological Association, Boston, MA.

Dornan, A., & Jane-Llopis, E. (2010). *The wellness imperative: Creating more effective organizations* (WEF publication No. 180110). Geneva, Switzerland: World Economic Forum. Retrieved from http://files.shareholder.com/downloads/MAN/849972748x0x347244/8dfb85fb-324e-4086-b04b-fc66c40cfd56/Right%20Management_The%20Wellness%20Imperative.pdf

Duncan, C. (1985). Job aids really can work: A study of the military application of job aid technology. *Performance + Instruction, 24*, 1–4.

Eby, L. T. (2011). Mentoring. In S. Zedeck (Ed.), *APA handbook of industrial and organizational psychology: Vol. 2. Selecting and developing members of the organization* (pp. 505–525). Washington, DC: American Psychological Association.

Ensher, E. A., Heun, C., & Blanchard, A. (2003). Online mentoring and computer-mediated communication: New directions in research. *Journal of Vocational Behavior, 63*, 264–288. http://dx.doi.org/10.1016/S0001-8791(03)00044-7

Flaherty, C. N. (2007). *The effect of tuition reimbursement on turnover: A case study analysis* (Working Paper No. 12975). Cambridge, MA: National Bureau of Economic Research. http://dx.doi.org/10.3386/w12975

Flynn, D., Eddy, E., & Tannenbaum, S. I. (2006). The impact of national culture on the continuous learning environment: Exploratory findings from multiple countries. *Journal of East-West Business, 12*, 85–107. http://dx.doi.org/10.1300/J097v12n02_05

Fortune. (2012). *Fortune 100 compare tool.* Retrieved from http://money.cnn.com/magazines/fortune/best-companies/2012/snapshots/1.html

Fowlkes, J., Dwyer, D. J., Oser, R. L., & Salas, E. (1998). Event-based approach to training (EBAT). *The International Journal of Aviation Psychology, 8*, 209–221.

Goldstein, I. L. (1986). *Training in organizations: Needs assessment, development, and evaluation.* Pacific Grove, CA: Brooks/Cole.

Goldstein, I. L. (1993). *Training in organizations: Needs assessment, development, and evaluation* (3rd ed.). Pacific Grove, CA: Cengage Learning.

Goldstein, I. L., & Ford, J. K. (2002). *Training in organizations: Needs assessment, development, and evaluation* (4th ed.). Belmont, CA: Wadsworth.

Graham, C. R., & Dziuban, C. (2008). Blended learning environments. In M. Spector, D. Merrill, J. Merrienboer, & M. Driscoll (Eds.), *Handbook of research on educational communications and technology: A project of the association for educational communications and technology* (3rd ed., pp. 269–276). New York, NY: Taylor & Francis.

Grawitch, M. J., Gottschalk, M., & Munz, D. C. (2006). The path to a healthy workplace: A critical review linking healthy workplace practices, employee well-being, and organizational improvements. *Consulting Psychology Journal: Practice and Research, 58*, 129–147. http://dx.doi.org/10.1037/1065-9293.58.3.129

Grawitch, M. J., Trares, S., & Kohler, J. M. (2007). Healthy workplace practices and employee outcomes. *International Journal of Stress Management, 14*, 275–293. http://dx.doi.org/10.1037/1072-5245.14.3.275

Gregory, J. B., Levy, P. E., & Jeffers, M. (2008). Development of a model of the feedback process within executive coaching. *Consulting Psychology Journal: Practice and Research, 60*, 42–56. http://dx.doi.org/10.1037/1065-9293.60.1.42

Hales, B. M., & Pronovost, P. J. (2006). The checklist—a tool for error management and performance improvement. *Journal of Critical Care, 21*, 231–235. http://dx.doi.org/10.1016/j.jcrc.2006.06.002

Haynes, A. B., Weiser, T. G., Berry, W. R., Lipsitz, S. R., Breizat, A. H., Dellinger, E. P., . . . Safe Surgery Saves Lives Study Group. (2009). A surgical safety checklist to reduce morbidity and mortality in a global population. *The New England Journal of Medicine, 360*, 491–499. http://dx.doi.org/10.1056/NEJMsa0810119

Hernez-Broome, G., & Hughes, R. L. (2004). Leadership development: Past, present, and future. *Human Resource Planning, 27*, 24–32.

Hesketh, B., & Ivancic, K. (2002). Enhancing performance through training. In S. Sonnentang (Ed.), *Psychological management of individual performance* (pp. 249–291). New York, NY: Wiley.

Huizing, R. (2012). Mentoring together: A literature review of group mentoring. *Mentoring & Tutoring: Partnership in Learning, 20*, 27–55. http://dx.doi.org/10.1080/13611267.2012.645599

Jarvis, P. (Ed.). (1995). *Adult & continuing education: Theory and practice* (2nd ed.). New York, NY: Routledge.

Judge, T. A., & Piccolo, R. F. (2004). Transformational and transactional leadership: A meta-analytic test of their relative validity. *Journal of Applied Psychology, 89*, 755–768. http://dx.doi.org/10.1037/0021-9010.89.5.755

Katz, D., & Kahn, R. L. (1952). Some recent findings in human relations research. In E. Swanson, T. Newcombe, & E. Hartley (Eds.), *Readings in social psychology* (pp. 650–656). New York, NY: Holt, Rinehart and Winston.

Kaye, B., & Jordan-Evans, S. (2008). *Love 'em or lose 'em: Getting good people to stay* (4th ed.). San Francisco, CA: Berrett-Koehler.

Kerr, R., & Booth, B. (1978). Specific and varied practice of motor skill. *Perceptual and Motor Skills, 46*, 395–401.

Knowles, M. S. (1973). *The adult learner: A neglected species.* Houston, TX: Gulf.

Knowles, M. S., Holton, E. F., & Swanson, R. A. (2005). *The adult learner: The definitive classic in adult education and human resource development* (6th ed.). Burlington, MA: Elsevier.

Kozlowski, S. W. J., Brown, K. G., Weissbein, D., Salas, E., & Cannon-Bowers, J. A. (2000). A multilevel approach to training effectiveness: Enhancing horizontal and vertical transfer. In K. J. Klein & S. W. J. Kozlowski (Eds.), *Multilevel theory, research, and methods in organizations: Foundations, extensions, and new directions* (pp. 9–30). San Francisco, CA: Jossey-Bass.

Kozlowski, S. W. J., Chao, G. T., & Jensen, J. M. (2009). Building an infrastructure for organizational learning: A multilevel approach. In S. W. J. Kozlowski & E. Salas (Eds.), *Learning, training, and development in organizations* (pp. 361–400). New York, NY: Routledge.

Kozlowski, S. W. J., Gully, S. M., Salas, E., & Cannon-Bowers, J. A. (1996). Team leadership and development: Theory, principles, and guidelines for training leaders and teams. In M. Beyerlein, S. Beyerlein, & D. Johnson (Eds.), *Advances in interdisciplinary studies of work teams: Team leadership* (Vol. 3, pp. 253–292). Greenwich, CT: JAI Press.

Kram, K. E. (1983). Phases of the mentor relationship. *Academy of Management Journal, 26*, 608–625. http://dx.doi.org/10.2307/255910

Kram, K. E. (1985). *Mentoring at work.* Lanham, MD: University Press of America.

Levine, C. I. (1997, August). On-the-job training. *American Society for Training & Development Infoline* (No. 9708). Retrieved from https://www.td.org/Store/Product?ProductId=17106

Levinson, D. J., Darrow, C. N., Klein, E. B., Levinson, M. A., & McKee, B. (1978). *Seasons of a man's life.* New York, NY: Knopf.

Manpower Inc. (2010). *Talent shortage survey: 2008 global results.* Retrieved from http://files.shareholder.com/downloads/MAN/292351486x0x189693/9adcf817-96cf-4bb3-ac68-038e79d5facf/Talent%20Shortage%20Survey%20Results_2008_FINAL.pdf

McIntosh, N. E. (1979). To make continuing education a reality. *Oxford Review of Education, 5,* 169–182. http://dx.doi.org/10.1080/0305498790050206

Mezirow, J. (1981). A critical theory of adult learning and education. *Adult Education Quarterly, 32,* 3–24. http://dx.doi.org/10.1177/074171368103200101

Mezirow, J. (Ed.). (2000). *Learning as transformation: Critical perspectives on a theory in progress.* San Francisco, CA: Jossey-Bass.

Morris, C. D., Bransford, J. D., & Franks, J. J. (1977). Levels of processing versus transfer appropriate processing. *Journal of Verbal Learning & Verbal Behavior, 16,* 519–533. http://dx.doi.org/10.1016/S0022-5371(77)80016-9

Noe, R. A. (1988). An investigation of the determinants of successful assigned mentoring. *Personnel Psychology, 41,* 457–479. http://dx.doi.org/10.1111/j.1744-6570.1988.tb00638.x

Parker, P., Hall, D. T., & Kram, K. E. (2008). Peer coaching: A relational process for accelerated career learning. *Academy of Management Learning & Education, 7,* 487–503. http://dx.doi.org/10.5465/AMLE.2008.35882189

Pearce, C. L., & Conger, J. A. (Eds.). (2003). *Shared leadership: Reframing the hows and whys of leadership.* Thousand Oaks, CA: Sage.

Piccolo, R. F., & Colquitt, J. A. (2006). Transformational leadership and job behaviors: The mediating role of job characteristics. *Academy of Management Journal, 49,* 327–340. http://dx.doi.org/10.5465/AMJ.2006.20786079

Ragins, B. R., & Cotton, J. L. (1999). Mentor functions and outcomes: A comparison of men and women in formal and informal mentoring relationships. *Journal of Applied Psychology, 84,* 529–550. http://dx.doi.org/10.1037/0021-9010.84.4.529

Ragins, B. R., Cotton, J. L., & Miller, J. S. (2000). Marginal mentoring: The effects of type of mentor, quality of relationship, and program design on work and career attitudes. *Academy of Management Journal, 43,* 1177–1194. http://dx.doi.org/10.2307/1556344

Reichard, R. J., & Avolio, B. J. (2005). Where are we? The status of leadership intervention research: A meta-analytic summary. In W. L. Gardner, B. J. Avolio, & F. O. Walumbwa (Eds.), *Authentic leadership and practice: Origins, effects, and development* (pp. 203–223). Amsterdam, The Netherlands: Elsevier.

Riggio, R. E. (2008). Leadership development: The current state and future expectations. *Consulting Psychology Journal: Practice and Research, 60,* 383–392. http://dx.doi.org/10.1037/1065-9293.60.4.383

Rossett, A. (Ed.). (2002). *The ASTD e-learning handbook*. New York, NY: McGraw-Hill.

Rossett, A., & Schafer, L. (2007). *Job aids and performance support: Moving from knowledge in the classroom to knowledge everywhere*. San Francisco, CA: Pfeiffer/Wiley.

Rost, J. C. (1991a). The nature of leadership. In J. C. Rost (Ed.), *Leadership for the 21st century* (pp. 97–128). New York, NY: Praeger.

Rost, J. C. (1991b). An overview of leadership studies. In J. C. Rost (Ed.), *Leadership for the 21st century* (pp. 13–36). New York, NY: Praeger.

Rothwell, W. J. (1999). On-the-job training (OJT). In D. G. Langdon, K. S. Whiteside, & M. M. McKenna (Eds.), *Intervention resource guide: 50 performance improvement tools* (pp. 243–250). San Francisco, CA: Jossey-Bass/Pfeiffer.

Salas, E., & Cannon-Bowers, J. A. (2001). The science of training: A decade of progress. *Annual Review of Psychology, 52*, 471–499. http://dx.doi.org/10.1146/annurev.psych.52.1.471

Salas, E., Wilson, K. A., Priest, H. A., & Guthrie, J. W. (2006). Design, delivery, and evaluation of training systems. In G. Salvendy (Ed.), *Handbook of human factors and ergonomics* (3rd ed., pp. 472–512). New York, NY: Wiley.

Sauter, S., Lim, S., & Murphy, L. (1996). Organizational health: A new paradigm for occupational stress research at NIOSH. *Japanese Journal of Occupational Mental Health, 4*, 248–254.

Schmidt, R. A., & Bjork, R. A. (1992). New conceptualizations of practice: Common principles in three paradigms suggest new concepts for training. *Psychological Science, 3*, 207–217. http://dx.doi.org/10.1111/j.1467-9280.1992.tb00029.x

Sherlock, J. J., & Nathan, M. L. (2008). How power dynamics impact the content and process of nonprofit CEO learning. *Management Learning, 39*, 245–269. http://dx.doi.org/10.1177/1350507608090876

Shute, V. J. (2008). Focus on formative feedback. *Review of Educational Research, 78*, 153–189. http://dx.doi.org/10.3102/0034654307313795

Sims, D. E., Burke, C. S., Metcalf, D., & Salas, E. (2008). Research-based guidelines for designing blended learning. *Ergonomics in Design: The Quarterly of Human Factors Applications, 16*, 23–29. http://dx.doi.org/10.1518/106480408X282764

Smith-Jentsch, K. A., Jentsch, F. G., Payne, S. C., & Salas, E. (1996). Can pretraining experiences explain individual differences in learning? *Journal of Applied Psychology, 81*, 110–116. http://dx.doi.org/10.1037/0021-9010.81.1.110

Smith-Jentsch, K. A., Scielzo, S. A., Yarbrough, C. S., & Rosopa, P. J. (2008). A comparison of face-to-face and electronic peer-mentoring: Interactions with mentor gender. *Journal of Vocational Behavior, 72*, 193–206. http://dx.doi.org/10.1016/j.jvb.2007.11.004

Society for Human Resource Management. (2013). *SHRM workplace forecast*. Alexandria, VA: Author. Retrieved from http://www.shrm.org/Research/FutureWorkplaceTrends/Documents/13-0146%20Workplace_Forecast_FULL_FNL.pdf

Stogdill, R. M. (1963). *Manual for the Leader Behavior Description Questionnaire—Form XII*. Columbus, OH: Ohio State University.

Tan, C.-M. (2012). *Search inside yourself*. Retrieved from http://www.mindful.org/mindfulness-practice/mindfulness-and-awareness/search-inside-yourself

Tannenbaum, S. I. (1997). Enhancing continuous learning: Diagnostic findings from multiple companies. *Human Resource Management, 36,* 437–452. http://dx.doi.org/10.1002/(SICI)1099-050X(199724)36:4<437::AID-HRM7>3.0.CO;2-W

Taylor, E. W. (2007). An update of transformative learning theory: A critical review of the empirical research. *International Journal of Lifelong Education, 26,* 173–191. http://dx.doi.org/10.1080/02601370701219475

U.S. Bureau of Labor Statistics. (2009). *Employer costs for employee compensation—September 2009*. Retrieved from http://www.bls.gov/news.release/archives/ecec_12092009.pdf

U.S. Government Accountability Office. (2000). *Human capital: A self-assessment checklist for agency leaders* (GAO publication No. GAO/OCG-00-14G). Washington, DC: D. M. Walker. Retrieved from http://www.gao.gov/special.pubs/cg00014g.pdf

Van Merrienboer, J. J. G., Kirschner, P. A., & Kester, L. (2003). Taking the load off a learner's mind: Instructional design for complex learning. *Educational Psychologist, 38,* 5–13. http://dx.doi.org/10.1207/S15326985EP3801_2

Van Merrienboer, J. J. G., & Sweller, J. (2005). Cognitive load theory and complex learning; Recent development and future directions. *Educational Psychology Review, 17,* 147–177. http://dx.doi.org/10.1007/s10648-005-3951-0

Venables, P. (1976). *Report of the Committee on Continuing Education*. Milton Keynes, England: Open University.

Wanberg, C. R., Welsh, E. T., & Hezlett, S. A. (2003). Mentoring research: A review and dynamic process model. In G. R. Ferris & J. J. Martocchio (Eds.), *Research in personnel and human resources management* (Vol. 22, pp. 39–124). Greenwich, CT: Elsevier Science/JAI Press.

Weick, K. E., & Roberts, K. H. (1993). Collective mind in organizations: Heedful interrelating on flight decks. *Administrative Science Quarterly, 38,* 357–381. http://dx.doi.org/10.2307/2393372

Winne, P. H., & Nesbit, J. C. (2010). The psychology of academic achievement. *Annual Review of Psychology, 61,* 653–678. http://dx.doi.org/10.1146/annurev.psych.093008.100348

Woods, P. A., Bennett, N., Harvey, J. A., & Wise, C. (2004). Variabilities and dualities in distributed leadership: Findings from a systematic literature review. *Educational Management Administration & Leadership, 32,* 439–457. http://dx.doi.org/10.1177/1741143204046497

4

EMPLOYEE GROWTH AND DEVELOPMENT: PERSPECTIVES FROM THE FIELD

RON DREW STONE

Organizations in the 21st century must manage their resources to compete in a global economy whose parameters are constantly redefined by changing international policy, unstable world economic conditions, shifting political influences, ethical issues, environmental protection issues, and diverse customer demands. Government, nonprofit, and charitable organizations are faced with similar challenges as they compete for resources and scarce funding to deliver goods and services that create sustained value. Although every industry or government agency is uniquely defined with numerous factors that shape the opportunities and threats in its marketplace, they all have one thing in common: their employees.

Organizations depend on employees to efficiently create and sustain the quality of products and services and deliver the ultimate customer experience. As employees take advantage of growth and development opportunities, their competence, confidence, and commitment increase while they engage in

http://dx.doi.org/10.1037/14731-005
The Psychologically Healthy Workplace: Building a Win–Win Environment for Organizations and Employees,
M. J. Grawitch and D. W. Ballard (Editors)

day-to-day work processes and deliver on the customer promise. By providing opportunities for growth and development, organizations contribute to the quality of employee work experience and realize the benefits of developing employees to their full potential. Growth and development opportunities also play a central role in talent management strategies to attract and retain the best and the brightest.

NATURE AND SCOPE OF EMPLOYEE GROWTH AND DEVELOPMENT INITIATIVES

It is useful to establish context by describing the nature and scope of employee growth and development initiatives. These initiatives often include objectives, strategies, and activities that fall into one of three categories. The three categories are less significant in the distinctions between them than as illustrations of the philosophical thinking of executives and line managers as they make decisions about funding, strategy, and priorities for training and employee development.

Category I: Industry-Specific Operational Skills Training

This category is often viewed as essential training because of its direct interface with business processes and the customer. Included is training in areas such as work processes and procedures, work quality, use of technology, customer service requirements, compliance, product knowledge, and sales. Generally speaking, without this knowledge and skill, employees could not do their jobs efficiently and effectively. Either employees possess these skills when hired or the employer provides opportunities to learn them through some form of formal training or on-the-job coaching activity.

Category II: Executive Development, Managerial and Supervisory Development, and Interpersonal Skills Training

Training in areas such as leadership, problem solving, decision making, communication, negotiation, and teamwork is often included in this category, along with initiatives that focus on new-employee orientation, coaching, mentoring, and high-potential employee development. Some of these could sometimes be included in Category I, depending on whether they are considered essential to day-to-day success. Some of these skills are often considered by management to be inherent or easy to learn and therefore can be developed in individuals over time with minimal negative consequences to the organization. If a lack of competency in any area of this category is viewed as a risk to the organization, then that competency and the associated program shift to Category I. Many organizations tend to assume that skills such as problem solving and decision making can be learned on the job, but this isn't necessarily the case.

Category III: Career Planning and Personal Development

This category includes programs such as tuition reimbursement, continuing education and career development courses, programs offered by professional associations, self-study, career counseling assistance, internal career advancement processes, and opportunities for promotion. Category III growth and development activities are usually not directly related to an immediate need associated with the current role of the employee. When money and other resources are scarce, satisfying current needs will usually prevail, and so programs in this category are generally viewed as longer term development initiatives. Funding for some of these types of initiatives is often shared by the employee and the organization (e.g., the employer pays some percentage of an employee's college tuition while the employee pays the rest). Some structure and resources are often available to employees who want to pursue personal development and realize career aspirations. Employees are generally expected to take the initiative in personal development, but processes sometimes exist that involve the supervisor or a counselor to guide and support the employee.

Executive leaders in companies that truly value employees as a strategic asset (the difference between success and failure) will often demand a more structured career development process including strong supervisor support and multiple avenues for development. For example, development may be encouraged through networking, mentoring, coaching, lateral moves to another position, temporary special assignments, and formal meetings with the immediate supervisor for career guidance. Such formalized activities provide supervisor and organizational support with the understanding that the employee is accountable for his or her own career development within the context of that support.

The three categories may occasionally overlap. For example, a course on negotiation skills may be considered Category I for the labor relations manager or for the employees in the purchasing department, whereas the same course may fall into Category II for employees whose jobs do not primarily require negotiating skills. New-employee orientation would typically be Category II;

however, if it includes training in specific work processes or engaging the customer, it will likely be in Category I. Hence, whether a particular development activity or training program falls into Category I, II, or III may be extremely context dependent.

THE EMPLOYEE TRAINING AND DEVELOPMENT PROCESS

The employee training and development process has seven key phases from beginning to end (Stone, 2009b). The entire process must function properly for employee needs to be met and to obtain the desired business contribution from any single employee development expenditure. Table 4.1 illustrates these seven phases and includes a synopsis of the role of key players during each phase. The roles in Table 4.1 speak principally to training and employee development activities that fit into Categories I and II. Most are also suited to Category III (career planning and personal development).

KEY QUESTIONS FOR SUCCESSFUL EMPLOYEE GROWTH AND DEVELOPMENT INITIATIVES

Organizations must grapple with seven key questions to successfully pursue and implement employee growth and development initiatives. The following subsections describe each issue, along with strategies organizations might use to successfully overcome these challenges.

Centralized or Decentralized Organization

Where should the employee training and development function report in order to optimize results? The central issues in determining reporting relationship are control, accountability, responsiveness, and cost-effectiveness. Those supporting a centralized approach point to a lack of cost-effectiveness when training is decentralized (i.e., when trainers report directly to the senior human resources officer rather than to an operational unit). They argue that training resources are suboptimized because there is usually duplication of resources, programs, and activities. Those supporting a decentralized function claim that training from the corporate ivory tower will not be responsive to the needs of line organizations. They argue that training requests often go unfilled or take too long to be fulfilled, and that training is often too generic and not relevant enough to meet organizational needs. The heart of the debate often focuses on Category I training that the operational line function

TABLE 4.1

Roles in the Training and Development Process

Phases of training and development process	Synopsis of roles and responsibilities (Categories I and II solutions)			
	Training function or training supplier	Trainee or participant	Client or immediate supervisor of trainee	Senior management
1. Identify the business opportunities and requirements, performance gaps, root cause, and needs	• Partner to identify business goal and need or opportunity • Partner to identify and communicate employee requirements, performance or opportunity gap, root cause of gap	• Provide input on needs and organization barriers to performance	• Partner to identify business opportunity and needs and to provide input and support • Make decisions on suitability of solution and how to influence success	• Provide funding that supports business purpose
2. Design the solution	• Partner to determine key components of effective and efficient solution that will influence execution in work setting	• Provide input on preferences	• Partner and approve the solution design that will best achieve desired results	• Provide funding • Demand and support a design that creates a partnership to get results
3. Develop or acquire content	• Match content to the approved solution design	• Provide input on learning preferences	• Provide input on preferences • Demand a results-centered solution	• Provide funding • Demand results-centered solutions
4. Initiate preengagement activity	• Initiate administration of the selected activity	• Complete the activity	• Partner to guide, support, and encourage the trainee	• Provide funding

(continues)

TABLE 4.1
Roles in the Training and Development Process   (Continued)

	Synopsis of roles and responsibilities (Categories I and II solutions)			
Phases of training and development process	Training function or training supplier	Trainee or participant	Client or immediate supervisor of trainee	Senior management
5. Deliver or accommodate delivery of the solution	• Deliver relevant solution and facilitate problem solving and deep thinking	• Participate and collaborate with others to facilitate learning	• Provide active support and reinforcement to guide and support trainee during and after delivery	• Provide funding • Provide visible support before, during, and after delivery
6. Follow up and execute in the work setting	• Partner with others to follow up and influence execution in the work setting	• Apply learning to work situations	• Visibly and actively follow up to reinforce employee execution and desired results	• Hold managers and supervisors accountable to reinforce desired outcomes
7. Verify or evaluate business outcome results	• Partner to determine if employee needs and business outcome are met	• Participate to determine if employee needs and business outcome are met	• Partner to support the activities to determine results and need for continuous improvement	• Support strategic sampling to determine if organization's objectives met

deems critical to its day-to-day success. Line functions are very protective of this type of training, primarily because it is often the first item to suffer budget cuts when company revenue falls short of expectations, which is especially problematic given that training budgets at the corporate level are sometimes arbitrarily cut as well.

Creating a Win–Win Reporting Structure

There is no easy way to determine whether a centralized or decentralized reporting structure is best for the training function of an organization. Over the course of an 8- to 10-year period, corporations often change the reporting structure of training units from centralized to decentralized and then change it back again, all in search of the elusive best approach or because new executives arrive with new philosophies. Some companies allow a centralized corporate training function to coexist with multiple decentralized training units in major departments such as sales, customer service, and manufacturing (e.g., specific sales training will report to the sales or marketing department). This can be an effective way to strike the balance between centralized and decentralized training functions. Mission, scope, and roles are then clearly defined to minimize duplication and optimize cost-effectiveness. For example, the training function within the sales department may have its scope limited strictly to sales skills training. Should the sales group require training in another area (e.g., effective communication), that training would be provided by the centralized training department. However, the best-laid plans often go awry as duplication and inefficiency ultimately may creep into such training operations.

Companies sometimes turn to a matrix type of organization to satisfy the needs of both corporate and line organizations while maintaining an acceptable level of cost-effectiveness. Executives often like the matrix because it allows the line departments such as sales and manufacturing to keep responsibility for delivering job-related skills training. At the same time, the skill and development needs that are common to the entire organization can be assessed and managed at the corporate level. This corporate management role is especially important in areas such as leadership development, supervisor training, and career development.

Figure 4.1 shows an example of a successful matrix structure. As shown in the figure, the operations training division reports directly to manufacturing operations support, which provides operations training for each of the three manufacturing divisions. Duplication and inefficiencies in operations and compliance training are minimized because all three divisions are supported by the same training unit. Because the type of skills required and the

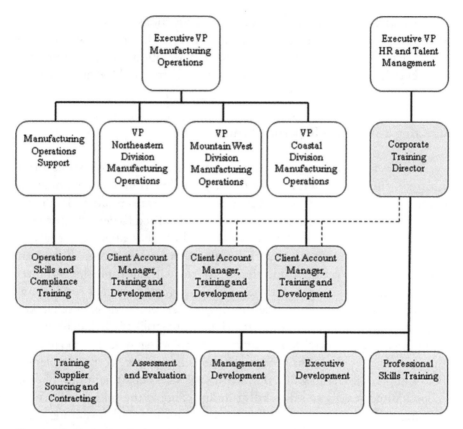

Figure 4.1. Example of win–win training organization structure.

compliance issues are similar within each division, this structure makes sense and reduces duplication and efficiency issues that would be of concern to the vice president of each operating division.

The corporate training director shown in Figure 4.1 is responsible for all employee training and development that is not related to operations skills and compliance training. To ensure that ongoing employee training and development needs are identified and met in a timely manner, client account managers report directly to the division operations structure and physically reside in the region. This reporting relationship and physical location allow account managers to concentrate exclusively on the needs of the division. A strong personal and professional relationship develops between the account managers and those they serve in the division. The dotted-line relationship to the corporate training director allows the account manager access to all of the resources of the corporate training function and minimizes duplication of effort and other inefficiencies that could develop.

The charter, role, and position description of the account manager specifies how the matrix reporting relationship functions. For example, the account manager coordinates the use of all outside sources with the training supplier sourcing and contracting group, which reports to the corporate function. Likewise, the other corporate training groups coordinate in the same way regarding the use of outside supplier sources. The account managers also go directly to each internal training group as necessary when they have needs that can be met by the group. For example, when account managers identify a need to provide communications skills training to a division client, they contact the professional skills training group at the corporate level. The professional skills group either delivers the training to the division client or assists the account executive with outsourcing as necessary.

The charter and mission of the corporate training function clearly spell out the responsibility to address all corporate programs (e.g., executive development, management development, and high-potential programs). The charter clearly describes operations skills and compliance training and specifies that all other training and employee development activities are the responsibility of the corporate training function. The charter specifically notes the responsibility to serve the needs expressed by the division client account manager in delivering programs and services within each division.

In short, the client account manager works with the corporate training function to identify needs, design and deliver effective solutions, and evaluate results. The person who occupies this position must be highly skilled in creating and sustaining partnerships, applying assessment and analysis, and using consultative approaches to negotiate alternative solutions. This individual must also become intimately familiar with division operations. The client account manager attends the corporate training director's staff meetings to share issues and routinely reports on training activities and needs. This individual is also a frequent attendee at division staff meetings and strategic planning sessions.

Effective and Efficient Training Delivery Methods

A few decades ago, training methods were limited to on-the-job training, small-group discussion, or a classroom facilitator. Media was limited to video, overhead transparencies, slides, and charts. Today, the Internet and the power of personal computers and mobile devices provide an array of methods for designing and delivering a learning experience. Learners now have the ability to selectively view content and make enhancements through technologies such as wikis, blogs, and social media platforms. These new technologies provide advantages of timeliness and convenience—learners can access what they need exactly when and where they need it. They are flexible, in that learners can access the content again at any time and as often as necessary, and the content can easily be made available to new audiences. Designers can create realistic scenarios in both classroom- and technology-delivered training through simulation. Technology also offers uniformity of content and delivery, which helps students gain consistent understanding and performance more consistently than they can via face-to-face instructor-led delivery. Designers can also easily customize and update software to keep content current. Finally, for all of these reasons, the technological approach tends to be cost-efficient, particularly in the long run, when compared with traditional methods.

On the other hand, the up-front development costs of technology can be very expensive. Some training solutions apply only to small populations and therefore are less cost-efficient overall. Technology cannot always enable human interaction and collaborative problem solving; rarely can it create realistic practice situations for learning purposes. Finally, many organizations do not have enough data to confirm whether technological delivery methods are in fact more effective than traditional methods.

In a given situation, traditional facilitator-led training may be the least expensive if not the most effective method, yet it may be the preferred method because that has been the way it has always been done. Neither of these two extremes is acceptable. Too many training professionals go along with what leaders in the organization want instead of demonstrating to them which method(s) will be the most effective, followed by a discussion and decisions about how to deliver learning efficiently. Many training professionals short-change consultative approaches with clients and organizational leaders that would employ systematic processes to determine the most effective delivery method. This may lead to quick but ineffective solutions.

Following the delivery of a particular solution, the reasons why performance does or does not improve as expected may not always be clear, as many factors in the work setting contribute to performance results. Identifying these factors is difficult, especially because everyone who has anything to do with business improvement tends to claim credit for successes (Stone, 2011). For example, when the marketing department launches a major promotion and advertising campaign during the same time frame as the delivery of sales training, each group is likely to claim that the sales improvement was due to their campaign. Likewise, when failure occurs, fingers often point in another direction (Stone, 2011). The reality is that the factors credited with an improvement may not be contributing at all. Table 4.2 lists the key deficiencies that often contribute to ineffective solutions (Stone, 2011). The table also suggests how training professionals can apply corrective actions so that solutions have the best opportunity for success.

TABLE 4.2
Key Issues in Designing Solutions and Recommendations

Key issue (deficiency)	Corrective action by training professionals
1. Needs assessment is lacking or, when conducted, addresses training needs with little or no consideration for management support or other nontraining issues.	Ensure sponsors identify the business purpose and the end-in-mind for each initiative. Use this as a stepping-stone to introduce and develop a needs assessment that quickly focuses on the desired business outcome to determine needs and surface a viable solution. Preassessments can also be administered to determine the readiness level of the targeted workforce. Ensure that training (if needed) and other actions are identified that will influence desired results. Ensure that the role of management reinforcement is clearly communicated to the sponsor and others as necessary.
2. Performance and outcome objectives are often nonexistent or do not include key measures of success.	When presenting the training or employee development solution to sponsors, focus on objectives that state the desired execution and business outcome. That is, what should employees do (performance or behavioral action) as a result of the solution, and how will the business benefit? Establish mutual agreement on how to measure these results, and build these objectives and measures into the program for everyone to see and accomplish.
3. Solutions are not reinforced through a partnership with the sponsor.	From the beginning, starting with the needs assessment, partner with sponsors to build a solution that includes the role and expected actions of sponsors and management in reinforcing the desired results. The training professional builds the solution with mutual agreement regarding the reinforcement role of sponsors and others. Be certain to focus on at least two key actions to be implemented by sponsors/managers: (a) communication of the objectives and expectations to the targeted employee group and (b) follow-up reinforcement and encouragement with employees in the work setting.

(continues)

TABLE 4.2
Key Issues in Designing Solutions and Recommendations *(Continued)*

Key issue (deficiency)	Corrective action by training professionals
4. Resources are not allocated for pilot experiments and to conduct some level of evaluation to determine how partnering on the solution contributes to business outcomes.	Training budgets and resources must be examined to determine the appropriate mix of needs assessment and evaluation activities. Each year, evaluation priorities and strategies must be addressed to determine where and how to allocate the fraction of budgeted resources to gain the most useful information for the organization. When evaluating solutions, focus on how the partnership and management reinforcement contribute to successful transfer and behavior change. Success is about the collaborative solution, not the learning event.
5. Training professionals behave like order takers instead of taking a consultative approach with sponsors and clients.	The road to effectiveness has more clarity when armed with (a) results from a sound needs assessment, (b) focused objectives and measures, (c) a clear sponsor involvement role and expectations for reinforcement, and (d) evidence from historical evaluations. Discovering what matters most and which delivery methods and solution design will be more effective in the environment is much easier for all to see. Hence, a partnership that includes collaboration, negotiation, and support is more likely to yield successful business outcomes. The bottom line: an effective and efficient solution.

Elaboration is required for a couple of the issues mentioned in Table 4.2. Issue 2 addresses the need to specify the desired execution and business outcomes. For instance, imagine that supervisors from a customer service center attend an 8-hour training program on how to effectively interact with customers. They then return to the work setting to coach their customer service representatives to execute the proper behavior. Their execution objectives are to apply the appropriate steps of the customer interaction process in every customer contact situation and to identify team members who lack confidence in the customer contact process and coach them in the application of the process. Meanwhile, their business outcome objectives are to maintain monthly customer satisfaction scores above 94% in the five major response categories of the customer satisfaction survey, and to reduce customer complaints to 10 per 100 contacts by end of first quarter.

Issue 5 in the table addresses the need for training professionals to use consultative approaches to convince managers and business leaders about the delivery methods that work best to achieve the goals of development initiatives or to correct performance problems. Training professionals must be observant and know when to shift roles from being listeners to being consultants (Stone, 2009a). Before this can be accomplished, they must develop their own skills to address the issues in Table 4.2 so as to build their confidence to use results-centered work processes to identify needs, develop conclusions, design the proper solutions, and approach clients in a consultative fashion to provide evidence and reasoning on which solutions and delivery methods will be the most effective.

When a training solution takes employees off the job and channels them to a learning activity, managers will rightfully expect results, and they will want to use the most efficient means of delivery. The burden is on the training function to provide compelling evidence about the best alternatives among methods (e.g., facilitator-led, e-learning, supported platforms for social media or other informal methods, or blended approaches) to achieve the desired result (Stone, 2011). If training professionals cannot provide such evidence or cannot at least provide sound reasoning, then they will have to default to client preferences, even though they may believe the desired outcome will not be achieved.

By allocating a percentage of training budgets to conduct follow-up evaluation, training professionals will have evidence to demonstrate which methods get results in specific situations and how partnering makes a significant contribution. These data will provide the best opportunity to present compelling evidence to influence the choices made by organizational leaders. More time and money need to be allocated to experimentation with a variety of delivery methods and designs with the goal of determining how each contributes to effective business outcomes. The lessons learned can then be used to influence better decisions about delivery methods and overall solution design.

Accountability for Talent Development Results

Accountability means delivering programs that meet three criteria: they get performance results, they show the contribution through some type of measurement sampling process (Spitzer, 2007), and the program designers take ownership regardless of the outcome. In many organizations, minimal effort is made to measure the contribution of employee development to business objectives. This lack of measurement contributes significantly to organizations' inability to optimize the performance, growth, and potential of human capital (Spitzer, 2007). Without effective measurement, it is difficult to know what causes a business outcome to occur when goals are met. Likewise, it is difficult to pinpoint how improvements can be made in partnering for employee development initiatives when limited evidence is available to aid in decision making.

Successful training departments have discovered a simple formula that gives them the best opportunity to succeed and sustain their contribution. That formula is partnering + identifying needs + management reinforcement = transfer of learning to the work setting and business outcomes (Kirkpatrick & Kirkpatrick, 2010). The benefit to the training department is an improved reputation, support from organizational leaders, and repeat business. Likewise, the employees who rely on these services to improve their skills and realize their potential are also beneficiaries.

Occasionally, breakdowns in roles and accountability present barriers to the success of employee training and development initiatives (see Table 4.2). These breakdowns tend to occur in three areas, which are discussed next: partnering to identify needs and effective solutions, transferring learning to behavior in the work setting, and demonstrating how partnering contributes to business outcomes.

Partnering to Identify Needs and Design Effective Solutions

Training managers and staff must meet the needs of the organization and its employees. However, training professionals sometimes get caught up in their own subject-matter expertise. They are so eager to contribute that they forge ahead with tunnel vision by thinking only about the delivery phase of the process. They sometimes neglect the important step of needs analysis, overlook performance issues unrelated to the learning (e.g., lack of management feedback, guidance, and recognition), and assume that learning equals results. The most common error is a failure to partner with leaders and clients and persuade them that some type of analysis, even if brief, should be done before identifying and designing a solution (Stone, 2009b). Many believe that needs analysis is time consuming. This may be true when dated and complicated processes are used to identify performance gaps and needs, but today's skilled training professionals know how to partner and use the right approach to quickly identify performance gaps, root causes, and learning and performance needs (Stone, 2009b).

No matter who sponsors a training or employee development initiative, the trainee's immediate supervisor should play a key role in terms of guidance, support, and reinforcement (Kirkpatrick & Kirkpatrick, 2010). This is true for performance solutions as well as for employee development and career planning. The responsibility of training professionals does not end with the learning event. They must consistently promote and nurture the involvement of supervisors so that knowledge and skills are transferred to the work setting and goals can be achieved. They must communicate this supervisory role to organizational leaders and clients and ensure that it is built into the design of solutions. Training should be about achieving performance success through a collaborative solution. This includes meeting the needs of the employee and the organization to influence business results. Successful training functions partner with organizational leaders and clients to determine employee execution requirements, analyze performance gaps and root causes, and identify the ultimate goal and solution. Then, members of the training function should proceed with a focus on managing partnerships and delivering consistent results. When results are consistently achieved over time, the training function develops a reputation of reliability throughout the organization.

Successful training functions also partner with supervisors to influence employee performance and counsel employees on career development and career advancement choices. They provide tools, coaching, and support to assist supervisors in performing their role. Both internal and external training suppliers should be assessed on their commitment to be accountable for results. Exhibit 4.1 is an assessment that can be used with training suppliers to gauge their commitment to accountability. Those who score high show a willingness to look beyond the event and work as partners to achieve business results. The assessment can be used by training professionals or it can be provided to supervisors, sponsors, and clients. The terms and language used can be modified to suit the situation.

Transferring Learning to Behavior in the Work Setting

Although performance breakdowns can and do occur at any part of the training process, a frequent area of breakdown is behavior change in the work setting after the training is delivered (sometimes called *failure to transfer*). Studies have shown that more than 70% of training failure comes after training is completed (Kirkpatrick & Kirkpatrick, 2009). Several authorities estimate that of the $400 billion spent on training annually in the United States, no more than 10% of those dollars result in improved performance. Other studies have suggested that close to 80% of the efforts of most training departments are wasted as transfer of learning to the job fails to occur (Brinkerhoff & Gill, 1994). Perhaps this is one reason why many executives view training as an expense and not an investment. Altogether, greater than 50% of training expenditures are wasted because trainees do not apply their new knowledge and skills on the job. The two reasons cited most by employees for this lack of follow-through are lack of management reinforcement following training and trainee difficulty in breaking away from old habits (Stone, 2009b).

EXHIBIT 4.1
Assessment: Training Supplier Commitment to Accountability

Supplier Commitment to Accountability	1	2	3	4

Using the scale below, ask the supplier these questions and rank their commitment to accountability based on your view of their response:

1 = unacceptable, 2 = borderline, 3 = acceptable, 4 = clearly superior

1. Performance issues and relevant needs
  a) How do you know what the performance gaps and needs are of our employees and our business (if you do not know, then how will you determine the answers)?
  b) How do you know that your program solution will meet these needs?
  c) If an off-the-shelf program is used, what will you do to customize the (fill in the blank) _____ program solution to make it relevant to our situation?

2. Solution design and delivery
  a) What key solution design components will influence the performance results we have targeted?
  b) Specifically, how will each of the above key design components contribute to the performance results we have targeted?

3. Business outcome
  a) How will your program solution contribute to improving the (fill in the blank with at least one key performance measure) _____business outcome?
  b) What evidence will you provide me to show that your program solution has influenced improvement in these key performance measures before?

4. Execution in the work setting
  a) What evidence will you provide me to show what my team will be able to do following delivery of the _____ program?
  b) What strategy do you recommend to ensure that my employees will actually execute in the work setting following delivery of the _____ program?

5. Supervisor support and reinforcement
  a) What is my role as a supervisor before, during, and after the program delivery?
  b) What specific suggestions, coaching, tools, or templates will you provide to help me fulfill my role?
  c) What will you do to help me conserve my time while guiding and supporting me in fulfilling my role?

6. Supplier follow-up and support before, during, and after delivery
  a) What services will you provide before, during, and after the program delivery?
  b) What specific actions will you take after delivery to determine if the solution is working effectively and what will be done if it is not effective?

Consider a study conducted by Brent Peterson at Columbia University (Kirkpatrick & Kirkpatrick, 2009) that found that the typical organization invests 85% of its resources in the training event, yet those events contributed only 24% to the learning effectiveness of the participants. The activities that led to the most learning effectiveness were follow-up activities that occurred after the training event. However, the training function typically allocates most of its resources to the learning event itself at the expense of sound strategies and practices for the preengagement and follow-up phases of the process. Yet, the follow-up phase is typically the weakest link in the training process. Training directors have the authority to alter this unproductive imbalance.

A good start would be to develop the right competencies in the professional training staff so that they are confident in how to approach and execute this follow-up responsibility. Next, trainers should cease using the end-of-session evaluation as the measure of success for facilitators, instructors, and the training event. As long as end-of-session evaluations are used as the most significant measure of success, then that is where training professionals will put their energy. Unfortunately, good end-of-session evaluations often mean little when it comes to the successful application of training content to the work setting. Most of the training that is delivered is not successfully applied in the work setting, no matter how positive the end-of-training evaluations. Therefore, as stated earlier, training professionals must partner with clients and others to achieve the intended business result. They must ensure that line managers and other important gatekeepers in the organization actively reinforce what was learned in training and encourage the application of learning on the job. The single biggest contributor to the success of employee training and development initiatives is the involvement of the client or immediate supervisor (Berger & Berger, 2004; Broad & Newstrom, 1992). A supervisor's words and actions carry significant weight in influencing employees' desire to learn and their willingness to execute following the learning.

Demonstrating How Employee Development Contributes to Business Outcomes

Historically, trainers have not adequately demonstrated how employee training and development initiatives actually contribute to business. More significant, training departments have often chosen the wrong path for demonstrating results. In the 21st century, training is rarely effective as a stand-alone performance solution (Stone, 2009b). Yet, trainers often continue to treat training and development initiatives as though they can work magic by implementing and evaluating them as stand-alone events. The problem with this approach is that the evaluation frequently serves to justify the existence of the training function itself, instead of focusing on achieving goals and continuous improvement. That is, by providing data that call attention to what the training achieved, the evaluation reinforces the notion that training can go it alone, with little support from business leaders or clients. In this scenario it is extremely difficult to gain support in the organization for the necessary data collection efforts to evaluate whether a specific training design is making a contribution. No one wants to help the training department toot its own horn and justify its existence.

So how can the significance of partnering be demonstrated? The appropriate organizational support and management reinforcement must be included in the design of every training and employee development initiative. Then, when we evaluate results, we evaluate the contribution of the complete design (including management support and reinforcement) and not just the contribution of the training event. When results are reported, the contribution of the complete design, not just the training event, should be emphasized. This sends the message that management support and reinforcement are needed to properly identify needs, design effective solutions, and influence the behaviors that drive business results.

To obtain evidence that shows the clear contribution of partnering, a pilot study could be conducted using an experimental design. Researchers would need to find two similar situations and work environments and deliver one solution that includes all the aspects of partnering (e.g., communication of expectations, follow-up reinforcement) and another solution that lacks the partnering activities. The learning event itself would be identical for both the experimental group and the control group. Then, the results of the training program that included partnering could be compared with the one that did not.

EFFECTIVE LONG-TERM TALENT DEVELOPMENT STRATEGIES

There are many types of strategies and various tactics for developing talent within the organization. Some organizations do a very effective job of allocating and managing the available resources to develop talent. However, in many organizations, talent development strategies and initiatives are misguided or nonexistent; they may even be incompatible with the needs of the organization. Figure 4.2 shows typical barriers to long-term effective talent development (Berger & Berger, 2004; Broad & Newstrom, 1992). Organizations that are successful in talent development are able to gain and sustain top management support by identifying clear program goals and outcomes that contribute to satisfying key business needs and measures (Adelsberg & Trolley, 1999).

Organizations generally have two types of long-term talent development programs. One type is career planning and development programs,

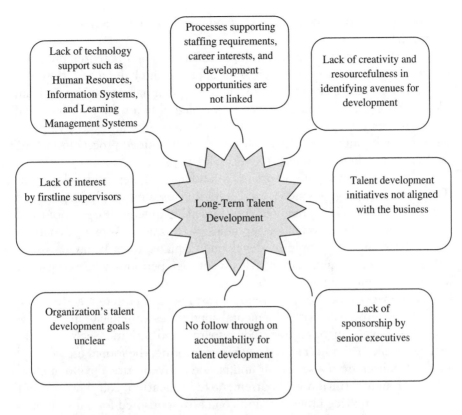

Lack of technology support such as Human Resources, Information Systems, and Learning Management Systems

Processes supporting staffing requirements, career interests, and development opportunities are not linked

Lack of creativity and resourcefulness in identifying avenues for development

Lack of interest by firstline supervisors

Long-Term Talent Development

Talent development initiatives not aligned with the business

Organization's talent development goals unclear

No follow through on accountability for talent development

Lack of sponsorship by senior executives

Figure 4.2. Typical barriers to long-term talent development.

which are typically associated with the general employee population, with a goal of growing talent from within and meeting employee satisfaction and retention goals. These programs usually include employee career planning coupled with opportunities for developmental movement and promotion within the organization. Career planning and development programs do not guarantee upward movement or job stability, but they do provide a formal channel for development and promotion. Developmental movement and promotion are usually based on employee aspirations, assessment of potential and current performance, and employee matching with the unique job requirements.

The other type of long-term development is high-potential programs, which are designed to retain top talent and increase the number of leaders ready to assume broader roles in the organization. This is sometimes referred to as developing bench strength. Participation in high-potential programs is usually limited to a small percentage of employees who are prescreened and assessed to match strict criteria. Many high-potential programs limit the pool of candidates to those identified and nominated by management (a top-down approach).

Organizations that have developed successful high-potential programs often use a three-tiered approach. This approach includes a selection process driven by management but also allows self-nomination and peer or team identification and assessment to determine eligibility for the high-potential candidate pool. Final selection is often determined by an executive panel with oversight authority, which follows a predetermined process in making decisions to include nominees in the candidate pool.

Assessing employee potential is a fundamental step in development. Typical tools or programs used for screening and assessing employee potential include core competency requirements, leadership inventories, psychological testing, traditional performance appraisals, multirater assessments, counseling, self-assessments, employee development plans, team behavior assessments, personal communication style inventories, performance management systems, and simulations.

Employees must also have avenues to express career interests and a means for development. Typical developmental approaches available to meet career and talent development goals include resources and activities such as coaching, certification and licensing programs, mentoring, the formal use of social media, feedback from assessments and personal inventories, developmental job assignments, tuition reimbursement for education, self-development resources, apprentice programs, and company-sponsored formal skills and leadership training to satisfy core developmental needs.

As indicated earlier, the skill of the planners and administrators in developing and executing an integrated strategy that links all of these tools, activities, and programs together is critical to successful talent development. Each of these processes, programs, and tools can be coordinated and administered with the assistance of state-of-the-art software, including human resources information systems and learning management systems.

The following examples of long-term talent development programs help to show how they are designed and administered in a concrete sense. Some ultimately failed and provided lessons learned, but most are success stories. These examples illustrate how the practical needs and constraints of an organization are paramount when designing and rolling out successful programs.

Case Example: A Failed Career Planning and Development Program

Several years ago, the senior vice president of human resources of a large aerospace company convinced the C-suite executives that a career planning program was an excellent and necessary tool to grow talent and allow employees more career choices. A permanent position of career planning manager was created to design and manage the effort. The new manager position was filled from within the company by promoting an inexperienced but highly regarded employee from the manufacturing unit. The new career planning manager spent several months visiting leading Fortune 500 companies to conduct research on how to design and implement a career planning program.

The final product was a lengthy process with slick brochures showing how the process worked and touting the benefits to employees and the organization. The roles and responsibilities of managers in administering the process were clearly articulated. Supervisors would be trained in how to administer the process, and information sessions were held for all employees. A website was created, containing downloadable career interest forms as well as additional information and details. The website allowed supervisors to enter employee assessment data, track employee interest in jobs, and track other important information.

Unfortunately, despite all their hard work, the career planning process floundered for 2 years while employees expressed dissatisfaction and supervisors became disinterested. Finally, management labeled the process a failure beyond repair, and a decision was made to abandon the process. Why did this happen? Several reasons were identified as major contributors to the failure. First, senior management and department heads had no major role in rolling out the process and demonstrating their support. Similarly, first-line and middle management had virtually no input into the design of the process and their role in administering it. More significant, the company had no long-term plan to identify future resource requirements and match the supply of workers to the availability of jobs at the organizational, regional, or national level. Hence, there was little management emphasis on employee career interests and no way to match those career interests with organizational needs. In addition, supervisors had no resources to identify job profiles outside their own units and, consequently, no way to guide employees toward broader career options. The company's formal job-posting program was not implemented until 16 months after the rollout of the career planning and development program, resulting in most job vacancies being filled with new hires. Finally, the resources for development from which employees could select were limited to existing formal training programs and self-development modules in the resource library available on the website.

The shortfalls in this career planning and development program need no elaboration as it is clear that this wound was self-inflicted. Nothing fails more easily than a program ill-planned and ill-conceived behind the closed doors of the corporate office. Organizations that are successful in developing talent for the long term have three things in common regarding their processes and programs: management support, an integrated program strategy, and customization to organization needs.

Case Example: A Successful High-Potential Program

With management commitment and creative design, high-potential programs can be successfully installed and executed. A high-potential program implemented 2 years ago by a large telecommunications company had the purpose of addressing the need for replacements and building bench strength to prepare for company growth and retirements. The profile of the program is shown in Table 4.3.

The design of the high-potential program includes two 5-day learning summits offered 6 months apart. Strategic projects are sandwiched between these summits. Each candidate is assigned to a senior leader of the organization to serve as his or her personal coach. The strategic projects are completed by teams through virtual teamwork and executive coaching. Periodic executive reviews provide feedback on the projects. After completion of the second learning summit, candidates transfer into a developmental job rotation assignment for a 5-month period with additional rotation assignments at future times as mutually determined by the executive coach and candidate. Figure 4.3 shows the design components of the high-potential program.

A highlight of the program is a personal dinner with the CEO. This dinner is completely unstructured with no agenda and is initiated by the CEO. A typical dinner includes light conversation about the candidate and discussion about the candidate's goals and company issues. Hence, the organization emphasizes the role of senior leaders in the development of high-potential employees, with senior leadership support extending all the way to the CEO.

TABLE 4.3
Profile of a Successful High-Potential Program

Business goals	Increase number of leaders who are ready to assume broader roles in the company
	Retain high-potential employees and future leaders
Program objectives	Accelerate development by developing leadership, strategic thinking, and decision-making capability
	Apply learning to real organizational challenges by engaging in regional strategic projects
	Develop and implement action plans to accelerate personal and organizational growth
	Establish a network with a variety of peers and functions across the organization to build relationships that enable collaboration and swift action
Time span	One-year structured program with a variety of developmental components designed to build leadership capability
Eligibility	High-potential candidates identified through succession planning and those employees who self-nominate and are certified by the executive selection panel

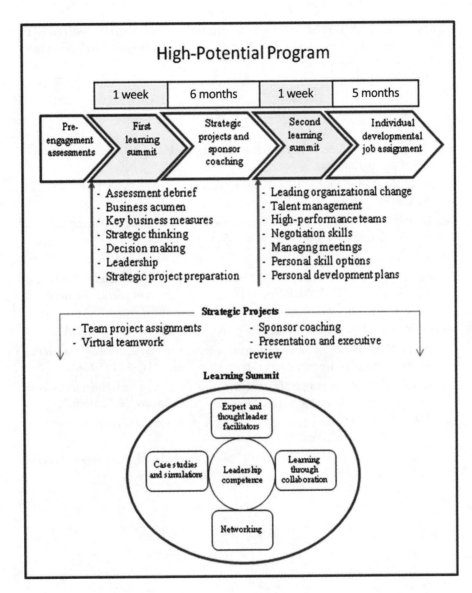

Figure 4.3. Design of successful high-potential program.

CLOSING THOUGHTS

Responsiveness, simplicity, flexibility, and convenience are additional keys to success in the new landscape of the 21st century. Training and talent development functions will likely need to adopt frugality as an operational value. They will need to demonstrate that they are good stewards of the company's money and resources. Even with limited budgets they will need to find a way to dedicate some funds to experiment with creative and new ideas, concepts, and approaches.

REFERENCES

Adelsberg, D., & Trolley, E. (1999). *Running training like a business*. San Francisco, CA: Berrett-Koehler.

Berger, L., & Berger, D. (2004). *The talent management handbook*. New York, NY: McGraw-Hill.

Brinkerhoff, R., & Gill, S. (1994). *The learning alliance: Systems thinking in human resource development*. San Francisco, CA: Jossey-Bass.

Broad, M., & Newstrom, J. (1992). *Transfer of training*. Reading, MA: Addison-Wesley.

Kirkpatrick, J., & Kirkpatrick, W. (2009). *The Kirkpatrick four levels: A fresh look after 50 years, 1959–2009*. Retrieved from http://www.kirkpatrickpartners.com/Portals/0/Resources/Kirkpatrick%20Four%20Levels%20white%20paper.pdf

Kirkpatrick, J., & Kirkpatrick, W. (2010). *Training on trial*. New York, NY: AMACOM.

Spitzer, D. (2007). *Transforming performance measurement: Rethinking the way we measure and drive organizational success*. New York, NY: AMACOM.

Stone, R. (2009a). Achieving results with a performance-centered design framework. *Performance Improvement, 48*(5), 37–44. http://dx.doi.org/10.1002/pfi.20077

Stone, R. (2009b). *Aligning training for results: A process and tools that link training to business*. San Francisco, CA: Pfeiffer.

Stone, R. (2011). *The real value of training: Measuring and analyzing business outcomes and the quality of ROI*. New York, NY: McGraw-Hill.

5

WORK–LIFE BALANCE: CONTEMPORARY PERSPECTIVES

LARISSA K. BARBER, MATTHEW J. GRAWITCH,
AND PATRICK W. MALONEY

Today's organizations are struggling with how to manage employees' growing demands for work–life balance while also improving productivity and the financial bottom line. Researchers have been steadily building a stronger business case for work–life initiatives over the past few decades. Contemporary research has gone beyond employee and organizational well-being indicators (e.g., strain, work–life conflict and facilitation, organizational climate) to also demonstrate effects of such initiatives on employee and organizational performance (Arthur & Cook, 2003; Clifton & Shepard, 2004; Konrad & Mangel, 2000; Stavrou, 2005; van Steenbergen & Ellemers, 2009). In addition, there is increasing interest regarding how organizations can provide social support systems via supervisors and organizational culture for employees to decrease conflict between work and nonwork domains (e.g., Greenhaus, Ziegert, & Allen, 2012; Hammer, Kossek, Anger, Bodner, & Zimmerman, 2011; Kossek, Pichler, Bodner, & Hammer, 2011). The focus

http://dx.doi.org/10.1037/14731-006
The Psychologically Healthy Workplace: Building a Win–Win Environment for Organizations and Employees,
M. J. Grawitch and D. W. Ballard (Editors)

111

on work–life balance initiatives is also prevalent in nonscholarly outlets. For example, the majority of 2012 winners featured in *Fortune's* "100 Best Companies to Work For" offer practices such as telecommuting (79 companies) and child care (33 companies). Thus, it appears that promoting work–life balance is a vital component of any effort to create a healthy and productive workplace.

Unfortunately, there is confusion surrounding conceptualizations of work–life balance (Eby, Casper, Lockwood, Bordeaux, & Brinley, 2005; Jain & Nair, 2013; Kalliath & Brough, 2008). Here we outline a working definition of work–life balance, along with an overview of recent criticisms regarding terminology and underlying assumptions. Then, we provide a brief overview of theory and research in work–life balance, including its application to workplace initiatives. Third, we explore a few key barriers that may prevent optimal work–life benefits for employees and the organization. Last, we discuss the role that work–life balance initiatives play in relation to other psychologically healthy workplace areas.

DEFINING *WORK–LIFE BALANCE*

There is some criticism of work–life balance in scholarly circles, centered on terminology and underlying assumptions. Some point to the vague, perhaps superficial distinction between work and life domains, insisting that work is a part of life, so perhaps it would be best to refer to managing demands across various personal pursuits (Grawitch, Barber, & Justice, 2010). Even the dichotomous distinction between work and nonwork activities can be problematic. There are many different activities associated with the nonwork domain (e.g., family, spiritual, leisure) that vary across individuals (Byrne, 2005; Grawitch et al., 2010; Keeney, Boyd, Sinha, Westring, & Ryan, 2013; Pichler, 2009).

The word *balance* also creates issues by implying equivalent resource allocation (e.g., time, money, energy) to both domains. Given the diversity of work arrangements and personal preferences for those arrangements, this is an inappropriate expectation. In fact, some researchers propose that *work–life fit* may be more appropriate terminology, or perhaps replacing the word *balance* with *interface* (e.g., Grawitch, Maloney, Barber, & Yost, 2011; Voydanoff, 2005). The use of the term *work–life balance*, however, is so ubiquitous that both scholarly and nonscholarly authors continue to use this term while admitting that its meaning is far from the traditional dictionary definition of *balance*.

Some have criticized the way that organizations approach work–life balance. For example, Eikhof, Warhurst, and Haunschild (2007) noted a number of assumptions in the work–life balance literature, such as the notion that the work domain is the source of the problem (work is bad), that individuals with caregiving (child care or elder care) responsibilities are in need of more interventions (work–family over work–life), and that the work domain should be separated from the nonwork domain (work–life integration is stressful). All of these assumptions overlook contradictory evidence showing that many individuals derive enjoyment and personal meaning from their work (Wrzesniewski, LoBuglio, Dutton, & Berg, 2013; Wrzesniewski, McCauley, Rozin, & Schwartz, 1997), individuals without families desire inclusion in work–life initiatives (Casper, Weltman, & Kwesiga, 2007; Ryan & Kossek, 2008), and some individuals prefer higher work–life integration than do others (Kossek & Lautsch, 2012; Rothbard, Philips, & Dumas, 2005).

In light of these nuances, it is important to incorporate employees' varied expectations toward their work and nonwork roles in creating a definition of work–life balance, including expectations about personal meaning (Eby et al., 2005; Kalliath & Brough, 2008). Thus, in this chapter we borrow from tenets of control theory (e.g., Carver & Scheier, 1982), self-determination theory (Ryan, Kuhl, & Deci, 1997), conservation of resources theory (Hobfoll, 1989), and other self-regulation perspectives that focus on individual success in managing finite resources with respect to goals. We define work–life balance as the extent to which one's perceived allocation of finite resources (physical, mental, and emotional) matches one's progress toward or achievement of meaningful goals or expectations across all life domains (both work and nonwork) at a given point in time (Grawitch et al., 2010). Some of the key assumptions regarding this definition are outlined in the following sections.

Work–Life Balance Is a Psychological State

Work–life balance is ultimately a psychological state, influenced by the person and the environment. Informed by person–environment fit theory (see Edwards, 1996, for a review), it is driven by personal preferences. For example, some employees like keeping their work and nonwork domains separate, some like to integrate these domains, and others like to alternate between periods of segmentation and integration (Kossek & Lautsch, 2012). However, it is worth noting that these preferences (and also subsequent behavior) may be affected by aspects of the social environment that include expectations and feedback from others (Grzywacz & Carlson, 2007). Therefore, changing aspects of the social environment is necessary but not sufficient to affect work–life balance, and the evaluations that people make about others' work–life balance can be confounded by their own expectations and preferences. In fact, recent research indicates that aligning one's preferences with the organizational environment is critical for reducing work–life conflict (Kossek & Lautsch, 2012).

Work–Life Balance Is Dependent on Successfully Managing Limited Resources

All individuals have a finite amount of resources (time, energy, money; Edwards & Rothbard, 2000) to devote to life pursuits. Although individuals differ in the amount of each of these resources (Hobfoll & Lilly, 1993), it is not possible to take up infinite pursuits with a finite amount of resources. From this perspective, conflict is experienced when one role requires a greater amount of resources than an individual wishes to allocate to that role or when one role demands a greater amount of resources than an individual currently possesses. On the other hand, facilitation is experienced when one role has a positive contribution to another role by requiring fewer resources than expected or when the resources expended in one role have a positive contribution to another role (Grawitch & Barber, 2010).

Work–Life Balance Requires Achievement of, or Progress Toward, Meaningful Goals

Individuals derive more meaning from goals that are congruent with their personal preferences, and greater meaning leads to improved well-being and performance. Thus, work–life balance is promoted when individuals perceive that they are achieving or making progress toward meaningful goals. Often, people expend their personal resources responding to life demands that do not correspond to their own personal goals. Though effectively managing those incongruent demands may prevent the experience of stress, it does not promote positive psychological states, such as engagement and personal growth (e.g., flourishing mental health; Fredrickson & Losada, 2005; Keyes, 2002). Through our definition of work–life balance, we argue that perceptions of balance are not achieved simply through the reduction of negative experiences (e.g., conflict) but also through role facilitation, personal growth, and development (Grzywacz & Marks, 2000; Kalliath & Brough, 2008).

Work–Life Balance Is a Dynamic State

The psychological state of balance is an outcome of a broader process that attempts to match one's expectations or resource capabilities with one's current situation. Like other self-regulatory processes (see Carver & Scheier, 1982, for an example), expecting individuals to merely achieve work–life balance is an inappropriate objective, given that role demands, goals, and expectations fluctuate over time. For example, research into personal projects (Little, 1983; Little, Salmela-Aro, & Phillips, 2006), personal strivings (Emmons, 1986, 1996), and the importance of certain types of goals over the life span (e.g., socioemotional selectivity theory; see Carstensen, Isaacowitz, & Charles, 1999) all suggest a more fluid approach to goals that can be influenced by numerous situational and personal factors. Thus, interventions addressing work–life balance should provide tools for increasing finite resources or allocating resources more efficiently to help employees manage their dynamic circumstances and personal goals.

THEORY AND RESEARCH

The underlying principles of contemporary work–life balance perspectives are based in role theory (Kahn, Wolfe, Quinn, Snoek, & Rosenthal, 1964); individuals assume multiple roles within a society, each with its own set of behavioral scripts, norms, and expectations. Most work–life balance research arose from tenets of role theory concerning the conflicting relationship among roles (interrole conflict; Kahn et al., 1964), though more recent research also examines ways in which they may enhance one another (interrole enrichment or enhancement; Greenhaus & Powell, 2006). Thus, work–life conflict occurs when engaging in one domain decreases functioning in another domain, whereas work–life facilitation occurs when engaging one domain promotes positive functioning in another domain (see Grzywacz & Marks, 2000, for a review). Researchers have also identified bidirectional conflict and facilitation (work-to-life vs. life-to-work; Frone, Russell, & Cooper, 1992; Frone, Yardley, & Markel, 1997; Grzywacz & Marks, 2000), which further pinpoints sources of conflict or facilitation.

Conflict and facilitation can occur via different linking mechanisms: spillover, compensation, segmentation–integration, resource drain, and congruence (Edwards & Rothbard, 2000; see Table 5.1). For example, conflict can occur due to one's behaviors or negative experiences in one domain interfering with those in another domain (e.g., via negative spillover or compensation) or time in one domain taking away from time in another domain (via resource drain and high segmentation). Likewise, facilitation would include behaviors or positive experiences complementing or enhancing another domain (e.g., positive spillover or congruence) as well as time spent simultaneously in both domains (e.g., high integration). Research suggests that each of these mechanisms may contribute to work–life balance, either across different situations or even simultaneously (Edwards & Rothbard, 2000; Lambert, 1990).

Some of the more recent perspectives that have informed linking mechanisms in the work–life balance literature are influenced by person–environment fit theory (Edwards, 1996). For example, Grzywacz and Marks (2000) couched the spillover model in ecological systems theory (Bronfenbrenner, 1979) to

TABLE 5.1
Linking Mechanisms Between Work and Nonwork Domains

Linking mechanism	Description/example	Examples of practices for managing linking mechanisms
Spillover	Positive relationship between domains. Satisfaction with home life increases job satisfaction, or dissatisfaction with home life decreases job satisfaction.	Nonwork support resources, such as dependent care, paid time off, family leave, and life management services
Compensation	Negative relationship between domains due to compensatory efforts. Job dissatisfaction may lead to more satisfaction in the nonwork domain.	Part-time work and phased transitions
Segmentation–integration	Separating domains leads to less relationship between domains; integrating domains leads to more relationship between domains. Job satisfaction is not likely to influence satisfaction in the nonwork domain with higher segmentation.	Work flexibility practices such as compressed work weeks and telecommuting
Resource drain	Resources spent in one domain are not available to use in another domain. Time and energy in the work domain leaves less of both for the nonwork domain.	Nonwork support resources, such as dependent care, paid time off, family leave, and life management services; part-time work and phased transitions
Congruence	Positive relationships between domains are due to a third factor that influences both.	Training and development programs targeted at knowledge, skills, and abilities affecting both domains (i.e., time management, organization/planning skills, interpersonal skills) can influence facilitation/enrichment

predict the degree to which role strain and role enhancement may occur based on individual factors (i.e., sex, age, education, ethnicity), environmental factors (family and organizational characteristics), and interactions between the two. Other researchers, in what can collectively be called *boundary theories* (Ashforth, Kreiner, & Fugate, 2000; Kossek & Lautsch, 2012; Kreiner, Hollensbe, & Sheep, 2009) have also suggested that individual characteristics (preferences, personality, meanings assigned to roles) and environmental factors (role contexts) influence one's choice of role transition strategies (spillover, compensation, segmentation–integration) that ultimately influence well-being. Grandey and Cropanzano (1999) also suggested drawing on conservation of resources theory (Hobfoll, 1989) to explore resource drain, which can also affect individual well-being due to person–environment fit. Thus, contemporary research has moved beyond a focus on general linking mechanisms in favor of more nuanced predictions in relation to individuals and their work and nonwork environments.

Work–Life Initiatives and Outcomes

Following theoretical perspectives outlining possible effects of work–life conflict and facilitation, organizations have been tasked with implementing policies and practices—collectively called *work–life initiatives*—that assist employees in managing their work and nonwork roles. Ideally, these initiatives should help employees manage multiple roles in a way that optimizes both employee and organizational well-being and performance to create a win–win scenario. Here we provide a more targeted overview of the relationship among work–life initiatives, conflict and facilitation, and outcomes. For simplicity, we do not specify relationships on the basis of linking mechanisms (spillover, compensation, segmentation–integration, resource drain, congruence) or directional influence (work-to-life, life-to-work).

Unfortunately, rigorous research exploring the effects of specific work–life balance initiatives on individual and organizational outcomes has been sparse (Eby et al., 2005; Kelly et al., 2008). Some studies indicate that adoption of work–life initiatives increases indicators of organizational performance (Clifton & Shepard, 2004; Konrad & Mangel, 2000) and perceptions of performance (Perry-Smith & Blum, 2000). Other research indicates that such initiatives may boost the organization's bottom line through other mechanisms, such as increasing the public's perceptions of the institution's value (Arthur, 2003), improving individual job performance (van Steenbergen & Ellemers, 2009; Witt & Carlson, 2006), creating a supportive work environment (Lambert, 2000; Ngo, Foley, & Loi, 2009), and improving employee recruitment and retention (Batt & Valcour, 2003; Casper & Buffardi, 2004; Honeycutt & Rosen, 1997).

Given the more immediate goal of work–life balance initiatives—to reduce work–life conflict or increase facilitation for employees—one would expect to see a clearer link between such initiatives and individual outcomes. Results are often complicated when considering the availability of such initiatives versus their utilization, with the latter leading to more consistent associations with lower conflict (e.g., Allen, 2001; Breaugh & Frye, 2008; Brough, O'Driscoll, & Kalliath, 2005; Butts, Casper, & Yang, 2013).

However, a recent review of studies found that program availability was positively associated with attitudinal outcomes such as job satisfaction, affective commitment, and intentions to stay in the organization (Butts et al., 2013). Studies have yet to examine effects of such initiatives on facilitation, though one study showed no relationship between availability of formal initiatives and facilitation (Taylor, DelCampo, & Blancero, 2009).

The necessity for drawing clear links between work–life initiatives and reduction in conflict or increases in facilitation is worth further exploration due to well-established relationships between conflict–facilitation and individual outcomes. For example, higher work–life conflict is associated with lower employee psychological well-being (e.g., Greenhaus & Powell, 2003; Rantanen, Kinnunen, Feldt, & Pulkkinen, 2008), job satisfaction (e.g., Allen, 2001; Balmforth & Gardner, 2006), and performance (e.g., Graves, Ohlott, & Ruderman, 2007; Witt & Carlson, 2006), as well as higher reports of turnover intentions (e.g., Allen, 2001; Nohe & Sonntag, 2014) and stress and burnout (e.g., Boyar, Maertz, Pearson, & Keough, 2003; Frone et al., 1992). Examples of outcomes associated with greater work–life facilitation include increased organizational commitment, job satisfaction, and effort (Balmforth & Gardner, 2006; Wayne, Musisca, & Fleeson, 2004) and decreased turnover intentions (Balmforth & Gardner, 2006). Research has also found that facilitation predicts objective measures of health, performance, and absenteeism (van Steenbergen & Ellemers, 2009).

Work Flexibility Versus Nonwork Support

Measurement issues concerning specificity may be a source of mixed findings with respect to the positive effects of work–life initiatives on individual and organizational outcomes (Kelly et al., 2008). Therefore, further categorizations concerning work–life balance practices may be warranted. Following contemporary theoretical perspectives and general linking mechanisms between work and nonwork roles, we propose that organizations may intervene by providing either (a) greater autonomy to help employees transition between roles or (b) additional resources for employees to manage the demands themselves. These strategies are represented by the terms *work flexibility* and *nonwork support*, respectively (Grawitch & Barber, 2010).

Work flexibility (e.g., Grzywacz & Marks, 2000) can refer to where employees work (e.g., telecommuting), the number of hours that they work (e.g., reduced hours, part-time options, job sharing), when employees work (e.g., flextime, compressed work weeks), and how they move in and out of work (e.g., phased retirement, phased return-to-work practices). Alternatively, nonwork support practices help employees manage nonwork demands by providing resources such as time or financial support. This includes paid time off (e.g., vacation, sick days), paid or unpaid leave (e.g., maternity, paternity, adoption), child care benefits, and life management resources (e.g., concierge services, discounts to local restaurants or health clubs, dry-cleaning services). Some studies separating aspects of the two have found differential effects on individual outcomes (Breaugh & Frye, 2008; Grawitch & Barber, 2010; Thomas & Ganster, 1995). Our own research suggests that when comparing work flexibility and nonwork support, work flexibility practices may demonstrate more direct and indirect effects on individual affective outcomes such as work-to-life conflict, work engagement, job strain, and life satisfaction (Grawitch & Barber, 2010).

Work flexibility is likely to affect work–life balance via multiple linking mechanisms, but the role of these linking mechanisms is dependent on employee preferences. With increases in autonomy for managing work and nonwork demands (Thomas & Ganster, 1995), individuals may choose optimal strategies for managing their work–life interface according to personal preferences (Kossek & Lautsch, 2012). For example, employees may opt to use flexibility to increase segmentation (compressed workweek), to increase integration (telecommuting), to compensate for increased nonwork demands or major life changes (part-time work, phased transitions), or merely to reduce conflict (flexible scheduling). Thus, work flexibility is not necessarily meant to affect work–life balance through a specific linking mechanism. Rather, it is an opportunity to provide individuals with the freedom to manage their demands in a manner that ensures optimal fit between the work and nonwork domains. Consistent with contemporary work–life perspectives promoting person–environment fit, this should lead to increased well-being and performance (e.g., Grandey & Cropanzano, 1999; Grzywacz & Marks, 2000).

Nonwork support, however, is likely to affect work–life balance through mechanisms focused on reducing negative spillover and resource drain. Increasing nonwork resources may affect well-being in the nonwork domain (because of successfully managing nonwork demands) that may also be associated with experiences in the work domain. For example, providing financial resources for dependent care may reduce stress experienced at home, thereby preventing negative emotions and behaviors from affecting work performance. In addition, increasing employee resources in the nonwork domain may help preserve resources in the work domain that would otherwise be drained by dealing with nonwork issues. For example, providing workers with personal time off to manage nonwork demands may help ensure that they are operating at their optimal performance when they return to work. However, targeting changes to the nonwork domain can be problematic. Research suggests stronger linkages between work antecedents and work outcomes (as well as family antecedents and family outcomes) rather than crossover effects (Amstad, Meier, Fasel, Elfering, & Semmer, 2011; Michel & Hargis, 2008).

Thus, practices designed specifically to increase work-related outcomes (e.g., job satisfaction) may be more cost-effective than practices that attempt to achieve indirect effects through nonwork-related outcomes.

Yet, this does not exclude the possibility that organizations benefit from nonwork support practices via other mechanisms. If they obtain additional resources to manage their nonwork demands, employees are more likely to see the organization as a better place to work than other organizations, which has been shown to aid in recruitment and retention (Batt & Valcour, 2003; Butts et al., 2013; Casper & Buffardi, 2004; Honeycutt & Rosen, 1997). In addition, prospective employees who are searching for jobs view organizations that offer schedule flexibility and dependent care assistance as potentially more supportive (Casper & Buffardi, 2004), which may help organizations in their recruiting efforts. Research also suggests that the provision of work–life policies is a signal to employees that the organization cares about their well-being, potentially motivating those employee to reciprocate this sentiment through greater organizational commitment and intentions to stay (Butts et al., 2013).

KEY FACTORS THAT FACILITATE OR INHIBIT WORK–LIFE BALANCE INITIATIVES

In light of person–environment fit theory (Edwards, 1996), the success of any work–life practice should be a function of both organizational and employee characteristics. As such, practice effectiveness is best achieved by ensuring that employees and organizational leaders are on the same page regarding the purpose of a practice, the ability of the practice to meet the needs of employees and the organization, and the ability of employees and the organization to meet the resource and competency demands of a practice. This entails an organizational development approach to work–life balance initiatives, which focuses on systemic issues surrounding assessment and development, implementation and utilization, and evaluation and refinement.

Assessment and Development

Key steps to consider during assessment and development of work–life initiatives include clarifying expectations, promoting inclusiveness, and setting appropriate measurement criteria to monitor effectiveness. First, clarifying expectations ensures that both the organization and employees are talking about the same goal and the same indicators for successfully achieving that goal. This helps alleviate dissatisfaction by setting realistic expectations for what the employee and the organization can attain via effective use of the programs. When these expectations are aligned, there is an increased chance that a given workplace practice will serve its intended purpose (e.g., increasing work–life balance without decreasing productivity; Kossek, Hammer, Kelly, & Moen, 2014). In line with expectancy theory (Vroom, 1964), this sort of alignment enhances motivation for employees to appropriately use a given practice because they can see (a) how a particular practice is consistent with their own values and (b) that the practice is consistent with organizational values. Effective top-down (management-driven) and bottom-up (employee-driven) communication strategies help to ensure that both parties will have similar, realistic expectations regarding the purpose of a particular workplace practice from both a well-being and performance perspective (Grawitch, Gottschalk, & Munz, 2006; Nielsen, 2013). Effective communication strategies can help prevent misunderstandings that may lead to frustration, cynicism, or resistance during the implementation stage.

Second, examining one's work–life balance terminology can reveal some underlying assumptions about who the program is targeting (or not targeting), which gives employers the opportunity to be more purposeful about types of employees they are attempting to attract or retain. Using the term *work–family* may indicate a focus on attracting female employees or employees with families, whereas *work–life* permits the inclusion of all employees, rather than focusing strictly on those with families or spouses (Casper et al., 2007). Other barriers to inclusiveness may include lack of universal access to certain practices (e.g., based on sex, geographic location, job level, or supervisory status), unfair negotiations to obtain certain practices, and miscommunication of practices to certain employees (Ryan & Kossek, 2008).

Finally, there are a few measurement issues to consider in assessing practice effectiveness. *Effectiveness* is often defined as improvements in employee and organizational well-being and performance. However, criteria should not be limited to expected impact of the practices on employee and organizational well-being or performance. Bardoel, De Cieri, and Mayson (2008) suggested that performance indicators should also be considered in terms of planning and alignment, customized initiatives, and supportive culture and leadership, in addition to value. Examples of assessment areas would include creating clearly defined objectives for the work–life initiatives (planning and alignment), identifying a match between work–life benefits and employee–organizational needs and capabilities (customization), and measuring level of involvement with work–life program development (supportive culture and leadership; Kossek et al., 2014).

Implementation and Utilization

A variety of contextual factors can influence whether a particular component of a work–life balance program is available and whether employees choose to use that particular component. These include aspects of the organizational environment and the work environment, as well as individual factors. Organizational constraints provide the greatest obstacle to practice implementation due to their large scope. An organization's internal environment (e.g., factors such as core business processes, human resources, organizational structure, technology support, strategy, and culture) often develops as a way to sustain a competitive advantage in its external environment (e.g., industry and general political–legal/economic/sociocultural/technological environments; Harrison & Shirom, 1999). Implementing practices that do not match an organization's internal–external alignment are likely to be ineffective or even impede the ability of the organization to meet external environmental demands, which may lead to abandoning the practice. Some of the specific organizational factors that may prevent proper implementation or utilization of work–life initiatives include work–life/family culture (e.g., Kossek et al., 2014), perceived organizational support (e.g., Casper & Buffardi, 2004; Witt & Carlson, 2006), justice perceptions (e.g., Greenberg, Roberge, Ho, & Rousseau, 2004; Rousseau, 2001), and quality of communication (e.g., Ryan & Kossek, 2008).

Work constraints can severely limit the ability of a particular practice to produce desired results because of aspects of an employee's more immediate work environment. Even though a workplace practice may be appropriately designed for the organization's environment (i.e., fits organizational values, needs, and capabilities), work constraints may arise in certain units of the organization as a result of work unit characteristics or attributes of a particular job. Work constraints may include coworker and supervisor support (e.g., Ryan & Kossek, 2008; Straub, 2012) and work demands and workload (e.g., Grzywacz, Casey, & Jones, 2007; Kossek et al., 2014). Interestingly, work environment factors more likely affect the use of workplace flexibility practices than do nonwork support practices (Straub, 2012). This is because having support from supervisors and colleagues serves as a key resource to help protect employees from stigma and other perceptions that may negatively affect advancement in the organization.

Although addressing organizational and work constraints is critically important for the successful implementation of work–life initiatives, managers must also be aware of individual factors associated with practice utilization. For example, socioeconomic characteristics (e.g., age, sex, marital status, ethnicity, living arrangements, number of children, medical history) and psychosocial characteristics (e.g., needs, interests, personality, self-identity) may influence preferences for certain work–life practices or vulnerability in experiencing conflict (e.g., Darcy, McCarthy, Hill, & Grady, 2012). Although no research has examined the role of personality variables influencing the use of practices, some researchers have examined their effects on perceptions of conflict and facilitation. For example, in a recent meta-analysis of the relationship between conflict/facilitation and personality, Michel, Clark, and Jaramillo (2011) demonstrated that neuroticism related moderately with work–nonwork conflict, whereas extraversion and openness related moderately to work–nonwork facilitation. These results indicate that employees high on neuroticism may be more vulnerable to experiencing conflict and those low on extraversion and openness may need more assistance in structuring these roles so that they facilitate one another.

Work-related aspects of the employee also may limit the utility of specific workplace practice primarily due to an inability to effectively use a practice. These aspects include employee knowledge, skills, and abilities (KSAs). When designing a work–life practice (e.g., telecommuting), organizations should specify relevant employee KSAs needed to effectively utilize that practice (e.g., computer proficiency). The identification of KSAs helps the organization identify training or equipment needed to increase appropriate utilization. For example, telecommuting arrangements require substantial logistic preparation and employee training to be optimally successful (e.g., Vega, 2003; Venkatesh & Johnson, 2002).

Feedback and Refinement

Simply putting a policy on paper does not ensure utilization or effectiveness. Numerous factors influence the success of work–life initiatives, which makes it exceedingly difficult to design programs that adequately meet the needs of all relevant stakeholders. Invariably, some changes will need to be made. Most research on the success of work–life initiatives has relied on cross-sectional designs, and there is little research linking changes in work–life initiatives to changes in desired outcomes (Glass & Finley, 2002). Fortunately, theory and research in organizational development as a broader discipline provide some guidance in this area.

There is no one prescribed method of policy analysis or feedback. Organizational decision makers must take into consideration the barriers they are likely to face in designing their data collection and feedback processes. However, research on survey feedback indicates that it can offer an effective and minimal-cost solution for a variety of organizational interventions. For instance, Bowers (1973) conducted a 5-year longitudinal study of 23 organizations involving more than 14,000 employees in a variety of positions. He found that survey feedback was the most effective treatment, as well as the only one associated with consistently large positive changes. Moreover, Neuman, Edwards, and Raju (1989) conducted a meta-analysis, finding that survey feedback significantly influences attitudes and perceptions of work situations. They concluded that this method effectively bridges the gap between the assessment of organizational problems and the implementation of problem-solving methods.

Before one engages in feedback, he or she should give careful consideration to preliminary planning of the data collection method. Once data are collected from relevant stakeholders and analyzed, the data may be fed back through bottom-up processes, top-down processes, or a combination of the two. Bottom-up approaches are driven by the employees and may be especially effective when data indicate that employees do not see value in the work–life initiatives offered by the organization. Top-down approaches are driven by top management and may be most effective when issues arise regarding systemic problems (e.g., issues of fit between initiatives and an organization's environment, strategy, or culture). Using a combination of the two (a bidirectional feedback process) can ensure that localized and systemic issues surrounding utilization and communication are both effectively addressed (Ryan & Kossek, 2008).

Last, institutionalizing behaviors may require developing organizational and departmental approaches to ensure that institutionalization includes support mechanisms and incentives (Kossek et al., 2014). Furthermore, Kossek et al. (2014) highlighted the importance of including both employees and managers in the process of sustaining the new behaviors and ways of doing things. Hence, the organization—and possibly individual departments or work units—needs to identify ways to encourage employees to effectively use specific practices and encourage managers to provide appropriate support to improve employee utilization. In addition, organizations may want to identify ways to recognize or reward employees who effectively utilize work–life initiatives, especially when considering practices that promote positive benefits for employees and for the organization (i.e., workplace flexibility initiatives).

Linking Work–Life Balance to Other Healthy Workplace Practices

As Grawitch and Ballard mentioned in the introduction to this volume, psychologically healthy workplace practices are not mutually exclusive. They can be integrated to produce more holistic programs that leverage the benefits of different practices. Unfortunately, there is a dearth of research focusing on ways in which employee involvement, growth and development, recognition, and health and safety intersect with work–life initiatives and outcomes. However, some research has provided a bit of guidance about how work–life research can be integrated with research in the other practice areas to produce more sustainable benefits for employees and the organization.

The effectiveness of work–life balance initiatives hinges on employee involvement during assessment and development, implementation and utilization, and evaluation and refinement. Research has shown that employee

involvement mediates the relationship between work–life balance practices and employee well-being (Grawitch, Ledford, Ballard, & Barber, 2009;
Nielsen, 2013). When considering employee growth and development,
research suggests that nonwork support benefits (e.g., time off for volun-
teerism, sabbaticals, financial resources to attend conferences) and work
flexibility benefits (e.g., flexible scheduling) can provide the resources and
autonomy employees need to improve workplace performance (Mazmanian
& Davis, 2002; Sima, 2000) and support involvement in activities outside of
work that bolster overall well-being (Thoits & Hewitt, 2001).

In terms of employee recognition, work flexibility and nonwork support practices can be a powerful recognition tool for outstanding employee
performance (Nelson, 2005), thus offering idiosyncratic work arrangements
(Rousseau, 2001) that, when properly managed, can create a recognition
system that is valued by employees and creates greater work–life balance.
Moreover, publicly recognizing high performers with alternative work arrangements may send a message to employees that such arrangements (a) are a
reward for consistent high performance, (b) are continued only given consistent performance results, and (c) do not prevent them from being seen as a
valuable asset to the organization.

Finally, with regard to health and safety, work–life interference is associated with specific health-related behaviors, including increased alcohol
and fatty food consumption and decreased physical activity (e.g., Allen &
Armstrong, 2006; Grzywacz & Marks, 2001) and, as discussed earlier, there are
strong empirical links between work–life balance and physiological and psychological health outcomes (e.g., Grzywacz & Marks, 2000; van Steenbergen
& Ellemers, 2009). Furthermore, psychological consequences of imbalance,
such as negative emotions and job dissatisfaction, not only decrease productivity but may even increase counterproductive work behaviors such as
theft, sabotage, withdrawal, production deviance, and interpersonal abuse or
incivility (Ferguson, Carlson, Hunter, & Whitten, 2012).

CONCLUSION

It is clear that research in the work–life arena has led to vast improvements in our knowledge of the interplay between organizational and individual health, well-being, and performance. Research is moving beyond a focus
on aspects of interference (e.g., role conflict) to incorporate strategies for promoting synergy (e.g., role enhancement) and personal growth in both the
work and nonwork domains. We are also shifting our attention from the individual to a more systemic perspective involving the organizational and home
environment, both of which affect and are affected by the employee's efforts to

obtain optimal fit across all domains. Finally, more recent research is attempting to draw causal links among organizational efforts to affect both individual and organizational well-being and performance via work–life initiatives.

Taken altogether, the literature reviewed in this chapter suggests that organizations' attention to carefully selected and implemented work–life balance programs can have a positive and widespread effect on employee recruitment, retention, well-being, and performance. Moreover, work–life balance may have a greater impact on these outcomes when integrated with other psychologically healthy workplace practices such as employee involvement, employee growth and development, employment recognition, and health and safety. Thus, work–life initiatives should not be considered just as fringe benefits to help increase employee well-being; they should be seen as a core component of an organization's competitive edge in both talent and productivity management.

REFERENCES

Allen, T. D. (2001). Family-supportive work environments: The role of organizational perceptions. *Journal of Vocational Behavior, 58,* 414–435. http://dx.doi.org/10.1006/jvbe.2000.1774

Allen, T. D., & Armstrong, J. A. (2006). Further examination of the link between work-family conflict and physical health. *American Behavioral Scientist, 49,* 1204–1221. http://dx.doi.org/10.1177/0002764206286386

Amstad, F. T., Meier, L. L., Fasel, U., Elfering, A., & Semmer, N. K. (2011). A meta-analysis of work-family conflict and various outcomes with a special emphasis on cross-domain versus matching-domain relations. *Journal of Occupational Health Psychology, 16,* 151–169. http://dx.doi.org/10.1037/a0022170

Arthur, M. M. (2003). Share price reactions to work-family initiatives: An institutional perspective. *Academy of Management Journal, 46,* 497–505. http://dx.doi.org/10.2307/30040641

Arthur, M. M., & Cook, A. (2003). The relationship between work-family human resource practices and firm profitability: A multi-theoretical perspective. *Research in Personnel and Human Resources Management, 22,* 219–252. http://dx.doi.org/10.1016/S0742-7301(03)22005-3

Ashforth, B. E., Kreiner, G. E., & Fugate, M. (2000). All in a day's work: Boundaries and micro role transitions. *Academy of Management Review, 25,* 472–491.

Balmforth, K., & Gardner, D. (2006). Conflict and facilitation between work and family: Realizing the outcomes for organizations. *New Zealand Journal of Psychology, 35,* 69–76.

Bardoel, E. A., De Cieri, H., & Mayson, S. (2008). Bridging the research–practice gap: Developing a measurement framework for work–life initiatives. *Journal of Management & Organization, 14,* 239–258.

Batt, R., & Valcour, M. (2003). Human resource practices as predictors of work-family outcomes and employee turnover. *Industrial Relations: A Journal of Economy and Society, 42*, 189–220. http://dx.doi.org/10.1111/1468-232X.00287

Bowers, D. G. (1973). OD techniques and their results in 23 organizations: The Michigan ICL study. *Journal of Applied Behavioral Science, 9*, 21–43. http://dx.doi.org/10.1177/002188637300900103

Boyar, S. L., Maertz, C. P., Pearson, A. W., & Keough, S. (2003). Work-family conflict: A model of linkages between work and family domain variables and turnover intentions. *Journal of Managerial Issues, 15*, 175–190.

Breaugh, J., & Frye, N. (2008). Work-family conflict: The importance of family-friendly employment practices and family-supportive supervisors. *Journal of Business and Psychology, 22*, 345–353. http://dx.doi.org/10.1007/s10869-008-9081-1

Bronfenbrenner, U. (1979). *The ecology of human development: Experiments by nature and design.* Cambridge, MA: Harvard University Press.

Brough, P., O'Driscoll, M. P., & Kalliath, T. J. (2005). The ability of "family friendly" organizational resources to predict work–family conflict and job and family satisfaction. *Stress and Health, 21*, 223–234. http://dx.doi.org/10.1002/smi.1059

Butts, M. M., Casper, W. J., & Yang, T. S. (2013). How important are work-family support policies? A meta-analytic investigation of their effects on employee outcomes. *Journal of Applied Psychology, 98*, 1–25. http://dx.doi.org/10.1037/a0030389

Byrne, U. (2005). Work-life balance: Why are we talking about it at all? *Business Information Review, 22*, 53–59. http://dx.doi.org/10.1177/0266382105052268

Carstensen, L. L., Isaacowitz, D. M., & Charles, S. T. (1999). Taking time seriously. A theory of socioemotional selectivity. *American Psychologist, 54*, 165–181. http://dx.doi.org/10.1037/0003-066X.54.3.165

Carver, C. S., & Scheier, M. F. (1982). Control theory: A useful conceptual framework for personality—social, clinical, and health psychology. *Psychological Bulletin, 92*, 111–135. http://dx.doi.org/10.1037/0033-2909.92.1.111

Casper, W. J., & Buffardi, L. C. (2004). Work-life benefits and job pursuit intentions: The role of anticipated organizational support. *Journal of Vocational Behavior, 65*, 391–410. http://dx.doi.org/10.1016/j.jvb.2003.09.003

Casper, W. J., Weltman, D., & Kwesiga, E. (2007). Beyond family-friendly: The construct and measurement of singles-friendly work cultures. *Journal of Vocational Behavior, 70*, 478–501. http://dx.doi.org/10.1016/j.jvb.2007.01.001

Clifton, T. J., & Shepard, E. (2004). Work and family programs and productivity: Estimates applying a production function model. *International Journal of Manpower, 25*, 714–728. http://dx.doi.org/10.1108/01437720410570036

Darcy, C., McCarthy, A., Hill, J., & Grady, G. (2012). Work–life balance: One size fits all? An exploratory analysis of the differential effects of career stage. *European Management Journal, 30*, 111–120. http://dx.doi.org/10.1016/j.emj.2011.11.001

Eby, L. T., Casper, W. J., Lockwood, A., Bordeaux, C., & Brinley, A. (2005). Work and family research in IO/OB: Content analysis and review of the literature (1980–2002). *Journal of Vocational Behavior, 66,* 124–197. http://dx.doi.org/10.1016/j.jvb.2003.11.003

Edwards, J. R. (1996). An examination of competing version of the person-environment fit approach to stress. *Academy of Management Journal, 39,* 292–339. http://dx.doi.org/10.2307/256782

Edwards, J. R., & Rothbard, N. P. (2000). Mechanisms linking work and family: Clarifying the relationship between work and family constructs. *Academy of Management Review, 25,* 178–199.

Eikhof, D. R., Warhurst, C., & Haunschild, A. (2007). What work, what life, what balance? Critical reflections on the work-life balance debate. *Employee Relations, 29,* 325–333.

Emmons, R. A. (1986). Personal strivings: An approach to personality and subjective well-being. *Journal of Personality and Social Psychology, 51,* 1058–1068.

Emmons, R. A. (1996). Striving and feeling: Personal goals and subjective well-being. In J. Bargh & P. Gollwitzer (Eds.), *The psychology of action: Linking motivation and cognition to behavior* (pp. 314–337). New York, NY: Guilford Press.

Ferguson, M., Carlson, D., Hunter, E. M., & Whitten, D. (2012). A two-study examination of work-family conflict, production deviance, and gender. *Journal of Vocational Behavior, 81,* 245–258. http://dx.doi.org/10.1016/j.jvb.2012.07.004

Fredrickson, B. L., & Losada, M. F. (2005). Positive affect and the complex dynamics of human flourishing. *American Psychologist, 60,* 678–686. http://dx.doi.org/10.1037/0003-066X.60.7.678

Frone, M. R., Russell, M., & Cooper, M. L. (1992). Antecedents and outcomes of work-family conflict: Testing a model of the work-family interface. *Journal of Applied Psychology, 77,* 65–78. http://dx.doi.org/10.1037/0021-9010.77.1.65

Frone, M. R., Yardley, J. K., & Markel, K. S. (1997). Developing and testing an integrative model of the work-family interface. *Journal of Vocational Behavior, 50,* 145–167. http://dx.doi.org/10.1006/jvbe.1996.1577

Glass, J. L., & Finley, A. (2002). Coverage and effectiveness of family-responsive workplace policies. *Human Resource Management Review, 12,* 313–337. http://dx.doi.org/10.1016/S1053-4822(02)00063-3

Grandey, A. A., & Cropanzano, R. (1999). The conservation of resources model applied to work–family conflict and strain. *Journal of Vocational Behavior, 54,* 350–370. http://dx.doi.org/10.1006/jvbe.1998.1666

Graves, L. M., Ohlott, P. J., & Ruderman, M. N. (2007). Commitment to family roles: Effects on managers' attitudes and performance. *Journal of Applied Psychology, 92,* 44–56. http://dx.doi.org/10.1037/0021-9010.92.1.44

Grawitch, M. J., & Barber, L. K. (2010). Work flexibility or non-work support? Theoretical and empirical distinctions for work-life initiatives. *Consulting Psychology Journal: Practice and Research, 62,* 169–188. http://dx.doi.org/10.1037/a0020591

Grawitch, M. J., Barber, L. K., & Justice, L. (2010). Rethinking the work-life interface: It's not about balance, it's about resource allocation. *Applied Psychology: Health and Well-Being, 2*, 127–159.

Grawitch, M. J., Gottschalk, M., & Munz, D. C. (2006). The path to a healthy workplace: A critical review linking healthy workplace practices, employee well-being, and organizational improvements. *Consulting Psychology Journal: Practice and Research, 58*, 129–147. http://dx.doi.org/10.1037/1065-9293.58.3.129

Grawitch, M. J., Ledford, G. E., Ballard, D. W., & Barber, L. K. (2009). Leading the healthy workforce: The integral role of employee involvement. *Consulting Psychology Journal: Practice and Research, 61*, 122–135. http://dx.doi.org/10.1037/a0015288

Grawitch, M. J., Maloney, P. W., Barber, L. K., & Yost, C. (2011). Moving toward a better understanding of the work and nonwork interface. *Industrial and Organizational Psychology: Perspectives on Science and Practice, 4*, 385–388. http://dx.doi.org/10.1111/j.1754-9434.2011.01357.x

Greenberg, J., Roberge, M., Ho, V. T., & Rousseau, D. M. (2004). Fairness in idiosyncratic work arrangements: Justice as an i-deal. In J. J. Martocchio & G. R. Ferris (Eds.), *Research in personnel and human resource management* (Vol. 23, pp. 1–34). San Diego, CA: Elsevier.

Greenhaus, J. H., & Powell, G. N. (2003). When work and family collide: Deciding between competing role demands. *Organizational Behavior and Human Decision Processes, 90*, 291–303. http://dx.doi.org/10.1016/S0749-5978(02)00519-8

Greenhaus, J. H., & Powell, G. N. (2006). When work and family are allies: A theory of work-family enrichment. *Academy of Management Review, 31*, 72–92. http://dx.doi.org/10.5465/AMR.2006.19379625

Greenhaus, J. H., Ziegert, J. C., & Allen, T. D. (2012). When family-supportive supervision matters: Relations between multiple sources of support and work–family balance. *Journal of Vocational Behavior, 80*, 266–275. http://dx.doi.org/10.1016/j.jvb.2011.10.008

Grzywacz, J. G., & Carlson, D. S. (2007). Conceptualizing work-family balance: Implications for practice and research. *Advances in Developing Human Resources, 9*, 455–471. http://dx.doi.org/10.1177/1523422307305487

Grzywacz, J. G., Casey, P. R., & Jones, F. A. (2007). The effects of workplace flexibility on health behaviors: A cross-sectional and longitudinal analysis. *Journal of Occupational and Environmental Medicine, 49*, 1302–1309. http://dx.doi.org/10.1097/JOM.0b013e31815ae9bc

Grzywacz, J. G., & Marks, N. F. (2000). Reconceptualizing the work-family interface: An ecological perspective on the correlates of positive and negative spillover between work and family. *Journal of Occupational Health Psychology, 5*, 111–126. http://dx.doi.org/10.1037/1076-8998.5.1.111

Grzywacz, J. G., & Marks, N. F. (2001). Social inequalities and exercise during adulthood: Toward an ecological perspective. *Journal of Health and Social Behavior, 42*, 202–220. http://dx.doi.org/10.2307/3090178

Hammer, L. B., Kossek, E. E., Anger, W. K., Bodner, T., & Zimmerman, K. L. (2011). Clarifying work-family intervention processes: The roles of work-family conflict and family-supportive supervisor behaviors. *Journal of Applied Psychology, 96*, 134–150. http://dx.doi.org/10.1037/a0020927

Harrison, M. I., & Shirom, A. (1999). *Organizational diagnosis and assessment: Bridging theory and practice.* Thousand Oaks, CA: Sage.

Hobfoll, S. E. (1989). Conservation of resources. A new attempt at conceptualizing stress. *American Psychologist, 44*, 513–524. http://dx.doi.org/10.1037/0003-066X.44.3.513

Hobfoll, S. E., & Lilly, R. S. (1993). Resource conservation as a strategy for community psychology. *Journal of Community Psychology, 21*, 128–148. http://dx.doi.org/10.1002/1520-6629(199304)21:2<128::AID-JCOP2290210206>3.0.CO;2-5

Honeycutt, T. L., & Rosen, B. (1997). Family friendly human resource policies, salary levels, and salient identity as predictors of organizational attraction. *Journal of Vocational Behavior, 50*, 271–290. http://dx.doi.org/10.1006/jvbe.1996.1554

Jain, S., & Nair, S. K. (2013). Research on work-family balance: A review. *Business Perspectives and Research, 2*(1), 43–58.

Kahn, R. L., Wolfe, D. M., Quinn, P. R., Snoek, J. D., & Rosenthal, R. A. (1964). *Organizational stress: Studies in role conflict and ambiguity.* New York, NY: Wiley.

Kalliath, T., & Brough, P. (2008). Work-life balance: A review of the meaning of the balance construct. *Journal of Management & Organization, 14*, 323–327.

Keeney, J., Boyd, E. M., Sinha, R., Westring, A. F., & Ryan, A. M. (2013). From "work-family" to "work-life": Broadening our conceptualization and measurement. *Journal of Vocational Behavior, 82*, 221–237. http://dx.doi.org/10.1016/j.jvb.2013.01.005

Kelly, E. L., Kossek, E. E., Hammer, L. B., Durham, M., Bray, J., Chermack, K., . . . Kaskubar, D. (2008). Getting there from here: Research on the effects of work-family initiatives on work-family conflict and business outcomes. *The Academy of Management Annals, 2*, 305–349. http://dx.doi.org/10.1080/19416520802211610

Keyes, C. L. M. (2002). The mental health continuum: From languishing to flourishing in life. *Journal of Health and Social Behavior, 43*, 207–222. http://dx.doi.org/10.2307/3090197

Konrad, A. M., & Mangel, R. (2000). The impact of work-life programs on firm productivity. *Strategic Management Journal, 21*, 1225–1237. http://dx.doi.org/10.1002/1097-0266(200012)21:12<1225::AID-SMJ135>3.0.CO;2-3

Kossek, E. E., Hammer, L. B., Kelly, E. L., & Moen, P. (2014). Designing work, family and health organizational change initiatives. *Organizational Dynamics, 43*, 53–63. http://dx.doi.org/10.1016/j.orgdyn.2013.10.007

Kossek, E. E., & Lautsch, B. A. (2012). Work-family boundary management styles in organizations: A cross-level model. *Organizational Psychology Review, 2*, 152–171. http://dx.doi.org/10.1177/2041386611436264

Kossek, E. E., Pichler, S., Bodner, T., & Hammer, L. B. (2011). Workplace social support and work-family conflict: A meta-analysis clarifying the influence of general and work-family specific supervisor and organizational support. *Personnel Psychology, 64*, 289–313. http://dx.doi.org/10.1111/j.1744-6570.2011.01211.x

Kreiner, G. E., Hollensbe, E. C., & Sheep, M. L. (2009). Balancing borders and bridges: Negotiating the work-home interface via boundary work tactics. *Academy of Management Journal, 52*, 704–730. http://dx.doi.org/10.5465/AMJ.2009.43669916

Lambert, S. J. (1990). Processes linking work and family: A critical review and research agenda. *Human Relations, 43*, 239–257. http://dx.doi.org/10.1177/001872679004300303

Lambert, S. J. (2000). Added benefits: The link between work-life benefits and organizational citizenship behavior. *Academy of Management Journal, 43*, 801–815. http://dx.doi.org/10.2307/1556411

Little, B. R. (1983). Personal projects: A rationale and method for investigation. *Environment and Behavior, 15*, 273–309. http://dx.doi.org/10.1177/0013916583153002

Little, B. R., Salmela-Aro, K., & Phillips, S. D. (2006). *Personal project pursuit: Goals, action and human flourishing.* Mahwah, NJ: Erlbaum.

Mazmanian, P. E., & Davis, D. A. (2002). Continuing medical education and the physician as a learner: Guide to the evidence. JAMA, 288, 1057–1060. http://dx.doi.org/10.1001/jama.288.9.1057

Michel, J. S., Clark, M. A., & Jaramillo, D. (2011). The role of the five factor model of personality in the perceptions of negative and positive forms of work-nonwork spillover: A meta-analytic review. *Journal of Vocational Behavior, 79*, 191–203. http://dx.doi.org/10.1016/j.jvb.2010.12.010

Michel, J. S., & Hargis, M. B. (2008). Linking mechanisms of work-family conflict and segmentation. *Journal of Vocational Behavior, 73*, 509–522. http://dx.doi.org/10.1016/j.jvb.2008.09.005

Nelson, B. (2005). *1001 ways to reward employees.* New York, NY: Workman.

Neuman, G. A., Edwards, J. E., & Raju, N. S. (1989). Organizational development interventions: A meta-analysis of their effects on satisfaction and other attitudes. *Personnel Psychology, 42*, 461–489. http://dx.doi.org/10.1111/j.1744-6570.1989.tb00665.x

Ngo, H.-Y., Foley, S., & Loi, R. (2009). Family friendly work practices, organizational climate, and firm performance: A study of multinational corporations in Hong Kong. *Journal of Organizational Behavior, 30*, 665–680. http://dx.doi.org/10.1002/job.606

Nielsen, K. (2013). Review article: How can we make organizational interventions work? Employees and line managers as actively crafting interventions. *Human Relations, 66*, 1029–1050. http://dx.doi.org/10.1177/0018726713477164

Nohe, C., & Sonntag, K. (2014). Work–family conflict, social support, and turnover intentions: A longitudinal study. *Journal of Vocational Behavior, 85*, 1–12. http://dx.doi.org/10.1016/j.jvb.2014.03.007

Perry-Smith, J. E., & Blum, T. C. (2000). Work-family human resource bundles and perceived organizational performance. *Academy of Management Journal, 43*, 1107–1117. http://dx.doi.org/10.2307/1556339

Pichler, F. (2009). Determinants of work-life balance: Shortcomings in the contemporary measurement of WLB in large-scale surveys. *Social Indicators Research, 92*, 449–469. http://dx.doi.org/10.1007/s11205-008-9297-5

Rantanen, J., Kinnunen, U., Feldt, T., & Pulkkinen, L. (2008). Work-family conflict and psychological well-being: Stability and cross-lagged relations within one- and six-year follow-up. *Journal of Vocational Behavior, 73*, 37–51. http://dx.doi.org/10.1016/j.jvb.2008.01.001

Rothbard, N. P., Philips, K. W., & Dumas, T. L. (2005). Multiple roles: Work–family policies and individual's desires for segmentation. *Organization Science, 16*, 243–258. http://dx.doi.org/10.1287/orsc.1050.0124

Rousseau, D. M. (2001). The idiosyncratic deal: Flexibility versus fairness? *Organizational Dynamics, 29*, 260–273. http://dx.doi.org/10.1016/S0090-2616(01)00032-8

Ryan, A. M., & Kossek, E. E. (2008). Work–life policy implementation: Breaking down or creating barriers to inclusiveness? *Human Resource Management, 47*, 295–310. http://dx.doi.org/10.1002/hrm.20213

Ryan, R. M., Kuhl, J., & Deci, E. L. (1997). Nature and autonomy: An organizational view of social and neurobiological aspects of self-regulation in behavior and development. *Development and Psychopathology, 9*, 701–728. http://dx.doi.org/10.1017/S0954579497001405

Sima, C. M. (2000). The role and benefits of the sabbatical leave in faculty development and satisfaction. *New Directions for Institutional Research, 2000*, 67–75. http://dx.doi.org/10.1002/ir.10506

Stavrou, E. T. (2005). Flexible work bundles and organizational competitiveness: A cross-national study of the European work context. *Journal of Organizational Behavior, 26*, 923–947. http://dx.doi.org/10.1002/job.356

Straub, C. (2012). Antecedents and organizational consequences of family supportive supervisor behavior: A multilevel conceptual framework for research. *Human Resource Management Review, 22*, 15–26. http://dx.doi.org/10.1016/j.hrmr.2011.08.001

Taylor, B. L., DelCampo, R. G., & Blancero, D. M. (2009). Work–family conflict/facilitation and the role of workplace supports for U.S. Hispanic professionals. *Journal of Organizational Behavior, 30*, 643–664. http://dx.doi.org/10.1002/job.605

Thoits, P. A., & Hewitt, L. N. (2001). Volunteer work and well-being. *Journal of Health and Social Behavior, 42*, 115–131. http://dx.doi.org/10.2307/3090173

Thomas, L. T., & Ganster, D. C. (1995). Impact of family supportive work variables on work-family conflict and strain: A control perspective. *Journal of Applied Psychology, 80*, 6–15. http://dx.doi.org/10.1037/0021-9010.80.1.6

van Steenbergen, E. F., & Ellemers, N. (2009). Is managing the work–family interface worthwhile? Benefits for employee health and performance. *Journal of Organizational Behavior, 30,* 617–642. http://dx.doi.org/10.1002/job.569

Vega, G. (2003). *Managing teleworkers and telecommuting strategies.* Westport, CT: Greenwood.

Venkatesh, V., & Johnson, P. (2002). Telecommuting technology implementations: A within-subjects longitudinal field study. *Personnel Psychology, 55,* 661–687. http://dx.doi.org/10.1111/j.1744-6570.2002.tb00125.x

Voydanoff, P. (2005). Toward a conceptualization of perceived work-family fit and balance: A demands and resources approach. *Journal of Marriage and Family, 67,* 822–836. http://dx.doi.org/10.1111/j.1741-3737.2005.00178.x

Vroom, V. H. (1964). *Work and motivation.* New York, NY: Wiley.

Wayne, J. H., Musisca, N., & Fleeson, W. (2004). Considering the role of personality in the work–family experience: Relationships of the big five to work–family conflict and facilitation. *Journal of Vocational Behavior, 64,* 108–130. http://dx.doi.org/10.1016/S0001-8791(03)00035-6

Witt, L. A., & Carlson, D. S. (2006). The work-family interface and job performance: Moderating effects of conscientiousness and perceived organizational support. *Journal of Occupational Health Psychology, 11,* 343–357. http://dx.doi.org/10.1037/1076-8998.11.4.343

Wrzesniewski, A., LoBuglio, N., Dutton, J. E., & Berg, J. M. (2013). Job crafting and cultivating positive meaning and identity in work. *Advances in Positive Organizational Psychology, 1,* 281–302. http://dx.doi.org/10.1108/S2046-410X(2013)0000001015

Wrzesniewski, A., McCauley, C., Rozin, R., & Schwartz, B. (1997). Jobs, careers, and callings: People's relation to their work. *Journal of Research in Personality, 31,* 21–33. http://dx.doi.org/10.1006/jrpe.1997.2162

6

WORK–LIFE BALANCE: PERSPECTIVES FROM THE FIELD

CALI WILLIAMS YOST, DONNA MILLER, AND JOANNE SPIGNER

In Chapter 5 of this volume, "Work–Life Balance: Contemporary Perspectives," Barber, Grawitch, and Maloney outlined what research tells us about work–life balance and its impact on employees and businesses. They further reviewed the challenges of implementation and utilization of work–life policies as part of the psychologically healthy workplace process. Our field experience is consistent with the research findings and the authors' conclusions about organizational challenges and success factors.

In this chapter, we focus on work–life balance in practice, when the goal is to make it achievable and impactful for a broad population of individuals and the organization. First, we provide a brief overview of traditional approaches to work–life balance and flexibility, which have historically tended to address primarily maternity-related issues that affect female employees. We then outline in detail the next-generation change and innovation process that helps organizations move work–life balance and flexibility from a traditionally

http://dx.doi.org/10.1037/14731-007
The Psychologically Healthy Workplace: Building a Win–Win Environment for Organizations and Employees,
M. J. Grawitch and D. W. Ballard (Editors)

siloed, programmatic employee benefit to a usable business strategy. This strategic approach has multiple, operational aspects that

- can be used by the organization no matter where it is on the work–life innovation continuum;
- unify employees around a shared vision for work–life balance in the organization;
- ensure that the needs of the organization and the employee are considered at all times;
- encourage inclusiveness and effective two-way communication up, down, and across the organization;
- affect important and varied organizational imperatives that include, but go well beyond, talent management; and
- can be measured, monitored, and refined at any time.

The change and innovation process used is not linear. Components are not taken in discrete steps that are done once and checked off the list forever. Instead, the process builds on itself, referencing what has come before, adapting to new information, and anticipating what is ahead. Though this change and innovation process can feel messy at times, if one understands the core principles and phases, it is, in fact, structured. Organizational patience and disciplined oversight render the process quite manageable.

And the payoff is substantial. Ultimately, flexibility becomes what practitioners and end users want: a real, accessible, high-impact strategy contributing to a psychologically healthy workplace in today's world. It also becomes what organizations need: a tool to help deal with a rapidly changing, demanding, global, technology-driven marketplace.

TRADITIONAL APPROACHES TO WORK–LIFE BALANCE

In our field experience, organizational work–life balance approaches and solutions follow a predictable innovation continuum. No particular points on the continuum are "good" or "bad" per se. They simply are, and they help practitioners identify a place from which to begin or advance the work–life conversation within their organizations (see Figure 6.1).

In the first stage, organizations meet the quiet demand for employee flexibility on an unofficial, ad hoc basis. People with a pressing need to change how, when, or where they work negotiate individual arrangements with their managers, who would prefer to accommodate rather than lose those employees. These case-by-case arrangements that center on individual needs tend to fly under the organizational radar screen. Such an "invisible" approach to work–life balance is deemed preferable to more transparent efforts because

Figure 6.1. Work–life flexibility innovation continuum. From Flex+Strategy Group/ Work+Life Fit, Inc. Copyright 2012 by Flex+Strategy Group/Work+Life Fit, Inc. Reprinted with permission.

it helps the individual avoid perceived career risks and the manager to avert the feared possibility of "me, too" requests. This invisible approach results in equally invisible solutions, none of which can be leveraged to more broadly promote well-being or monitored to assess business impact.

As awareness of employee need grows, work–life balance efforts and flexibility become more visible and formalized. Historically, this means a move from ad hoc solutions to broader, human resource–based approaches. This approach typically begins with benefits-oriented programs that include, but are not limited to, resource and referral services, on-site child care, parental leave, and dependent care assistance plans.

As an organization becomes increasingly comfortable with the individual employee need for flexibility, it uses its human resource function to continue layering on more sophisticated work–life balance solutions. The impetus for developing a stronger set of programs and policies is often driven by (a) a recommendation from a women's initiative and/or (b) a desire to be recognized as a preferred employer on one or more of a growing roster of lists and awards. The resulting solutions usually center on a set menu of formal, flexible work arrangement policies (e.g., flextime, telecommuting, job sharing, compressed workweeks, part-time hours, paid or unpaid leave).

The human resource stage of the innovation continuum demonstrates an organization's good faith efforts toward promoting and supporting a psychologically healthy workplace. It is straightforward to manage and can provide work–life relief for individuals. In many instances, it renders the organization attractive to prospective employees. However, the solutions it creates have their limits. They may inadvertently support the misperception that flexibility is a woman's or a parent's issue and minimize—or ignore—the flexibility needs of men and nonparents. They tend to create rigid and limiting, one-size-fits-all options for individuals that do not always allow clear, workable solutions tailored to unique work and personal circumstances. Furthermore, they encourage a bias toward the individual's needs and underemphasize the needs of the organization. These limitations can thwart utilization or lead to flexibility applications that are misaligned with business realities and, therefore, are hard to rewind and rework for better impact. Traditional work–life programs and policies are simply too narrow and cookie-cutter to create sustainable impact on their own (Yost, 2009).

A NEW STAGE IN WORK–LIFE BALANCE INNOVATION

A next-generation approach to work–life balance has added another stage to the innovation continuum, and it is robust and strategic. Work–life considerations and flexibility are not ends in themselves; rather, they are a means to an end. That end is the ability for individuals and organizations to thrive in the new realities of a global, 24/7, technologically dependent society in which rapid change is the norm. Change management and innovation methodologies (e.g., Hamel, 2000; Kelley & Littman, 2001; Kotter, 1996) are used to minimize the recognized limitations within more traditional approaches without losing the knowledge gained from them. It uses specific protocols and terminology to

- reshape and expand the work–life discourse,
- encourage ownership for flexibility across the organization,
- tailor solutions to the organization, and
- tirelessly integrate them into existing systems and routines.

In our client organizations, we have consistently observed a broad range of high-impact outcomes that result from this cutting-edge approach to work–life balance and flexibility. They support other components of a psychologically healthy workplace (i.e., employee involvement, health and safety, recognition, growth and development) and contribute to operating and business outcomes (e.g., cost containment, resource maximization, productivity improvement, client service excellence, diversity advancement, environmental sustainability, disaster preparedness, recruitment and retention; see Table 6.1).

NEXT GENERATION IN WORK–LIFE FIT: FIVE UNDERLYING PRINCIPLES

Five underlying principles guide the next-generation approach to work–life innovation. These principles pertain throughout the entire process and are applied in varying degrees depending on the aspect of the process under consideration and the organization's current situation or context. They minimize the typical obstacles a practitioner would confront within a work–life initiative, which distinguishes this more innovative approach from traditional efforts. These underlying principles state that

- individual and business needs drive flexibility;
- flexibility is a process, not a program or a policy;
- language matters;

TABLE 6.1
Strategic Work–Life Flexibility Impacts

Working better/smarter	Managing talent	Improving customer/ client service
• Increasing employee engagement/involvement • Improving productivity • Making workflow and communication efficient	• Providing nonmonetary rewards/recognition • Attracting talent • Retaining talent • Developing leaders • Increasing diversity	• Retaining knowledge-able, consistent staff • Providing global client coverage
Containing and reducing costs, including	**Improving individual work–life fit**	**Improving environmental sustainability**
• labor • operating • real estate • health care • safety costs • technology investments	• For everyone, day-to-day • For parents • For eldercare providers • For millennials • For pre-retirees	• Reducing carbon footprint • Lowering energy-related costs
		Increasing disaster preparedness
		• For planned crises (e.g., hurricanes, snow storms) • For unforeseen crises (e.g., H1N1, terrorism)

Note. From Flex+Strategy Group/Work+Life Fit, Inc. Copyright 2012 by Flex+Strategy Group/Work+Life Fit, Inc. Reprinted with permission.

- business ownership and cross-functional involvement create traction; and
- alignment and integration support sustainability (Eaton, 2010).

Although every work–life initiative must be unique in conception, creation, and implementation, these principles can be applied across organizations and situations. The difference between a strategy that is well used and meaningful and one that is not depends on understanding these principles and their phased application.

INDIVIDUAL AND BUSINESS NEEDS DRIVE FLEXIBILITY

The next-generation approach positions flexibility as a strategic business tool for individuals and organizations. Practitioners are often more familiar with and focused on the benefits of flexibility to the individual end user and should continue pursuing those. However, a dual application of flexibility creates a process designed to benefit the business and the employee.

We have found that positioning flexibility as a business tool (with broad effects on operations and on people) creates wide interest, understanding, and buy-in from employees, line managers, and leaders. It also bolsters the use of more flexible ways of working. In our experience, this work flexibility contributes not only to recruitment and retention but also to productivity, cost containment, and resource utilization. This change and innovation process integrates flexibility into the business toolbox, making it available to address a variety of business imperatives—including those related to traditional talent management. This dual application of flexibility underlies all that is described and discussed in the remainder of this chapter.

Flexibility Is a Process

Flexibility is more effective when viewed as an ongoing process adaptable to the unique circumstances in a job and in a person's life rather than as a standardized set of policies and programs. Giving everyone equal access to a consistent process addresses a practitioner's need to create and implement a sustainable and fair approach to work–life balance.

At first, this process-based approach may seem counterintuitive. Typically, practitioners reason that policies and programs provide the necessary fairness and consistency by offering a delineated set of protocols and options. This may be attractive to practitioners, but individuals and organizations pay a significant price for this presumption. For example, consistent utilization suffers when an employee cannot flexibly tailor a rigid program or policy to his or her unique set of work–life circumstances. Delivering consistent fairness can be a challenge when an organization tries, in vain, to apply a one-size-fits-all policy equally to everyone in its diverse ranks. In short, policies and programs alone are not the answer.

Proponents of the next-generation approach to work–life understand that flexibility is a resource-rich tool that includes, but is not limited to, flexible work arrangements. It uses a clearly understood, organization-wide process that can be initiated by any individual, team, or organization wanting to change how, when, or where work gets done. With a process, everyone has equal access to flexibility, but no single outcome is prescribed or guaranteed. The range of flexibility choices—from ad hoc, day-to-day flexibility in how, when, or where work is done that requires no pre-approved plan to the most formally documented leave of absence and all points in between—allows flexibility to be creatively applied for myriad business and personal challenges and opportunities. An effective process will be supported by training, coaching resources and templates so that it is uniformly understood and consistently applied to meet both individual and organizational needs. For individuals, those needs focus on managing their work and life, whereas for organizations, the needs may include talent management, cost containment, and resource management (see Table 6.1).

LANGUAGE MATTERS

Another important principle centers on language. How we speak about flexibility and work–life balance matters insofar as it will either reinforce or undercut the mind-sets critical to success. At the outset of our culture change and development work with an organization, we discuss and agree on language that reflects the values and characteristics of a strategic, business-based approach to flexibility.

For example, like many involved in the work–life sphere (e.g., Grawitch, Maloney, Barber, & Yost, 2011), we were troubled by work–life vernacular and its constraints on a practical and broader use of flexibility. As a result, over the past decade, we have purposefully shifted our language choices to better articulate the next-generation approach, starting with our decision to make work–life "fit" our preferred term. The word *fit* is more appropriate than the typical word in use, *balance*. Though work and life can be theoretically balanced when each sit in perfect equilibrium, our experience tells us that finding such equilibrium is highly unlikely—and for some, undesired. One side of the equation, either work or life, tips and disrupts the delicate balance achieved. "Balance" therefore becomes an unattainable goal that frustrates those who pursue it.

"Fit," however, replaces the unattainable with the possible. It communicates that there is no single way in which to unite and manage one's personal and professional being. It allows for a large range of acceptable, satisfying solutions that can be altered depending on one's stage of life, goals, unique work realities, mix of commitments, and other factors. It validates and celebrates every possible combination of work and life and, in doing so, is better suited to a more innovative, real-world approach.

We are also disciplined about other terms, in an effort to set the appropriate tone and mind-set. For instance, as noted earlier, we always refer to flexibility as a process and never as a program. We prefer to say that flexibility is a tool or a strategy, rather than a benefit or perk. We speak of helping individuals manage their work–life fit, rather than creating flexible work arrangements. We have found these language alterations, though subtle, to be transformational.

OWNERSHIP AND CROSS-FUNCTIONAL INVOLVEMENT CREATE URGENCY AND TRACTION

In the next-generation approach, responsibility for work–life and flexibility strategies is placed within the group or groups best positioned to set a strong tone and drive success within the day-to-day operating model of the business (Yergler, 2011). Historically, Human Resources (sometimes in conjunction with a Diversity or Women's Initiative team) has been the primary owner of work–life efforts. However, in a recent national survey of Top 100 chief financial officers, 65% of respondents felt that work–life flexibility could not be successful with the HR department as the only champion (Yost, 2009). Therefore, practitioners should explore which facet(s) of the business can best drive strategy development and implementation into the organizational culture and operations and what role HR can play to support the effort.

Strong ownership by the frontline business alone, however, is not enough. It is also critical to enlist an expanding circle of support across functions throughout the entire process. Traditional work–life initiatives often do not invest the time and effort to do this. Wider scale involvement can feel too time consuming and difficult to manage. Therefore, organizations often choose to have the same group of people involved from concept to rollout.

There are benefits to having a small, well-versed core team dedicated to strategy development and implementation. In fact, we strongly urge all practitioners to assemble the best team possible up-front. However, the core team must continually broaden its circle by enlisting a wide range of people into the process while maintaining manageability and momentum. This can be accomplished by conducting interviews, serving in leadership roles as task force members or rollout leaders, soliciting individuals from across the organization to provide input during feedback loops and pilots, to name just a few. The five-phase practitioner framework described later in this chapter offers a variety of specific opportunities for broad-based involvement.

ALIGNMENT AND INTEGRATION SUPPORT SUSTAINABILITY

Finally, this more innovative business-based approach to work–life fit and flexibility assumes that all solutions will be fully aligned with existing systems and routines. Practitioners recognize that simply layering new ideas on top of practices that do not support them leads to trouble. Historically, disconnects between the desired process-based flexibility strategy and unsupportive organizational realities are either ignored or quickly glossed over (Mescher, Benschop, & Doorewaard, 2010). Without an appropriate sense of urgency and focus and attention to how flexibility fits with the organization's overall psychologically healthy workplace philosophy, even diligent attempts to address misalignments can be thwarted in an organization.

To ensure utilization and impact, alignment must be given full attention. From the outset and throughout strategy development, practitioners should pay particular attention to workflow practices, productivity measures, performance tools, recognition, and reward systems. In our experience, these are common sources of misalignment. When a mismatch is identified and carefully addressed, flexibility is integrated more deeply and seamlessly into business operations. This ultimately embeds flexibility into the organizational culture.

In sum, the new approach to work–life fit and flexibility relies on ongoing tweaks to both the flexibility strategy and the organization's processes and practices until both intersect in a way that supports desired employee and organizational outcomes. With these principles understood, practitioners can use the following framework to tailor a strategy with impact and sustainability.

NEXT-GENERATION IN WORK–LIFE FIT: A FRAMEWORK FOR PRACTITIONERS

The next-generation approach to flexibility focuses on a comprehensive strategic process that helps organizations achieve broad business goals and helps individuals manage their work–life fit. As organizations increasingly recognize the limits of their traditional models to meet the complex demands of the changing workplace and business environment, this more innovative business-based approach to work–life fit and flexibility will receive serious attention by practitioners.

The process, which we call the *Flex+Strategy process*, is framed in the following five phases that build on and refer back to one another:

- Discovery
- Vision and Strategy Development
- Readiness
- Orientation and Ongoing Learning
- Evaluation and Improvement

The Flex+Strategy model builds on the traditional approaches highlighted earlier and aligns with the systemic process described in the Chapter 5. For example, the Flex+Strategy model adds a phase of extensive up-front

TABLE 6.2
Flex+Strategy Approach—Comparative Analysis

Traditional approach	Flex+Strategy approach	Objectives
	Discovery	• To engage a significant cross-section of people in process • To assess and articulate the current state of flexibility • To build a compelling business case
Policies and programs	Vision and Strategy Readiness	• Create a shared flexibility vision • Articulate pillars of the flexibility strategy • Prepare all levels for change • Anticipate, acknowledge, plan for bumps in road
Communication rollout	Orientation and Ongoing Learning	• Engage and educate everyone in organization • Introduce tools and resources
Measurement (utilization and effectiveness)	Evaluation and Improvement	• Measure and learn • Experiment with innovation • Respond to changing business realities • Keep information flowing

Note. From Flex+Strategy Group/Work+Life Fit, Inc. Copyright 2012 by Flex+Strategy Group/Work+Life Fit, Inc. Reprinted with permission.

discovery about the business case and current state of the operation, market, and flexibility. It also includes robust vision and strategy development and readiness-building throughout all levels of the organization. This is done prior to the formal introduction of the flexibility strategies and tools. It also invests in ongoing learning and evaluation to optimize work–life fit and flexibility use and impact over time (see Table 6.2).

The following section elaborates on each phase of the next-generation process. To illustrate the process, we share highlights of the experience of Next Generation Corp. (NGCorp), a composite of multiple clients supported by the authors. NGCorp, a growing mid-sized company with offices across the country, has operated successfully in highly competitive global markets. It began investigating a more formalized approach to flexibility through its women's initiative, which identified balance and flexibility as priorities to address.

DISCOVERY

Discovery kicks off the Flex+Strategy process. Whether an organization is just starting to develop a flexibility strategy or is reviewing and enhancing an existing approach, it is important to ask and answer key questions before formulating solutions.

The objectives of discovery are to do the following:

1. Build a compelling business case for flexibility as a business tool for the organization.
2. Assess and articulate the current state of flexibility.
3. Immediately engage a cross-section of employees.

Discovery inquiries are aimed at clarifying the business case and current state of flexibility in the organization. For example, business-focused questions include the following: What are the organization's core strategies and priorities? How do you see fit and flexibility contributing to business success? What specific prices and payoffs do you anticipate realizing from a successful flexibility strategy?

Questions that deepen understanding about the current state include the following: What is your organization's current approach to flexibility? What is your individual approach to finding your work–life fit? Where do you see pockets of success and points of resistance in your organization?

To engage people in dialogue and reflection, we use a mix of the following techniques:

- Organization-wide surveys give everyone a voice and serve to collect data from across the organization. Interviews with the CEO, senior leaders, and early adopters who successfully use or manage flexibility sharpen insights and provoke new questions to explore.
- Flexibility workshops attended by a cross-section of employees and managers test out flexibility principles. We recommend interactive workshops rather than traditional ask-and-answer focus groups. This more experience-based approach unearths both the leverage points and roadblocks in the organization, generates useful feedback, begins to introduce new language and concepts, and provides participants with practical information they can apply immediately and appropriately on their own.

Each line of inquiry and technique solicits a tremendous amount of information that informs how the following phases develop. Practitioners can use each communication touch point to convey key messages, broaden ownership, and model the type of dialogue that is critical to long-term success.

How Discovery Worked for NGCorp

Though somewhat skeptical that more information was needed to supplement data gathered by its women's initiative, the executive team agreed that further information could help NGCorp advance the organization's flexibility to the next stage of the innovation continuum. They enlisted outside consultants to conduct a discovery process in partnership with their internal team. The goal was to ensure that outside expertise informed the straight talk about the potential application and impact of work–life fit and flexibility in their culture and operation.

Through a series of interviews, workshops and dialogues conducted across levels and functions, NGCorp leaders realized that what they "already knew" was but a small slice of the previously undetected whole. Discovery unearthed a need for flexibility that touched every employee segment, not just women and not just parents. Discovery also identified potential ways in which a more flexible approach to work could solve business challenges that had not been originally associated with flexibility (e.g., improving already-strong client service, containing growing real estate costs, managing varied labor costs).

Flexibility began to be viewed as a "must have" for future NGCorp success, not a "nice to have" means of attracting and retaining women (which is what originally started the company on its journey of discovery). Involving senior leaders from the outset generated buy-in and focus, and leveraging a cross-section of support from across the organization grounded the information in NGCorp's current operating realities. In short order, flexibility became a more compelling investment of time, energy and capital as a business-driven priority.

VISION AND STRATEGY DEVELOPMENT

With a clearer understanding of the business case and current state, an organization begins to create a road map for action.

The objectives of the Vision and Strategy Development phase are as follows:

1. Create a shared flexibility vision.
2. Articulate the pillars of the flexibility strategy.

Creating a compelling shared vision is an important element of any meaningful change process. It unifies many views into one clear, widely owned and known picture of the future that inspires people, informs strategic direction, and focuses effort. In our experience, however, traditional approaches to work–life fit and flexibility rarely include time to develop a shared vision. This critical aspect is either skipped over, done superficially (e.g., a tag line is created to place on posters, coffee mugs, and notepads), or created by a small group in charge of the flexibility initiative without further input.

The Flex+Strategy process avoids this mistake by incorporating a wide-scale visioning element prior to developing and implementing a strategy. Though visioning processes can vary, the consistent underpinning is a structure that gets many voices in play and funnels them into a concrete, relevant, and forward-looking picture of success that resonates across the organization.

The strategy to achieve the vision is as follows:

- identify the key pillars needed to align flexibility to the organization's core business and its place in the market,
- integrate it internally, and
- place it in the hands of those who will use and manage it.

This vision-driven strategy development process typically includes the following:

- Core flexibility frameworks that support individuals and managers who want to apply flexibility to themselves or their business. Practitioners will want to outline the consistent processes and guidelines that will support the creation of flexibility solutions tailored to business and personal realities. This may include templates, tools and other supporting resources, as well as the preferred language employees and managers will use to describe elements of the strategy.
- Communication plans that disseminate key information at appropriate times and shine a favorable spotlight on flexibility and weave it into ongoing messaging. Considerations should include identifying target audiences, priority messages, key communicators and influencers, and effective vehicles (e.g., print, electronic, video, face-to-face, social media).
- Alignment plans that identify where and how to close gaps between the ideals embedded in the vision and the current organizational realities. These plans must address the aspects of the strategy that will affect utilization. Areas to review include, but are not limited to, performance management, compensation and benefits, paid time off, and productivity measures.
- Direct employee supports that help individuals flexibly manage their unique work–life fit. At this point, practitioners consider what additional supports are needed to achieve the vision. This may include child and eldercare resources, parental leave, financial planning, and leave and time off policies.
- Metrics that truly evaluate flexibility's effects on employees and the business as outlined in the shared vision and provide actionable information to support ongoing evaluation, learning, and

improvement. Metrics can be both quantitative and qualitative. The source of baseline data, the evaluation timeline and the vehicles (e.g., interviews, focus groups survey) must be agreed on by the internal and external members of the flexibility strategy team.

Typically, there are many interdependent strategy elements to tackle. Some are small and easy; others are large and challenging. The Flex+Strategy process helps tie all aspects together into a cohesive plan. Together, discovery, vision, and strategy create momentum and set the stage to boost readiness for a larger scale rollout (Jahani, Javadein, & Jafari, 2010).

How Vision and Strategy Were Developed in NGCorp

Leveraging the exciting discovery developments fresh in their collective experience, NGCorp set out to articulate what its "flexible future" looked like. With great care, they assembled a task force of respected individuals from different parts of the business and tasked them with taking a first stab at NGCorp's flexibility vision. After a day of concentrated work, a vision began to emerge. Thereafter, NGCorp conducted small group visioning meetings with hundreds of people throughout the organization. These visioning meetings were facilitated by the members of the task force and resulted in a refined vision that linked directly to the information that emerged in discovery: "Flexibility touches everything we do at NGCorp. It provides every one of our people with work–life fit, every client with excellent service, and every part of the business with smart painless ways to help manage budgets." The words may seem straightforward to an outsider. But the involvement and shared leadership of many people in addition to the contextual use of the vision to anchor goals, plans and communication, made it an inspiring catalyst to support change.

To develop the strategy, the flexibility team literally drew a map of all the important issues and areas that had been identified to date, and they tapped into the key groups and individuals needed to address them. Discussions were held with colleagues from human resources, information technology, communication, finance, and operations. There were also regular cross-functional conversations to spot connect-the-dots opportunities that might otherwise have been missed. These teams had been included in discovery and visioning work; therefore, a shared understanding and common goals contributed to strong partnering and constructive problem-solving. The result was a strong plan with joint ownership of goals, roles and responsibilities and a commitment to contributing to successful outcomes. It was time to turn to ensuring broad-based readiness.

Readiness refers to the ability of individuals and the organization to deliver on the commitments created in the flexibility vision and strategy. Readiness objectives are to do as follows:

1. Prepare all levels for the changes that the flexibility strategy will bring.
2. Anticipate, acknowledge, and plan to address the inevitable bumps in the road.

Vision and strategy development create excitement and confidence throughout an organization. This can result in a very strong urge to "pull the switch" and roll flexibility out broadly. But at this juncture, practitioners must enforce organizational discipline. You must first understand where individuals are on the learning curve and then help them prepare to accept the changes that a flexibility strategy will require. Doing so optimizes overall success.

Senior leaders benefit from this preparation phase. From the beginning, the organization relies on them to positively model and message. People watch this group to see if they "really mean it" when it comes to flexibility. Yet, as individuals they are on their own real-time learning curve that must be respected. They may have personal, often unconscious, biases that undercut the vision and strategy. They may behave in habitual ways that can be viewed as devaluing flexibility. They may be willing but unclear about how to reset a culture that values "face time." Getting this group ready to be supporters and leaders of flexibility is important.

Employees and managers also benefit from preparation. Employees may fear that flexibility proposals will be denied, cause resentment, hurt their careers, or threaten their jobs. Managers may fear that the process will be abused or subject their department to an unmanageable flood of requests. They may also wonder how work will get done, and to what level of excellence, and may fear that if they give employees greater work flexibility, they will find themselves alone and responsible for getting the work done.

The Flex+Strategy process acknowledges these readiness issues without judgment and addresses them. It reviews data collected during discovery, vision, and strategy development for red flags and recurring themes that will be barriers to success. It then uses proven change management techniques to raise awareness about fears and barriers and help work through them in advance. This phase of the process is not a silver bullet—individual mind-sets and organizational culture cannot be altered overnight—but it does offer a forum for roadblocks to be productively addressed, which leads to stronger results.

How NGCorp Built Readiness

Four key audiences were identified that needed to be introduced to, or refreshed on, the work–life fit and flexibility business case, vision, and plans. We helped them work through potential barriers that they could each control or influence in the following venues:

1. The executive team held a full-day meeting dedicated to the flexibility strategy.
2. The top 300 people discussed flexibility at the annual leadership meeting.
3. Human resources managers allotted time on a series of conference calls.
4. A cross-section of employees piloted orientation sessions, including segments designed to confront individual and manager fears.

All these discussions incorporated constructive dialogue and problem solving. They modeled a culture that would support the company's vision and strategy. Follow-up surveys and interviews with these audiences indicated a promising level of optimism and commitment to actively championing flexibility. NGCorp was ready to give flexibility the company-wide "green light."

ORIENTATION AND ONGOING LEARNING

With preparations complete, flexibility plans and tools can be launched throughout the organization. The purposes of Orientation and Ongoing Learning are to do the following:

1. Engage and educate everyone in the organization about the work–life fit and flexibility strategy.
2. Introduce tools and resources that will support initial and ongoing learning.

This phase requires the same level of planning and thoughtfulness that have been present in the other phases. It is similar to the rollout phase in traditional approaches to flexibility with some key differences. First, it is viewed primarily as a communication phase rather than a training phase. Second, it is framed as an orientation—a new beginning rather than the end of the work. It strongly emphasizes the continued focus, work, and learning that must follow. Finally, it reinforces key principles, the organization's business case for flexibility as a strategic lever, and the vision throughout.

Every single person participates in the orientations. A good deal of orientation time is spent communicating (yet again) the business case for flexibility and describing how the strategy is a tool for both individuals and the business. Participants are offered the knowledge, skills, and resources that support the strategy, including the core flexibility frameworks guiding the day-to-day implementation within the business. Individuals walk through how to access and use the varied forms of flexibility, including how to manage day-to-day flexibility and how to develop and propose a formal flexibility plan. Managers also receive the same orientation on the individual applications of flexibility. This is later augmented by management-level information that describes how to create an environment that supports the discussion and innovation related to flexibility and how to successfully use flexibility as a strategic lever to run their business.

Orientation methods vary and can include large-group, small-team, or one-on-one vehicles. The tools and resources presented during orientation are equally varied and can include the following:

- Tools and templates that provide a clear road map of the flexibility process, including roles, responsibilities, tips for successful planning and implementation for different types of tailored solutions.
- Training opportunities (live and virtual) that give people a chance to gather further information, and learn or reacquaint themselves with skills relevant to using flexibility.
- Communication tools that keep flexibility ideals and messages alive. These can include the introduction of or reminders about web pages, newsletters, town halls, brown bag lunch sessions and other forums that maintain the cross-functional connections that have been established around flexibility throughout the process. Marketing materials can also be introduced at this time. In the Flex+Strategy process, organization-wide marketing around flexibility happens later than in traditional approaches. That way marketing is used to support the organization's vision and strategy rather than to create them.

NGCorp's Orientation and Ongoing Learning

Enthused about its flexibility vision and strategy, NGCorp created a flexibility orientation session to communicate key information. It wanted to ensure that everyone in the organization had a consistent understanding of how to access and use flexibility successfully. The plan included the following:

- Orientation sessions in every office to launch flexibility. These were facilitated by a pairing of a line manager with a human resources leader. Together they introduced the core framework, tools, and templates. The information in this session was later adapted and expanded for specialized webinars and e-learning resources and integrated into other relevant programs.

- Promotional campaigns that highlighted a range of successful flexibility applications were introduced and included a flexibility chat room, a high-quality poster campaign, newsletters, and a series of office-based presentations. A video created for the initial orientation meetings was repurposed for internal and external audiences.
- A dedicated website on the NGCorp portal that was launched to house all flexibility information and tools has been updated regularly.

The orientation sessions moved NGCorp closer to its vision while reinforcing that this was only the beginning in terms of making its flexibility strategy come to life.

EVALUATION AND IMPROVEMENT

As noted earlier, change and innovation are not static processes that have an end. They continue to evolve. The purposes of evaluation and improvement are to help an organization

- measure and learn from experience,
- experiment with new innovations,
- respond to changing business objectives and market realities, and
- keep information and dialogue flowing.

Historically, organizations considered themselves finished when the "national rollout" of flexibility was complete. The Flex+Strategy approach recognizes that, like any important business strategy that remains relevant to individuals and the organization, flexibility needs to be measured and nurtured consistently over time. During this stage of the process, basics are reinforced as needed to maintain the integrity of the vision and the strategy. The strategy and its tactics are evaluated using the metrics and timelines that were articulated earlier. These evaluations recognize and broadcast new success and further serve to highlight tactics to refine, clarify, or rework. With the vision as an anchor, the organization can begin to realize the return on its significant investment: flexibility that supports the individual and the organization so that both can thrive.

How NGCorp Continues to Evaluate and Improve

The company is proud of the progress it has made in a relatively short amount of time. Flexibility has become a strategic tool that can be used by individuals and businesses to achieve broad operating and individual objectives. As an integrated part of the operating model, the positive impact is clear. In fact, the company has received numerous well-publicized awards. Despite this exciting success, NGCorp knows that continual improvement and ongoing vibrancy of flexibility require effort. For example, its recent annual employee survey identified places to amplify and clarify messaging. A change in market conditions provided a perfect opportunity to shift focus of the strategy to the cost savings and productivity improvements outlined in the guiding vision.

It is interesting to note that the additional benefit to NGCorp includes broader organizational learning about change and innovation. Elements of the approach used to advance flexibility have been applied to subsequent initiatives. And these same lessons can drive the considerations for other organizations and managers interested in advancing work–life fit and flexibility as part of a psychologically healthy workplace.

NEXT GENERATION IN WORK–LIFE FIT: PRACTITIONER CONSIDERATIONS

Practitioners interested in exploring this next-generation change and innovation-based approach to work–life fit and flexibility have much to consider (Erwin & Garman, 2010). While every organization will have a unique list of issues to consider before starting, the following questions are fundamental:

- Is it feasible for my organization to engage in this process now in this business environment and cycle? If yes, is there a willingness to devote the time, people, and money required for success; and
- if we want to move ahead, what types of resources can we commit?

Feasibility and willingness considerations are the starting points. No time will ever be perfect, but there are moments that will feel more "right" than others. As a practitioner you can start the feasibility discussion by asking one or two discovery-type questions (refer to the "current state" questions in the Discovery section).

Feasibility has little to do with willingness. If your organization feels the time is right, then it should quickly ask if there is broad-based willingness to devote time and energy to the process. Like any worthwhile endeavor, the Flex+Strategy process achieves the greatest result when an organization acknowledges and accepts what it truly requires to achieve the positive outcomes for employees and the organization. Again, practitioners can begin the willingness conversation by asking one or two discovery-type questions (refer to "building the business case" questions in the Discovery section).

Feasibility and willingness determine your organization's most basic readiness. However, feasibility and willingness mean little when not backed with actual resources. Determining types and amounts of real support moves the organization from a philosophical conversation to a practical one. We have seen resources allocated in different ways with success. But make no mistake, resources must be dedicated. Consider the number and level of people who will lead and staff the process. Would you benefit, for example, from a senior executive sponsor, a strategy leader and a team of dedicated developers and implementers? Do you need external support to provide deep and broad expertise, and to ensure the work advances at an effective pace?

Consider also your budget for the process. What can you legitimately afford to staff, develop, and implement a strategy that will achieve results? At the outset, your organization may be unable to definitively answer these questions; however, it will certainly be able to generally assess whether or not it is willing to shift resources to work–life strategy advancement.

If feasibility, willingness, and resource questions undeniably lead to your organization taking robust next steps, then the Flex+Strategy process can begin. Keep in mind, however, that the approach need not be all or nothing. Your organization can benefit from using aspects of the framework that meet your organization's needs and realities, wherever you are on the innovation curve. Practitioners can help connect feasibility–willingness–resource considerations to the best-suited aspects of the Flex+Strategy process.

CONCLUSION

In this chapter, we focused on a change and innovation process that develops work–life fit and flexibility strategies that benefit both the business and employees. This next-generation process can be invoked by individuals, teams, and organizations interested in changing how, when, or where work gets done for broad operational and individual impact. It helps create a psychologically healthy workplace, which helps individuals thrive and organizations compete in the global, 24/7, technology-driven business environment. Practitioners can guide their organizations through or around the obstacles and roadblocks that so often plague flexibility initiatives by using the principles and framework described here. The payoffs to practitioners, end users, and organizations alike can be significant.

REFERENCES

Eaton, M. (2010). Why change programs fail. *Human Resource Management International Digest, 18*(2), 37–42. http://dx.doi.org/10.1108/09670731011028492

Erwin, D. G., & Garman, A. N. (2010). Resistance to organizational change: Linking research and practice. *Leadership & Organization Development Journal, 31,* 39–56. http://dx.doi.org/10.1108/01437731011010371

Grawitch, M. J., Maloney, P. W., Barber, L. K., & Yost, C. (2011). Moving toward a better understanding of the work and non-work interface. *Industrial and Organizational Psychology: Perspectives on Science and Practice, 4,* 385–388. http://dx.doi.org/10.1111/j.1754-9434.2011.01357.x

Hamel, G. (2000). *Leading the revolution.* Boston, MA: Harvard Business School Press.

Jahani, B., Javadein, S. R. S., & Jafari, H. A. (2010). Measurement of enterprise architecture readiness within organizations. *Business Strategy Series, 11,* 177–191. http://dx.doi.org/10.1108/17515631011043840

Kelley, T., & Littman, J. (2001). *The art of innovation.* New York, NY: Doubleday.

Kotter, J. P. (1996). *Leading change.* Boston, MA: Harvard Business School Press.

Mescher, S., Benschop, Y., & Doorewaard, H. (2010). Representations of work–life balance support. *Human Relations, 63,* 21–39. http://dx.doi.org/10.1177/0018726709349197

Yergler, J. D. (2011). Beyond strategy: The leader's role in successful implementation. *Leadership & Organization Development Journal, 32,* 102–104. http://dx.doi.org/10.1108/lodj.2011.32.1.102.4

Yost, C. W. (2009). CFOs see business impacts of work–life flexibility, but they can't execute for strategic benefit. *World at Work Journal, 18*(2), 59–67.

7

YOU GET WHAT YOU REWARD: A RESEARCH-BASED APPROACH TO EMPLOYEE RECOGNITION

BOB NELSON

It seems that not a month goes by without the emergence of some new surefire management fad, "guaranteed" to increase employee performance, improve morale, and cure whatever ails an organization. Most of these fads are soon discarded by those who implement them—much to the chagrin of the employees who feel like ping pong balls, bounced from one new management approach to the next.

There are, however, certain basic truths in management. One is, "You get what you reward"—sometimes referred to as the "greatest management principle in the world," first coined by Michael LeBoeuf (1985) in a book by the same name. We know from extensive research that human behavior is shaped by its consequences and that providing positive consequences for employee performance is one of the most powerful ways to enhance that performance (Podsakoff, Todor, & Skov, 1982). If a specific behavior is noticed, recognized, or rewarded, that behavior tends to be repeated.

http://dx.doi.org/10.1037/14731-008
The Psychologically Healthy Workplace: Building a Win–Win Environment for Organizations and Employees, M. J. Grawitch and D. W. Ballard (Editors)

Given that positive reinforcement is one of the most validated principles in management and psychology (Appelbaum, Bregman, & Moroz, 1998; Podsakoff, Bommer, Podsakoff, & MacKenzie, 2006), it is surprising how few managers use it on a regular basis. It is common sense but far from common practice in business today. Yet it needs to become common practice if an organization is to thrive, let alone survive. Most employees like to be recognized and appreciated (Brun & Dugas, 2008), but how many managers consider "appreciating others" to be a major function of their job? Indeed, how many managers are expected by their organizations to recognize employees when they do good work?

At a time when employees are being asked to do more than ever before, to make suggestions for continuous improvement, to handle complex problems quickly, and to act independently in the best interests of the company, most companies have fewer resources to commit to such practices, given the challenging economic environment in recent years. Budgets are tight, salaries are often frozen, layoffs are rampant, promotional opportunities are on the decline, and employees feel unappreciated and stuck. In a survey conducted by the American Psychological Association (2013), only 39% of working Americans said they had sufficient opportunities for internal career advancement and just over half (51%) reported feeling valued at work. More than ever, employees need to be told by their managers that their efforts are appreciated and that they play an important role in their organizations.

In today's business environment, however, managers tend to be too busy and too removed from their employees to notice when they have done exceptional work and to thank them for it. Looking at a computer screen has replaced many personal interactions. Futurist John Naisbitt (1988) predicted this would happen almost 30 years ago. He said the more highly technical our work environments become, the greater the employee need would be for human contact. He called this emerging need "high-tech/high-touch."

The widespread lack of rewards and recognition programs at a time when they are most needed is particularly ironic because what motivates people the most takes so little time and money to implement. Nonmonetary incentives actually rank higher in importance for employees than traditional organizational rewards. In multiple studies conducted first in the 1940s (Lindahl, 1949), later in the mid-1990s (Kovach, 1995), and most recently in 2012 (Kowalewski & Phillips, 2012), employees have consistently ranked items such as "full appreciation for work done," "feeling 'in' on things," and "interesting work" as being more important to them than more traditional incentives. Stajkovic and Luthans (1997) identified seven classes of reinforcement related only to interventions, including financial, nonfinancial, and social reinforcement, of which no class of reinforcement produced effects that were significantly different from those of nonfinancial interventions. Therefore, it does not take a fat bonus check, a trip to the Bahamas, or a lavish annual awards banquet to get the best out of people. It just takes a little time, thoughtfulness, and energy to make a difference in an employee's job; rewards and recognition are tools that can be used by any manager or leader in any organization to help realize enormous business benefits.

DEFINING EMPLOYEE RECOGNITION

I define *employee recognition* as a positive consequence provided to a person for a behavior or result. Recognition can take the form of acknowledgment, approval, or the expression of gratitude. It means appreciating someone for something he or she has done for an individual, a group, or an organization. Recognition can be given as one strives to achieve a certain goal or behavior or on completion of that goal or behavior. It comes in all shapes and sizes, but the major categories of recognition include *interpersonal* recognition (Nelson, 2001), which can take the form of a personal or written thank you from one's employee or peers; *social* recognition—acknowledgement, public praise, or the granting of elite status, such as being made a part of a special group or team; *tangible* recognition—a certificate, plaque, trophy, paperweight, coffee mug, or other memento; and *intangible* recognition—the awarding of more involvement in decision making, more autonomy, flexibility, or choice of working assignment. Other terms that relate to recognition that are discussed in this chapter include *motivation*, which is something that energizes, directs, and sustains behavior (Steers & Porter, 1983). A *motivator* is anything that increases motivational energy, whereas a *demotivator* reduces motivational energy or triggers negative behaviors. A *reward* is an item or experience that has monetary value, is given for desired behavior or performance, and is often accompanied by recognition. Kanter (1986) defined a *reward* as something employees can receive for going above and beyond, and an *incentive* is a reward that is planned, agreed upon in advance, or a future reward that is anticipated (Spitzer, 1995). Incentives create anticipation and excitement and thus can result in stronger, clearer motivation.

THE FUNDAMENTALS OF MOTIVATION

Motivation is a diverse, well-established area of the management and psychology literature, and no single theory is capable of fully explaining the complexities of human behavior. Three important theories of motivation that relate to issues of employee recognition are as follows: (a) *reinforcement theory*, which attempts to explain behavior as a function of the environment, particularly the consequences of specific behavior; (b) *social learning theory*, which attempts to explain behavior as a function of the person and his or her social environment, and the interaction between both; and (c) *expectancy theory*, which attempts to explain behavior as a function of the person and his or her internal cognitive processes.

Reinforcement Theory

Reinforcement theory (Skinner, 1953) states that behavior is a function of its consequences and their frequency. Consequences that provide rewards increase a behavior, whereas consequences that provide undesired outcomes decrease a behavior. The effectiveness of rewards can be traced back to fundamental principles of positive reinforcement. Under conditions of positive reinforcement, the response produces a consequence that results in an increase in the frequency of the response. Such consequences are typically rewarding, pleasing, or drive-reducing for the individual. Reinforcers can come from many sources such as positive, intrinsic feelings that result from the receipt of valued nonmonetary recognition.

Positive reinforcement is effective for several reasons. First, it increases the probable occurrence of the desired response by associating rewarding consequences with certain behaviors; and second, it creates the desire for these consequences in the future by incenting particular behaviors. In addition, the adverse emotional responses associated with negative reinforcement are apt to be reduced, and in fact, favorable emotions may be developed (Nord, 1974).

Principles

Positive reinforcement is most effective when some simple guidelines are followed. According to Nord (1974), "the crucial variable in distributing any reward is contingency" (p. 398); that is, the reward needs to be clearly given in response to the desired behavior, and it must be given as soon as possible after the desired behavior occurs. As Nord explained,

> most rapid conditioning results when the desired response is "reinforced" immediately. In other words, the desired response is followed directly by some consequence. In simple terms, if the outcome is pleasing to the individual, the probability of his repeating the response is apt to be increased. The process of inducing such change in the response rate is called operant conditioning. In general, the frequency of a behavior is said to be a function of its consequences. (p. 385)

To be effective, consequences also need to be valued and meaningful to the individuals who receive them. It is necessary that rewards dependent on results are sufficiently meaningful such that other incentives employees might have to act contrary to the corporation's best interest are offset (Merchant, 1989). An example of this is the personal delivery of praise to the employee from the manager. Because time is a limited resource for virtually every manager, taking time to recognize or praise an employee underscores the importance of the activity to the employee and thus tends to have value to the employee. Finally, behaviors that are reinforced frequently are more likely to become established as habit (Podsakoff, Podsakoff, & Kuskova, 2010). In the long term, intermittent reinforcement tends to be the most effective at sustaining desired behavior.

Implications

The use of reinforcement theory by management to shape desired behavior of employees seems as though it would be a given: The manager, whether consciously or not, is constantly shaping subordinate behavior through the use of rewards, thereby modifying the behavior patterns of the work group (Haire, 1964). Yet as Steers and Porter (1983) observed,

> one of the primary reasons that managers fail to 'motivate' workers to perform in the desired manner is due to a lack of understanding of the power of the contingencies of reinforcement over the employee and of the manager's role in arranging these contingencies. (p. 122)

As Wiley (1997) explained,

> employees are motivated by feedback and recognition for the work they do. Herein lies the problem. Most employers think they know how to express appreciation for a job well done. Yet, research shows that employers seldom acknowledge appreciation for employees' work; and, when they do, it is done poorly. More than 80 per cent of supervisors claim they frequently express appreciation to their subordinates, while less than 20 per cent of the employees report that their supervisors express appreciation more than occasionally. (p. 263)

Social Learning Theory

Social learning theory builds on reinforcement theory to suggest not only that behavior stems from its consequences but also that it includes constant learning from and adapting to one's environment and that most learning probably occurs vicariously through observation of others. Bandura (1971) went so far as to say that "most of the behaviors that people display are learned either deliberately or inadvertently, through the influence of example" (p. 5).

Principles

Bandura's (1977) work on social learning theory contributes several important elements. Modeling, observational learning, or vicarious learning through observation and imitation modeling, the most prominent aspect of this theory, involves four components: (a) *attention*—the observer must pay attention to the behavior that is modeled; (b) *retention*—when behavior has been observed, it must then be retained through cognitive processes; (c) *reproduction*—the observer must be able to reproduce the observed behavior; and (d) *motivation*—there must be sufficient incentive for the observer to repeat the modeled behavior (Grusec, 1992).

Although modeling is often considered a straightforward imitation process, research suggests that it is very complex, often involving links to cognitive schemata or scripts (Manz & Sims, 1986). Bandura (1977) observed that "cognitive factors partly determine which external events will be observed, how they will be perceived, whether they leave any lasting effects, what valence and efficacy they have, and how the information they convey will be organized for future use" (p. 160).

Self-regulation governs the transfer of behavior from external sources to internal ones. This mechanism operates through three principal subfunctions: (a) self-monitoring of one's behavior, its determinants, and its effects; (b) judgment of one's behavior in relation to personal standards and environmental circumstances; and (c) affective self-reaction (Bandura, 1991). Like modeling, self-monitoring is not simply a mechanical audit of one's performances. Preexisting cognitive structures and self-beliefs exert selective influence on which aspects of one's functioning are given the most attention, how they are perceived, and how performance information is organized for memory representation (Bandura, 1991). Regarding self-control processes, Bandura (1977) observed that

> behavior can, and is, extensively self-regulated by self-produced consequences for one's own actions. . . . Because of their great representational and self-reactive capacities, humans are less dependent upon immediate external supports for their behavior. The inclusion of self-reinforcement phenomena in learning theory thus greatly increases the explanatory power of reinforcement principles as applied to human functioning. (p. 28)

Self-efficacy is a major determinant of self-regulation. Self-efficacy theory argues that a person's self-beliefs about his or her ability to perform specific tasks will strongly influence his or her ability to perform (Appelbaum & Hare, 1996). Individuals develop and strengthen beliefs about their efficacy in the following four ways: (a) mastery experiences or enactive mastery; (b) modeling or observational learning; (c) social persuasion, including persuasive discussions and specific performance feedback regarding a person's ability to perform a task; and (d) judgments of their own physiological states (Boyd & Vozikis, 1994). Empirical studies confirm that self-efficacy has a strong, positive relationship with employee performance (Earley, 1994; Pescosolido, 2001) and grows stronger over time as the employee successfully performs tasks and builds the confidence necessary to fulfill his or her role in the organization (Gist & Mitchell, 1992; Pescosolido, 2001).

Next, *reciprocal determinism* represents the interrelationship among the individual, the environment, and the behavior. Bandura argued that behavior, the environment and cognition, and other personal factors operate as interacting determinants that have a bidirectional influence on each other (Grusec, 1992). This concept served as the basis for social cognitive theory, which includes cognitive constructs such as self-regulatory mechanisms that extend beyond issues of learning or modifying behavior. In social cognitive theory, human behavior is extensively motivated and regulated by the ongoing exercise of self-influence, and learning is viewed as knowledge acquisition through cognitive processing of information (Stajkovic & Luthans, 1998).

Implications

It stands to reason that social learning theory would have abundant application in any organizational setting, given the social nature of work. Outside of the application of interpersonal skills training, however, the use of social learning theory in an organizational environment is less well-documented. Modeling has been shown to be effective in developing communication skills of managers and supervisors with subordinates as well as the training of supervisors to improve interpersonal skills in dealing with their employees (Latham & Saari, 1979). Focused training can also help build self-efficacy and result in important motivation and performance gains (Brown, Cron, & Slocum, 1998; Lankau & Scandura, 2002).

Expectancy Theory

Expectancy theory helps to explain why people choose one action out of many possible actions (Locke & Henne, 1986). It suggests that people implicitly or explicitly are involved in a cognitive process of asking themselves, "What's in it for me?" when deciding whether to engage in a certain behavior to determine the likelihood that the effort expended will lead to something they value (Landy & Trumbo, 1980). It assumes that people make choices between alternative modes of behavior or between different levels of effort, depending on the attractiveness they attach to the various outcomes. The theory provides a framework for explaining motivation and under which circumstances motivation leads to performance (Benkhoff, 1997). Georgopoulos, Mahoney, and Jones (1957) proposed that if a worker sees high productivity as a path leading to the attainment of one or more personal goals, then that worker should tend to be a high producer. Conversely, if low productivity is seen as a path to the achievement of goals, low production will result.

Principles

Vroom (1964) and later Porter and Lawler (1968), among others, expanded the theory by suggesting that any behavior is a function of a person's expectations regarding the following three relationships (Locke & Henne, 1986): *expectancy*, or the subjective belief that exerting a given level of effort will lead to successful performance of the act; *instrumentality*, or the subjective belief that successful performance will result in some specific outcome; and *valence*, the subjective value (positive or negative) individuals place on that specific outcome.

Determinants of an individual's expectancy include self-esteem or self-efficacy, the perceived availability or accessibility of training or developmental opportunities, and trusting that the environment is safe enough to take interpersonal risks (Murray & Gerhart, 1998). Determinants of a manager's instrumentality might include his or her past experience with similar behaviors, his or her perceptions of other managers in the organization, and cultural dimensions of the organization.

Implications

The three aspects of expectancy theory can be applied to managerial use of employee recognition. There is *expectancy:* Does the manager believe his or her efforts to provide recognition are successful? What is easy for one person may be difficult for another. This is especially true when the behavior is new and unfamiliar to the person practicing it (e.g., a shy manager who is uncomfortable with interpersonal communication). There is *instrumentality:* Do managers who use recognition expect to receive the results they were seeking for its use? Managers who frequently use recognition will generally believe it is worth the effort and will lead to desired rewards, although the rewards received may not be immediate or directly align with the activity. Low-frequency recognition users, however, likely feel the use of recognition definitely will not lead to desired outcomes, achieving significant goals is not possible through the use of recognition, and the use of recognition will likely lead to negative outcomes that are undesirable to them. Finally, there is *valence:* Are the outcomes managers receive for using recognition valued (i.e., are they rewarding), and will they lead to the achievement of their own personal goals?

Although a comprehensive review of motivation theories is beyond the scope of this chapter, readers are directed to additional resources for more in-depth exploration, including the history of work motivation theory (Steers, Mowday, & Shapiro, 2004), goal setting and task motivation (Locke & Latham, 2002), self-determination theory (Gagné & Deci, 2005), and the integration of various perspectives (Eccles & Wigfield, 2002).

THE SEVEN ASPECTS OF EFFECTIVE RECOGNITION

The act of recognizing an employee, when done well, has to take into account seven considerations (Nelson & Spitzer, 2003). The first is *contingency*, which refers to how closely the recognition is tied to the behavior recognized. Contingent recognition is given only when an employee exhibits some sort of desired behavior or performance—for example, it can be given when an employee handles a difficult customer request or completes a project on time. Noncontingent recognition is generalized and is given, for example, when an organization holds a company picnic for all employees or celebrates an employee's birthday.

Second is *timing*. Recognition is the most meaningful when it is given as soon as possible after the desired behavior or performance (Nord, 1969). Recognition loses meaning (or can even become alienating to the recipient) when it is not timely, which means that saving up individual recognition for an annual performance appraisal or rewards banquet can be counterproductive.

Third is *frequency*. Positive reinforcement is most effective in shaping desired behavior or performance when it is frequent, at least until the behavior becomes established (Daniels, 1989). For recognition to reinforce performance, the recognition itself has to be reinforced. Frequency should always be considered when designing a rewards and recognition program.

Organizations typically use nonmonetary recognition on a formal yet infrequent basis around specific "events," such as one to celebrate a record sales quarter. To institutionalize nonmonetary recognition, companies often establish "programs," such as an employee-of-the-month program or a safety awards program. Or they might make this kind of recognition a daily part of management "practices," as with daily feedback on performance, personal one-on-one praising, and the frequent use of thank you notes.

Fourth is *formality*. A formal reward is one that stems from a planned and agreed-on program of incentives (Dalton, 1959). Formal rewards include employee-of-the-month programs, years-of-service awards, and attendance awards. An informal reward is more spontaneous and flexible, often stemming from the relationship between the parties involved (Dalton, 1959) and might include a personal word of thanks for a job well done or recognition in a staff meeting for excellent customer service. Formality leads to a pattern of defined behaviors, whereas informality leads to a pattern of interacting roles (Nord, 1969).

Fifth is *recognition setting and context*. Recognition can be given to an employee privately or in front of some or all of the company's personnel. Although many people like a spontaneous personal word of thanks, formal praise tends to be more highly valued by recipients (Nelson, 2001), although shy individuals often prefer private and less formal displays of gratitude. This suggests that individual differences among employees need to be taken into account. Recognition can be presented impersonally (e.g., by mail), or it can be very personal, even anecdotal and emotional. But most employees prefer recognition that is presented with a personal touch, no matter what size the audience.

Sixth is the *significance of the provider*. In general, manager-initiated recognition is highly valued by employees (Graham & Unruh, 1990). But who should provide the recognition? Should it be the individual with the most status or the one with a special relationship to the recipient? There is a trade-off when the person with the most emotional significance to the recipient (e.g., a workplace friend) does not also have power within the organization hierarchy. The preferred recognition provider will thus vary from individual to individual.

Last is the *value to the recipient*. Recognition is more meaningful when the form it takes is highly valued by the recipient (Nelson, 2001). One individual may value rewards that relate to his or her job, such as a specialized work tool, a software upgrade, or an educational opportunity, whereas another individual may value rewards that relate to his or her personal and family life and that can be shared with others. Such rewards might include dinner out with a significant other, a weekend getaway, a barbecue set, or tickets to a sporting event. Hence, rewards and recognition should be customized for the individual recipient. This may include considering whether the recipient would most value tangible recognition, intangible recognition, or both. Tangible recognition might be a trophy or plaque, whereas intangible or symbolic recognition includes ceremonies, public announcements, time off, or the gift of more responsibility or more space, as in a corner office.

Managers today need to consider a range of tools for getting results from their employees, such as personal thanks, active listening, and consensus building, which only a few years ago might have been considered too fuzzy, abstract, and ill-defined to be taken seriously. Although the best managers may have always been skilled at providing recognition to employees, organizations today need every manager to be rewards-and-recognition savvy and to create the kind of workplace in which we all would like to work.

KEY FACTORS THAT FACILITATE OR INHIBIT EMPLOYEE RECOGNITION EFFECTIVENESS

Employees expect to be recognized when they do good work. This statement is supported by dozens of studies and surveys, including the following:

- 84% of employers agree that providing nonmonetary recognition when employees do good work helps to increase employees' performance levels.
- 85% of today's employees feel overworked and underappreciated.

Thanking employees for doing good work increases the likelihood that they will be motivated to perform, which can subsequently serve as a catalyst for attracting talented, new recruits.

The Recognition and Performance Link

A key benefit of nonmonetary recognition is its impact on improving job performance of employees. At the same time, the impact of the employees' improved performance serves to reinforce the manager's decision to continue to provide additional recognition. Nelson's (2001) doctoral dissertation found evidence to support the recognition–performance link in at least three ways.

First, several performance-related variables were found to have broad support by all managers in the study, the majority of whom agreed or strongly agreed. Second, almost 73% of managers reported that they received the results they expected when they used nonmonetary recognition either immediately or soon after performance, and 98.8% said they felt they would eventually obtain the desired results. Third, of the 598 employees who reported to managers in this study, 77.6% said that it was very or extremely important to be recognized by their manager when they do good work. Employees expected recognition to occur immediately (20.0%), soon thereafter (52.9%), or sometime later (18.8%). (See Table 7.1.)

For these reasons alone, it might be expected that the use of recognition would be standard operating procedure in today's organizations, but it is not. In fact, the opposite is most often the case. In a 3-year study as part of my doctoral work in conjunction with the Peter F. Drucker Graduate Management Center of the Claremont Graduate University, I sought to answer a simple question: Why is it that so few managers recognize employees when they do good work? Specifically, I wanted to determine what factors encouraged and inhibited the use of employee recognition by managers. I considered 140 different variables in the study, ranging from the individual (e.g., awareness, skills, demographics) to the organizational (e.g., age, size, culture). The results were illuminating and often surprising.

TABLE 7.1
Managerial Recognition Behavior and Percentage of Managers in Study Who Supported the Behavior

Recognition behavior	Percentage
Recognizing employees helps me better motivate them.	90.5
Providing nonmonetary recognition to my employees when they do good work helps to increase their performance.	84.4
Recognizing employees provides them with practical feedback.	84.4
Recognizing my employees for good work makes it easier to get the work done.	80.3
Recognizing employees helps them to be more productive.	77.7
Providing nonmonetary recognition helps me to achieve my personal goals.	69.3
Providing nonmonetary recognition helps me to achieve my job goals.	60.3

A group of managers were drawn from 34 organizations, representing seven industries: health care, financial services, insurance, hospitality/restaurant/retail, information technology, manufacturing, and government. Within each organization, managers identified as frequent users of recognition were matched against managers identified as infrequent users of recognition. A broad-based survey was then conducted of all managers, exploring their motivations for using recognition, which ranged from past experience with it, to present reinforcement of recognition, to future expectations from the behavior. Open-ended questions were also used to collect each manager's perceptions of the primary factors that help or hinder use of recognition. The validity of inferences made from the survey results was enhanced by a response rate of 69%.

Why Managers Do Not Use Recognition

First and most simply, low-use managers felt strongly that recognition was not important and therefore did not use the behavior. They did not know how to effectively provide recognition and felt strongly that its use would lead to undesired outcomes. Older managers (over age 50) who had worked many years in the same job or for the same organization were more likely to feel that recognition was not an important behavior to practice. In fact, age was the only highly significant demographic factor that distinguished the group of high-use managers from the group of low-use managers; other demographic factors such as gender, ethnicity, nationality, and educational level had no significant impact on the giving of recognition. This suggests that older managers may be reluctant to use recognition and thus need additional convincing and encouragement to make it happen.

Organizations must meet low-use managers at their own level if they are going to make recognition a personal, practical, and positive experience. Misperceptions and constraints must be overcome, objections and obstacles must be removed, and excuses must be confronted. The following paragraphs depict the six leading "excuses" for not using recognition, as reported by low-use managers themselves (see Nelson & Spitzer, 2003, pp. 37–40).

"I Don't Feel Providing Recognition Is an Important Part of My Job"

Organizations need to set the expectation that providing recognition is not an optional activity but an integral part of the organization's strategies, specifically tied to achieving the company's goals. Managers need to be evaluated on the success of their efforts at providing recognition in a frequent and meaningful way. Recognition should be made to be an important part of the ongoing planning of organizational, team, and individual goal setting and not "management by announcement," in which an initiative is announced once and then never heard of again. A vice president at the American Automobile Association of Southern California personally writes notes of thanks to individuals in field offices, demonstrating to all managers reporting to him that if he can find time to acknowledge employees, they can as well.

"I Don't Have Time to Recognize My Employees"

Perhaps surprisingly, high-use managers actually tend to rate time as a facilitator for conducting recognition because some of the best forms of recognition (e.g., personal or written praise, public recognition, positive voicemail or e-mail messages) require very little time to initiate and accomplish. Thus, low-recognition managers who say they do not have enough time are really just offering an excuse. Such excuses can be countered with techniques that can be readily applied, even by busy managers. All managers and supervisors at Busch Gardens in Tampa, Florida, are provided tokens inscribed with the words "thank you" to use as an on-the-spot form of recognition for any employee caught demonstrating one of the organization's core values.

"I'm Unsure How Best to Recognize My Employees"

Most low-use managers consider giving recognition a difficult task. They need to have an increased awareness of the importance of recognition, to be trained in the skills of recognition, to be provided with individual feedback, and to be shown positive examples and techniques that they can actually do, no matter their time and resource constraints. To get buy-in, managers should discuss potential recognition strategies with their staff and seek feedback on their own recognition behaviors. At BankBoston (now a part of Bank of America), managers give employees a blank index card on their first day of work and ask them to make a list of those things that motivate them. The manager ends up with an individualized motivation checklist for every employee.

"I'm Afraid I Might Leave Somebody Out"

Another common concern of managers is the possibility of leaving out someone who is deserving of recognition. Whereas low-use managers take this concern and interpret it as an excuse for not recognizing employees at all, high-use managers translate this concern into a greater commitment to recognize everyone who deserves it. This might, for example, mean checking with a team leader to determine whether you have all the names of people who assisted with a successful project before commending the team in public. If at any time someone deserving is left out, it is perfectly acceptable to simply apologize and make amends as appropriate. I attended a corporate awards program in which several employees were flown to the corporate headquarters in New York solely to be recognized at the presentation. Unfortunately, business was first conducted, which cut back on the available time for the recognition at the end of the meeting, and the disgruntled employees had to return home without having been recognized.

"Employees Don't Value the Recognition I Have Given in the Past"

Instead of being put off by what might not have worked in the past, low-use managers should make a fresh start and seek to find out what forms of recognition their employees would most value. Managers can talk with employees one-on-one, have a group discussion about potential rewards and incentives, or ask each to bring two suggested motivators to share at the next staff meeting. By involving employees in decisions that affect their own motivation, managers increase the employees' commitment and buy-in and the likelihood that what is done will be successful.

A manager at the Hyatt Corporation asked her employees at a staff meeting what ideas they had for increasing recognition. One of the employees suggested that the department rotate the responsibility for recognition throughout the group so that each week one person would be responsible for finding an individual or group achievement and then recognize it in some way of their own choosing. Creativity flourished; recognition skyrocketed.

"My Organization Does Not Help Facilitate or Support Recognition Efforts"

Although recognition efforts can flourish even in the absence of formal organizational support, such support, if made available, can help managers maintain their commitment. Information, training, tools, budget allowances, and programs that reinforce recognition activities should be made available on an ongoing basis—even if all managers do not use these resources—to support recognition efforts and the expectation that the organization has for every manager to take the responsibility of providing recognition seriously.

At each morning's plant-wide meeting at a chemical plant in Moncure, North Carolina, employees were allowed to publicly exchange thanks and acknowledgments with other employees. On hearing of an achievement from one of his managers, the plant manager would suggest possible recognition awards or activities for that manager to consider doing for his people.

THE CYCLE OF RECOGNITION

The continued use of recognition—or not—by any manager tends to become a reinforcing loop, as illustrated in the following paragraphs. In this study, high-use managers tended to have a positive experience with recognition, which made them more likely to use recognition with those they managed. The managers were reinforced for the use of recognition (in descending order of importance) by their employees, themselves, other colleagues, suppliers, and their own managers. They also obtained the results they desired in using recognition, which included increased performance and morale on the part of their employees. On the basis of this success, managers were more likely to use the behavior again and again to the point that it became a part of their daily behavioral repertoire (see Figure 7.1).

Low-use managers, on the other hand, did not have a positive experience with the use of recognition and thus had little or no chance of being reinforced for the behavior. No benefits were derived from the use of recognition, and any concerns or fears about the behavior became excuses for not doing the behavior. The result was that neither skills nor confidence were enhanced, and the behavior was avoided (Nelson & Spitzer, 2003, p 33; see Figure 7.2).

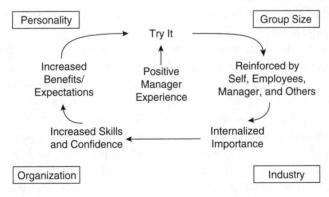

Figure 7.1. The experience of high-use managers.

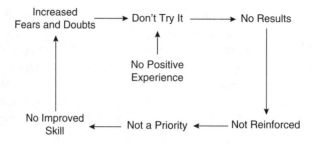

Figure 7.2. The experience of low-use managers.

These findings further suggest that when it comes to triggering a positive cycle of recognition, a positive personal experience is more important than the ready availability of programs, tools, budget allowances, or other resources.

CONVERTING LOW-USE MANAGERS
INTO HIGH-USE MANAGERS

Can a low-use manager ever become a high-use manager? If the answer to this question is yes, will the change last? How can a change agent raise managers' awareness of recognition and its benefits, help them learn the relevant skills to use recognition, and encourage managers to make the first step in recognizing others?

The trick lies in finding a catalyst—an event or trigger mechanism that will help low-use managers personally experience recognition in a positive, meaningful way. Such a stimulus as watching an admired mentor or role model recognize someone, personal feedback, a rational discussion, or even an article that persuades the individual to act differently can lend immediate credibility to the behavior and start the person on a journey toward increased usage of recognition (Nelson & Spitzer, 2003). A seemingly small step can make a profound difference.

Likewise, simple techniques may be most effective—placing a stack of thank-you cards on a manager's desk and getting his commitment to write a few notes to deserving employees at the end of each day or listing all direct reports on a weekly "to do" list and checking off each employee once they have been caught doing something right. Techniques such as these can go a long way toward making recognition simple and doable. Managers may need to personally experience the behavior and its potential and then systematically build on its use and subsequent successes. Once they are convinced of the value of recognition, tools, resources, and encouragement can help to make the identification of recognition opportunities and the practice of recognition routine. By creating a cycle of behavior and response that leads to the escalating use of recognition on the part of managers, as illustrated in the following section, it may be possible to initiate a low-use manager at any point of the cycle, converting him or her to a high-use manager.

IMPLICATIONS FOR THE READER

If you are a manager, recognition giving is well within your abilities. It depends far more on your internal sense of competence and your simple commitment to try than on formal organizational efforts, programs, tools, and resources. Opportunities to recognize your employees and make recognition part of your behavioral repertoire are all around you on a daily basis and can even extend to how you delegate assignments.

At American Express, all managers are taught a concept they call *label and link*, in which every manager who provides a development opportunity to an employee is asked to explain why he or she thought the project would be a good for the employee, what the employee can expect to learn from it, and how it will lead to other opportunities and responsibilities.

If you are a human resources professional, you can be a leading advocate for the use of recognition in your organization. Consider asking managers to use and discuss recognition behaviors, activities, tools, and programs with those who report to them; establishing a cross-functional recognition task force to deal with recognition recommendations and concerns of the organization; and examining ways of targeting low-recognition managers (many of whom are likely to be older, upper level managers) for individualized attention.

At BankBoston (now Bank of America), for example, a member of the recognition committee tasked those managers who did not use the organization's programs with explaining and updating them, often inviting them to discuss the use and impact of the programs with other managers who were more active users.

If you are an executive, you set the tone for what everyone else in your organization feels is important. What you notice, they notice; what you model, they model. Look to determine what employees in your organization value, and then support doing more of those things, leading the charge with your own actions.

A general manager at Xerox Corporation goes around the room at the end of each of his management team meetings and asks everyone to share one thing that they had done to recognize someone on their staff since the group was last together. Not only does the energy level rise, but managers often take note of each other's ideas and plan to use those ideas themselves.

If you are a consultant who works in employee motivation, you should articulate remedies for improved employee recognition efforts. You should also explain and defend such recommendations to both upper and middle management. And you should help managers and executives tie recognition to desired performance as much as possible and to link it to the strategic objectives of the organization.

The legal firm Perkins Coie showed drastic improvements in employee survey data after they implemented a number of new recognition processes and programs, which was instrumental in getting them listed as one of *Fortune*'s (2014) "100 Best Companies to Work For."

Recognizing employees is one of the most important things a manager can do to build morale and enhance performance in today's fast-moving, competitive workplaces. It is also essential to an organization's ability to attract and retain talent and get the most out of the investment being made in that talent. Managers cannot control their age or upbringing, but they can learn to understand their biases and overcome those beliefs that hamper their effectiveness and learn new behaviors that will help them—and the organizations for which they work—to be successful.

INDIVIDUAL VERSUS GROUP-BASED RECOGNITION

Recognition works with individuals when it is immediate, sincere, specific, and based on performance. It works best when it is personal and comes from an employee's immediate manager or from others in the workplace who are held in high regard.

The same principles hold true for teams. The best forms of team recognition are personal, whether it's a manager thanking group members for their work or sending a letter to all team members thanking them for their contributions. A manager can also take a personal interest in a team project by attending its first meeting, to help emphasize the importance of the group's purpose. Managers can conduct informal retreats for team members to set goals, stimulate communication, or focus on problems. They might order in special food as a way to celebrate a team's progress, express appreciation, and encourage their continued energy. And, at the end of the project, managers can send the project team on an outing.

That said, the task of recognizing teams differs in many respects from that of recognizing individuals, and this presents a dilemma. In recognizing a team as a group, a manager runs the risk of alienating those members who contributed most to the team's work while unintentionally reinforcing the slack behavior of team members who contributed little or nothing to the team's efforts. *Jelly bean motivation*—giving equal recognition for unequal performance—is detrimental to the sustained performance of the group. The best performers will feel underappreciated and might quit the group (or the organization) or cut back their efforts, reducing their productivity to match the team's norm. Recognizing everyone in the same way serves to reinforce even marginal performance. Rarely do all members of a team contribute equally to the group's work; instead, each participant brings a different degree of skill, knowledge, experience, and enthusiasm to the work at hand. Still, that cannot serve as an excuse to recognize no one.

One way to resolve this conflict is to ensure that each team leader can and does recognize individual members of the group when performance warrants it. As the group develops into a team, each member can assume this leadership role of recognizing others. By the time the group becomes a high-performing team, all members are skilled at recognizing and praising each other, and the overall manager's job is that much easier.

Another solution is to recognize both individual and team contributions simultaneously. For example, when a team's project is finished, they can be publicly praised as a group for their work, and additional individual praise can be given to top performers. At First Chicago (now Bank One Corporation), management recognized team achievements by inviting the honored team on an outing—dinner, theater, or a sports event—and presenting them with a plaque commemorating the achievement (Nelson, 2005).

A team challenge or contest can be created in which a team competes to achieve its own goals or competes with another group. When the team is successful, the members decide how to celebrate, perhaps by going bowling, playing laser tag, visiting a state fair, going to a movie, having a pizza party, a potluck dinner, or a catered lunch.

Of course, although money is not the only motivator in the workplace, it can be used effectively as a facet of team recognition. In the team program at Cal Snap & Tab, located in the City of Industry, California, everyone can win, but one team wins big. They use a combination spoilage/attendance program in which they put $40,000 into a fund for each team, from which costs for mistakes are deducted. At the end of the program, each team gets to keep its kitty (Nelson, 2005).

At Boston's Beth Israel Deaconess Medical Center, the PREPARE/21 program has increased employee involvement, teamwork, and creativity. Under PREPARE/21—which stands for Participation, Responsibility, Education, Productivity, Accountability, Recognition, and Excellence for the 21st Century—employees are encouraged to organize teams to study ways to cut costs and improve the organization. However, Beth Israel Deaconess goes a step further by allowing employees to share in the monetary savings that accrue as a result of team suggestions. In the first year of the program, participating employees split $1 million—half of the $2 million that Beth Israel Deaconess saved as a result of employee suggestions (Nelson, 2005).

CONCLUSION

Employees expect to be recognized when they do good work. Although many managers feel it is their responsibility to recognize their employees' accomplishments, this sentiment is hardly universal across organizations. Older managers (over age 50) are less likely to believe that recognition is an important behavior. Even those managers who do appreciate the importance of recognition are often unsure how best to go about recognizing their employees. Therefore, when working to convince low-use managers of the utility and importance of recognition, small steps tend to work best.

REFERENCES

American Psychological Association. (2013). *APA survey finds U.S. employers unresponsive to employee needs.* Retrieved from http://www.apa.org/news/press/releases/2013/03/employee-needs.aspx

Appelbaum, S. H., Bregman, M., & Moroz, P. (1998). Fear as a strategy: Effects and impact within the organization. *Journal of European Industrial Training, 22,* 113–127.

Appelbaum, S. H., & Hare, A. (1996). Self-efficacy as a mediator of goal setting and performance: Some human resource applications. *Journal of Managerial Psychology, 11*(3), 33–47. http://dx.doi.org/10.1108/02683949610113584

Bandura, A. (1971). *Social learning theory.* Morristown, NY: General Learning Press.

Bandura, A. (1977). *Social learning theory* (2nd ed.). Englewood Cliffs, NJ: Prentice-Hall.

Bandura, A. (1991). Social cognitive theory of self-regulation. *Organizational Behavior and Human Decision Processes, 50,* 248–287. http://dx.doi.org/10.1016/0749-5978(91)90022-L

Benkhoff, B. (1997). Ignoring commitment is costly: New approaches establish the missing link between commitment and performance. *Human Relations, 50,* 701–726. http://dx.doi.org/10.1177/001872679705000604

Boyd, N. G., & Vozikis, G. S. (1994). The influence of self-efficacy on the development of entrepreneurial intentions and actions. *Entrepreneurship: Theory and Practice, 18*(4), 63–76.

Brown, S. P., Cron, W. L., & Slocum, J. W., Jr. (1998). Effects of trait competitiveness and perceived intraorganizational competition on salesperson goal setting and performance. *Journal of Marketing, 62,* 88–98. http://dx.doi.org/10.2307/1252289

Brun, J. P., & Dugas, N. (2008). An analysis of employee recognition: Perspectives on human resources practices. *The International Journal of Human Resource Management, 19,* 716–730. http://dx.doi.org/10.1080/09585190801953723

Dalton, M. (1959). *Men who manage.* New York, NY: Wiley.

Daniels, A. C. (1989). *Performance management: Improving quality productivity through positive reinforcement* (3rd ed., pp. 95–96). Tucker, GA: Performance Management.

Earley, P. C. (1994). Self or group? Cultural effects of training on self-efficacy and performance. *Administrative Science Quarterly, 39,* 89–117. http://dx.doi.org/10.2307/2393495

Eccles, J. S., & Wigfield, A. (2002). Motivational beliefs, values, and goals. *Annual Review of Psychology, 53,* 109–132. http://dx.doi.org/10.1146/annurev.psych.53.100901.135153

Fortune. (2014). *100 best companies to work for.* Retrieved from http://archive.fortune.com/magazines/fortune/best-companies/2014/list/

Gagné, M., & Deci, E. L. (2005). Self-determination theory and work motivation. *Journal of Organizational Behavior, 26,* 331–362. http://dx.doi.org/10.1002/job.322

Georgopoulos, B. S., Mahoney, G. M., & Jones, N. W., Jr. (1957). A path-goal approach to productivity. *Journal of Applied Psychology, 41,* 345–353.

Gist, M. E., & Mitchell, T. R. (1992). Self-efficacy: A theoretical analysis of its determinants and malleability. *The Academy of Management Review, 17,* 183–211.

Graham, G. H., & Unruh, J. (1990). The motivational impact of nonfinancial employee appreciation practices on medical technologists. *The Health Care Supervisor, 8*(3), 9–17.

Grusec, J. E. (1992). Social learning theory and developmental psychology: The legacies of Robert Sears and Albert Bandura. *Developmental Psychology, 28,* 776–786.

Haire, M. (1964). *Psychology in management* (2nd ed.). New York, NY: McGraw-Hill.

Kanter, R. M. (1986). Kanter on management—Holiday gifts: Celebrating employee achievements. *Management Review, 75*(12), 19–21.

Kovach, K. A. (1995). Employee motivation: Addressing a crucial factor in your organization's performance. *Employment Relations Today, 22,* 93–107. http://dx.doi.org/10.1002/ert.3910220209

Kowalewski, S. J., & Phillips, S. L. (2012). Preferences for performance-based employee rewards: Evidence from small business environments. *International Journal of Management and Marketing Research, 5,* 65–76.

Landy, F., & Trumbo, D. (1980). *Psychology of work behavior* (2nd ed.). Homewood, IL: The Dorsey Press.

Lankau, M. J., & Scandura, T. A. (2002). An investigation of personal learning in mentoring relationships: Content, antecedents, and consequences. *Academy of Management Journal, 45,* 779–790. http://dx.doi.org/10.2307/3069311

Latham, G. P., & Saari, L. M. (1979). Application of social learning theory to training supervisors through behavioral modeling. *Journal of Applied Psychology, 64,* 239–246. http://dx.doi.org/10.1037/0021-9010.64.3.239

LeBoeuf, M. (1985). *The greatest management principle in the world.* New York, NY: Putnam.

Lindahl, L. G. (1949). What makes a good job? *Personnel, 25,* 263–266.

Locke, E. A., & Henne, D. (1986). Work motivation theories. In C. L. Cooper & I. T. Robertson (Eds.), *International review of industrial and organizational psychology 1986* (pp. 1–35). Chichester, England: Wiley.

Locke, E. A., & Latham, G. P. (2002). Building a practically useful theory of goal setting and task motivation. A 35-year odyssey. *American Psychologist, 57,* 705–717. http://dx.doi.org/10.1037/0003-066X.57.9.705

Manz, C. C., & Sims, H. P., Jr. (1986). Beyond imitation: Complex behavioral and affective linkages resulting from exposure to leadership training models. *Journal of Applied Psychology, 71,* 571–578. http://dx.doi.org/10.1037/0021-9010.71.4.571

Merchant, K. A. (1989). *Rewarding results: Motivating profit center managers.* Boston, MA: Harvard Business School Press.

Murray, B., & Gerhart, B. (1998). An empirical analysis of a skill-based pay program and plant performance outcomes. *Academy of Management Journal, 41,* 68–78. http://dx.doi.org/10.2307/256898

Naisbitt, J. (1988). *Megatrends: Ten new directions transforming our lives.* New York, NY: Grand Central.

Nelson, R. B. (2001). *Factors that encourage or inhibit the use of non-monetary recognition by U.S. managers.* (Unpublished doctoral dissertation). Claremont Graduate University, Claremont, CA.

Nelson, R. B. (2005). *1001 ways to reward employees.* New York, NY: Workman.

Nelson, R. B., & Spitzer, D. (2003). *The 1001 rewards & recognition fieldbook.* New York, NY: Workman.

Nord, W. R. (1969). Beyond the teaching machine: The neglected area of operant conditioning in the theory and practice of management. *Organizational Behavior & Human Performance, 4,* 375–401. http://dx.doi.org/10.1016/0030-5073(69)90017-8

Nord, W. R. (1974). Beyond the teaching machine: Operant conditioning in management. In H. L. Tosi & W. C. Hammer, *Organizational behavior and management: A contingency approach* (pp. 385–397). Chicago, IL: St. Clair Press.

Pescosolido, A. T. (2001). Informal leaders and the development of group efficacy. *Small Group Research, 32,* 74–93. http://dx.doi.org/10.1177/104649640103200104

Podsakoff, N. P., Podsakoff, P. M., & Kuskova, V. V. (2010). Dispelling misconceptions and providing guidelines for leader reward and punishment behavior. *Business Horizons, 53,* 291–303. http://dx.doi.org/10.1016/j.bushor.2010.01.003

Podsakoff, P. M., Bommer, W. H., Podsakoff, N. P., & MacKenzie, S. B. (2006). Relationships between leader reward and punishment behavior and subordinate attitudes, perceptions, and behaviors: A meta-analytic review of existing and new research. *Organizational Behavior and Human Decision Processes, 99,* 113–142. http://dx.doi.org/10.1016/j.obhdp.2005.09.002

Podsakoff, P. M., Todor, W. D., & Skov, R. (1982). Effects of leader contingent and noncontingent reward and punishment behaviors on subordinate performance and satisfaction. *Academy of Management Journal, 25*, 810–821. http://dx.doi.org/10.2307/256100

Porter, L. W., & Lawler, E. E., III. (1968). *Managerial attitudes and performance*. London, England: Irwin.

Skinner, B. F. (1953). *Science and human behavior*. New York, NY: The Free Press.

Spitzer, D. R. (1995). *Supermotivation: A blueprint for energizing your organization from top to bottom*. New York, NY: AMACOM.

Stajkovic, A. D., & Luthans, F. (1997). A meta-analysis of the effects of organizational behavior modification on task performance, 1975–95. *Academy of Management Journal, 40*, 1122–1149. http://dx.doi.org/10.2307/256929

Stajkovic, A. D., & Luthans, F. (1998). Social cognitive theory and self-efficacy: Going beyond traditional motivational and behavioral approaches. *Organizational Dynamics, 26*(4), 62–74. http://dx.doi.org/10.1016/S0090-2616(98)90006-7

Steers, R. M., Mowday, R. T., & Shapiro, D. L. (2004). The future of work motivation theory. *The Academy of Management Review, 29*, 379–387.

Steers, R. M., & Porter, L. W. (1983). *Motivation and work behavior* (3rd ed.). New York, NY: McGraw-Hill.

Vroom, V. H. (1964). *Work and motivation*. New York, NY: Wiley.

Wiley, C. (1997). What motivates employees according to over 40 years of motivation surveys. *International Journal of Manpower, 18*, 263–280. http://dx.doi.org/10.1108/01437729710169373

8

EMPLOYEE RECOGNITION: PERSPECTIVES FROM THE FIELD

ROY SAUNDERSON

For most organizations, employee recognition is viewed at least as the "right" thing to do—even if its primary purpose is to reinforce and motivate higher performance and improved productivity. Emerging research (as highlighted in Chapter 7, this volume), as well as the experiences of employers and consultants, certainly reveals the psychological benefit gained from showing employees their contributions are truly valued and appreciated (Aberdeen Group, 2013; American Psychological Association, 2014). Furthermore, a lack of recognition can create a stressful situation. For example, Brun, Biron, Martel, and Ivers (2003) reported that lack of recognition by peers in the workplace was the second highest cause of workplace stress right after workload.

In 2013, nearly 90% of companies stated that they had recognition programs in place (WorldatWork, 2013). Some develop their own internal recognition programs, whereas others acquire vendor-supported

http://dx.doi.org/10.1037/14731-009
The Psychologically Healthy Workplace: Building a Win–Win Environment for Organizations and Employees,
M. J. Grawitch and D. W. Ballard (Editors)

recognition, incentive, and reward programs under the auspices of "giving employee recognition." Yet, many of these programs present challenges in implementation. Some recognition programs are just that, programmatic systems that are in place to provide recognition across the board. However, others provide resources that management can use to practice the art of acknowledging and recognizing the employees who work for them. Recognition programs should assist managers and employees, and not be the sole focus or method for providing meaningful acknowledgement of people and their actions (Bersin, 2012; Towers Watson, 2009). Even with the prevalence of recognition programs, the Gallup Organization suggests they may not always be effective. Of 4 million workers surveyed on the topic of recognition and praise by the Gallup organization, 65% reported receiving no job-related recognition in the year prior to the survey (Rath & Clifton, 2004).

Whether they are practitioners in human resources (HR), compensation and benefits, marketing and communications, or simply a manager of employees, those commissioned with the responsibility of instilling recognition programs and initiatives must use programs that have a solid foundation built on psychological principles and business knowledge. Best practice standards from the recognition industry cover various facets of recognition programs and can be helpful in building a structural framework for understanding recognition practices and their practical application in the workplace. Following are the best practice standards formulated by Recognition Professionals International (RPI) to gauge an organization's practices and programs.

RECOGNITION STRATEGY

This is a written statement and plan with specific program objectives, addressing how recognition is aligned with an organization's culture (i.e., vision, mission, and values) and its business strategy and objectives using a 3-dimensional recognition approach. This approach focuses on formal, informal, and day-to-day recognition practices. A recognition strategy document typically outlines the procedures and processes used and the program delivery methods for the various types of recognition adopted.

Management Responsibility

Responsible management will steer a sound recognition strategy to success. This requires senior leaders to be involved in developing strategy, creating clearly articulated objectives, supporting and advocating for recognition resources and budgets, developing policies and procedures, planning communications, educating and training managers, and ensuring account-ability for recognition practices and program results. Saunderson (2004) found that 93% of managers indicated that senior leader involvement in recognition programs was very or extremely important, and 75% of the 93% stated that senior leader participation was extremely important. However, the same research revealed that only 21% of senior leaders were actually involved in recognition programs Therefore, if recognition practices are going to work, managers at all levels must become exemplary practitioners of giving meaningful and effective recognition.

Recognition Program Measurement

RPI's best practice standard of recognition program measurement uses metrics to gauge the impact of recognition practices and programs using both quantitative and qualitative measures. Besides measuring program participation and frequency of employee recognition, employers must also evaluate whether the recognition given is meaningful in the minds of recipients while also meeting organizational objectives. Hence, organizations must assess whether recognition practices are serving their intended purpose.

Communication Plan

Having a well-articulated, strategic recognition communication plan goes beyond the lead-up to and launch of a new recognition program. It should also establish goals and plans for ongoing communication efforts, reinforcement of recognition practices, and educational resources. A solid communication plan also includes branding information, messaging, identification of target audiences, the types of media to be used, and the frequency of distribution.

Recognition Training

Recognition training teaches executives how to administer recognition programs (whether provided by vendors or developed in house) while also educating managers and employees and developing their recognition skills. An orientation to the recognition system is often delivered through online webinar tutorials. This education can be delivered through a variety of media (e.g., classroom, online, blended learning platform delivered through a learning management system). Various methodologies (e.g., pre- and postevaluation, quizzes, learning application journals, surveys, estimation analysis) may be used to collect and report data on learning outcomes, return on investment (ROI), and transfer of learning into the workplace.

Recognition Events and Celebrations

Most organizations have ongoing recognition events and celebrations. Written processes, policies, and procedures for the various formal and informal events and celebrations help establish organizational expectations, budget controls, alignment with business objectives, and standards for measurement and accountability. Organizations should demonstrate how responsibility for event planning is coordinated, outline the involvement and participation of management, and demonstrate accountability for the review and improvement of planned events.

Program Change and Flexibility

Recognition programs and practices must be continually evaluated to monitor success and identify opportunities for refinement and revitalization and also to ensure they are aligned with, and achieve and promote, the organization's goals and values. No recognition program is perfect after it is launched, so there must be a commitment to adjust, modify, and even eliminate elements of programs (or programs in their entirety) if they do not fulfill their original mandate. Every output and touch point of recognition given to employees has to be measured, so the recognition's effectiveness can be demonstrated and managed.

The best practice standards are shown graphically in Figure 8.1. Recognition strategy, management responsibility, and measurement form the core foundation of an effective recognition program. The remaining four best practice standards perform a supporting role to these essential foundation standards.

INDUSTRY CONUNDRUM: REWARDS VERSUS RECOGNITION

Besides a lack of strategic focus toward recognition and reward programs, many leaders and organizations struggle with how they view and understand employee recognition. Having conducted numerous assessments of the recognition practices that exist in organizations, it is evident that managers and employees have some difficulty understanding the differences between rewards and recognition. This dilemma is inadvertently perpetuated by many professional and industry trade associations because there is no uniform interdisciplinary vocabulary with clear operational definitions (WorldatWork, n.d.). For instance, the Incentive Marketing Association (IMA) defined *recognition based solely on incentives* as "something, such as the expectation of reward, that induces action, or motivates effort" (IMA, n.d.). Meanwhile, The Society for

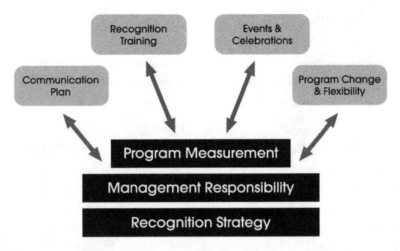

Figure 8.1. Refocusing Recognition Professionals International (RPI) best practice standards. From Recognition Management Institute. Copyright 2008 by Recognition Management Institute. Reprinted with permission.

Human Resource Management (SHRM) suggested that *employee recognition* is "an acknowledgment of employee achievement" (SHRM, 2008). Whereas SHRM states that recognition can be public or private, it can also involve either a monetary or a nonmonetary reward. This can appear confusing when coupling the words recognition and rewards. Definitions from RPI (2006) clearly differentiate between rewards and recognition:

- *Incentive:* Contingent reward based on achievement of predetermined results within a specific time frame
- *Award:* Item to commemorate specified achievement (nonmonetary)
- *Reward:* Item for meeting predetermined goal (sometimes monetary)
- *Recognition:* After-the-fact appreciation for desired behavior, effort, or result that supports goals and values

Rewards–Recognition Continuum

With these definitions in mind, it is critical for practitioners to understand the differences between rewards and recognition and how to use each of them effectively. It is also important to understand the impact each can have on employee attitudes and behaviors. For example, in a financial services company, employees providing direct financial sales services to clients are usually rewarded with cash bonuses for reaching sales targets and may be given

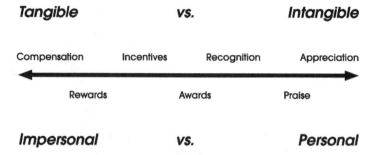

Figure 8.2. Rewards-to-recognition continuum. From Recognition Management Institute. Copyright 2008 by Recognition Management Institute. Reprinted with permission.

additional cash or tangible noncash rewards if they earn the highest total revenues generated within a specified time period. However, such rewards are really just a part of the compensation structure, where if you produce *x* results you will receive *y* rewards. Rewards, in this case, tend to be much more transactional in nature in that you do *this* and you know you will receive *that*. In Figure 8.2 on the reward–recognition continuum, such bonuses are categorized as rewards and can be seen as more tangible in nature and having less personal interaction in their delivery. Such bonuses most often end up on the paycheck with no fanfare or long-lasting trophy value. For the "best of the best" types of awards in this financial service sector scenario, individuals may receive monetary rewards, or a travel award, or may receive formal acknowledgement at an annual, semiannual, or quarterly awards event.

Awards tend to straddle the reward–recognition continuum. They typically include a celebratory event, a presentation of a tangible award, and social accolades and recognition from colleagues and leaders. In this way awards can be both tangible and intangible in nature and combine impersonal and personal attributes. Meanwhile, support staff for these salespeople, who are instrumental in helping with the client interactions, getting necessary paperwork off for client signatures, and assisting sales staff in all tactical and clerical operations, are often ineligible for rewards and excluded from receiving any recognition. Hence, these essential personnel are rarely acknowledged for their contributions through recognition, whether in tangible or intangible form.

Case Study: Cargill, Inc.

Cargill, Inc. is an international producer and marketer of food, agricultural, financial, and industrial products and services (Cargill, 2012a). More than 70 different businesses, operating in 65 countries with over 142,000 employees (Cargill, 2012b), fulfill customer needs for these products and service areas. How could such a large company achieve this honor?

It Starts at the Top

Cargill senior leaders are committed to employee recognition. Few organizations in North America, let alone global organizations, include a chief recognition officer (CRO) in their managerial ranks. Bill Buckner is CRO at Cargill, and he is also one of the senior executive vice presidents within the company. He heads the Global Recognition Steering Committee, which is responsible for both the development of the company recognition strategy and corresponding recognition programs, practices, and initiatives. This is a cross-functional group of representatives composed of members from various business units with differing levels of responsibilities and representing different countries. The cross-functional composition ensures a diversity of involvement and input from employees. Senior leaders also sponsor Chairman awards, for which functional areas and business units can be nominated for outstanding achievement in areas of Business Excellence, Innovation, High Performance, Customer Focus, Leadership, Safety, Environment and Health, or Best Plant, which creates a strong leadership and ownership connection so critical for the success of any formal recognition program (Karen Sachs, Global Human Resources Leader, Cargill, Inc., personal communication, November 15, 2012).

A Clearly Written and Visually Depicted Recognition Strategy

Cargill's Global Recognition Team wrote a well-articulated purpose statement regarding its recognition programs and practices, along with specific objectives for implementing employee recognition throughout the global organization. Cargill's strategy is to "[e]nhance high performance by growing our global culture of recognition ('culture' includes the collective actions and behaviors of all of us)" (RPI, 2008, p. 3). Using this purpose statement, all Cargill businesses around the world can design their programs and provide education on recognition practices to meet this philosophy and purpose.

For Cargill employees worldwide, *recognition* is defined as "[a]cknowledging people in a way that is both meaningful and motivational" (RPI, 2008, p. 3). This simple and straightforward description encompasses individual and cultural differences across all business areas. Strategically, Cargill is instilling a global recognition culture in the workplace by building greater awareness of the importance of recognition, modeling appropriate recognition behaviors, and integrating recognition into daily work.

Cargill has used two visual graphics to help reinforce the importance and understanding of employee recognition to accompany these written statements. The first visual is of a four-tiered recognition pyramid showing the typical types of recognition that RPI refers to as day-to-day recognition, then informal recognition above that, with formal recognition at the apex. However, Cargill knew it had to go further to be able to instill recognition as a more universal practice. Drawing on a values-based approach to cover all cultures, Cargill leaders placed the principles of common courtesy and respect at the base of the pyramid underneath day-to-day recognition.

Without the daily display and presence of genuine common courtesy and respect, the provision and receipt of recognition cannot be authentic. After all, addressing people by their preferred name when greeting them and treating them in a kind manner every day is a necessary foundation for effective recognition. If no courtesy and respect is demonstrated, then no amount of recognition, whether formal, informal, or day-to-day, will ever have any real meaning for employees. Managers are taught to focus most of their time on the bottom two tiers of the pyramid, namely, common courtesy and respect, along with day-to-day recognition giving.

The second visual is an icon for Cargill's global business strategy and depicts a view of a three-pillared Acropolis-like building. The foundation block is titled "Leadership" and the three pillars are from left to right: "High Performance," "Customer Focus," and "Innovation." The triangular roof represents "Creating Distinctive Value," which is the ultimate customer-focused goal of all Cargill's businesses. Woven between the three pillars are two ribbons, one labeled "Collaboration" and the second "Recognition." Through this symbolic imagery, all managers and employees can visualize the culture of recognition and how recognition should be "woven" into business goals.

Cargill is careful to communicate key messages and successes using social media, including Cargill's definition of recognition, the strategic business case for recognition, and the recognition pyramid. They also equip managers and employees with the tools, training, and other resources required to drive recognition practices and successes throughout the organization and to make recognition readily accessible and easy to implement for leaders, managers, and employees by providing ideas, best practices, training, tools, and resources.

Cargill demonstrates continuous improvement processes toward recognition and has reviewed and revamped how nominations are made and how awards are presented. Instead of being given only at the biannual conference, awards are now presented by senior leaders who travel to the location of the winners, so celebrations are shared locally and can be tailored to local customs. This change further strengthens Cargill's desire to formally communicate the importance of living the values of courtesy and respect (Karen Sachs, personal communication, November 15, 2012).

Varied Types of Recognition

Every 2 years, Cargill requests nominations for its formal recognition awards. These formal awards have evolved out of the typical industry safety awards from years past. Now, however, the awards given are far more strategic and business focused than they have ever been. Current awards focus on the areas of business excellence; innovation; high performance; customer focus; leadership; safety, environment, and health; and best plant. Recently, Cargill added a Spirit of Cargill Award in memory of the company's founder, William Wallace Cargill. This award builds on the legacy of the company and honors the finest volunteers who serve their communities. Recipients receive a plaque, and a cash donation is made to the organization the volunteers serve. These formal awards are made through nominations and then evaluated using a formal selection process. The goal is to recognize the highest achievers globally throughout the company in a public way.

For day-to-day and informal recognition, each business and functional area develops its own programs and activities that are aligned with the company recognition strategy and purpose. Recognition practices can range from the typical acts of verbal acknowledgement and handwritten thank-you notes to giving meal vouchers or time off from work, as well as other no-cost and low-cost ideas.

Each business area takes responsibility for developing its own award program so that recognition can be given on a smaller scale. For example, Human Resources created an Excellence Award, Information Technology created a Circle of Pride Award, and other business groups developed their own award categories. This allows specific recognition practices to be tailored to the preferences, norms, cultural variations, and purposes that most affect each business area and geographic location. In this way, local and functional needs are met while staying true to the company mission, vision, and values and the objectives of the recognition strategy.

Education and Communication

Changing people's behaviors to align with a strategy requires not only strong leadership, which is present from top to bottom at Cargill, but also ongoing education and training and regular communication about the importance of employee recognition. These materials are accessible online to all employees and managers. Cargill also has its own corporate university, known as NourishingU, which provides specific recognition courses beyond management and supervisory training programs and the core course offerings available to all employees.

The Global Recognition Steering Committee has a subcommittee that is responsible for developing and implementing a communication plan to support all recognition initiatives. A member on the steering committee is also a manager of the company news magazine, *Cargill News*. The Steering committee uses a variety of communication tools to reinforce the importance of employee recognition.

There are many materials, online tools, and resources on the topic of recognition housed on the recognition web portal on the company website. The Intranet site houses all recognition related content, reinforces the message that recognition is more than just a biennial formal awards process, lists new and alternative ways to provide day-to-day recognition, and helps functional and business unit managers with ideas for creating a culture of recognition in their work areas. It also enables users to recognize one another through internal social media, and through online eThank-you cards that can be sent to managers, peers, and teams, in multiple languages.

Implications of Cargill's Recognition Practices

Many organizations and the employees responsible for recognition practices report an ongoing struggle getting the executive leaders or C-suite to buy in to recognition. Many of these organizations view employee recognition in a very transactional manner—simply spending financial resources to buy a recognition program, pay for communication branding, training, and other tactical approaches. If references to rewards and recognition are reduced solely to budget lines and the means of paying for them, then recognition will always be seen as an expense or cost that can be easily cut.

Rather than buy-in, what is really needed is senior leader commitment. Commitment takes a leader from a transactional approach to a transformational one and then toward transcending what is presently being done. It is an individual act of committing oneself to becoming engaged and dedicated to a cause—whether it is employee recognition practices and programs or any other corporate strategy. Recognition is thereby seen as an investment. By this standard, Cargill leadership is committed to employee recognition practices and programs.

GAINING SENIOR LEADER COMMITMENT

Obtaining full commitment from senior leaders and making any initiative a success requires involvement, leadership, and accountability. The following five strategies are needed to make this happen.

- *Get senior leaders involved in recognition strategy development.* Leaders of companies know the big picture. They are intimately aware of and well-informed about the business objectives and financial targets to be reached and can see or learn how recognition can be a powerful tool to assist with these goals. They must provide the organizational strategic directives and suggestions for how recognition can be aligned with these objectives and best leveraged to achieve them.

- *Find an executive sponsor to advocate for the proposed recognition strategy.* Ideally, you will be able to find a leader who can be an ally for all those responsible for recognition programs and practices. That leader must be passionate about the value and contribution recognition initiatives bring to the table and supportive toward practitioners, managers, and employees at large. An executive sponsor brings recognition out of HR's domain and into the corporate boardroom. An executive sponsor ensures all recognition practices and programs are performance focused and relationally and emotionally driven.
- *Create quarterly and annual accountability meetings with leaders.* There can be no progress until we become good at measuring recognition outcomes and being held accountable for the results. Senior leaders are adept at knowing both the financial and HR metrics that are relevant. They understand how recognition practices can affect employee engagement, customer satisfaction, and financial results. If there is no accountability, then there will be no progress.
- *Make friends with finance executives.* Chief financial officers, accountants, and business analysts can help measure the monetary costs and benefits associated with recognition programs and practices. They can help determine the organizational impact and the dollar values of various metrics and even how to measure certain indicators. The goal is to show that recognition is an investment and not just an expense. ROI indicators can be determined for many recognition outputs and HR metrics. For example, in the food services industry it is not uncommon to have at least a 50% turnover rate. A restaurant with 50 employees may have a recognition strategy goal to save 20% of its turnover costs, or retain 10 employees, at a savings of $125,000 annually. A restaurant could design a recognition program targeting outstanding demonstration of customer service and allow peer-to-peer recognition for exemplary actions at a cost of $60 per employee (50 total employees) for an annual cost of $36,000. If the program achieved its target, a savings of $125,000 would be produced at a cost of $36,000 for an ROI of 3.47:1.
- *Continually educate senior leaders and promote recognition.* Senior leaders are in their positions because of their strong leadership, decision-making, and administrative skills. However, they cannot be expected to know everything about employee recognition research or best practices. It is important to keep them informed

and educated on the research findings from scientific journals and professional associations or through online searches, along with the data from your own programs, so they are able to promote and defend recognition efforts as necessary.

CHALLENGES WITH THE TYPES OF RECOGNITION

Many organizations report having at least three types of recognition practices: *everyday, informal*, and *formal* recognition (see Figure 8.3). However, if an organization does not create a recognition strategy, as Cargill has, it can fall into a trap of seeing each type of recognition in isolation from other types of recognition, rather than as a part of a systemic whole.

Formal Recognition

Formal recognition is at the apex of the pyramid in Figure 8.3. The model also shows that recognition efforts typically reach only 1% to 10% of the employee base. More typically, the number of employees receiving formal recognition may be as low as 1% to 3% (RPI, n.d.).

Formal recognition most often can be described as company-wide awards (typically given annually). An *award* can be defined as something bestowed to commemorate an achievement or as the result of a contest as judged by specific criteria (mostly nonmonetary in nature). They can be earned in the sense that if a salesperson is the top producer in a given year, there can be no argument that he or she merits receiving the particular award on the basis of those measures.

Figure 8.3. Three-tiered recognition pyramid. From Recognition Management Institute. Copyright 2007 by Recognition Management Institute. Reprinted with permission.

In another type of award, individuals are nominated in various categories and their detailed written nomination is evaluated against a specific set of criteria by a committee. Sometimes, the nominations are more subjective in content, whereas others are weighted against performance-based metrics or other measures (e.g., business strategy goals, organizational values). Using both quantitative and qualitative criteria, the judging committee determines the best of the best for these types of awards.

Formal recognition can also include career or service milestone awards, in which companies honor employees for the service and contributions made at various selected milestones, typically at 5-year increments. These awards are bestowed on employees by managers and the company and may consist of plaques, pins, heritage gift items, or lifestyle items that the employee chooses from a catalog of gifts. Lifestyle and heritage award gift items are usually of different monetary value that increases dependent on the length of service.

Informal Recognition

This type of recognition is usually more performance-based and meets the needs of departments or business units, or it can be an outgrowth of corporate-wide initiatives. It is multifaceted and can include awards, incentives, and point-based systems rewarding and recognizing employees for carrying out certain actions and behaviors. These can be given by managers, supervisors, and/or peers. Informal recognition can also include more social celebrations like births, birthdays, marriages, and retirements and team or departmental acknowledgements of projects and goal completion. Informal recognition is much more frequent in occurrence than formal recognition and affects a greater number of employees, typically anywhere from 30% to 50% of the employees within an organization (RPI, n.d.).

Everyday Recognition

This type of recognition includes the tangible or intangible expression of acknowledgement for an individual's contribution, achievements, or observed behaviors. The focus is on expressing thanks and acknowledging work done or appreciation of the individual. Such acts can be given by all levels of employees. Although findings reveal manager-to-employee recognition elevates employee engagement (Towers Watson, 2009), a majority of employees seek more readily available peer-to-peer recognition (Bersin, 2012).

Everyday recognition, as the term implies, can happen on a weekly or daily basis and can affect anywhere from 80% to 100% of employees (RPI, n.d.).

The exact percentage depends on how integrated the recognition practices are within management competencies and the organizational culture.

As previously mentioned, Cargill has also added a value-based level of common courtesy and respect to this typical three-tier recognition pyramid to create four levels. By so doing, the company has created a tool to emphasize the need for clear actions around common courtesy and respect before it addresses recognition at the day-to-day level. This places greater importance on managers greeting employees by name each day, truly listening to employee needs, and demonstrating genuine caring and concern for each person with whom they interact.

CONSIDERATIONS IN IMPLEMENTING AN EFFECTIVE RECOGNITION PROGRAM

In emphasizing how recognition can contribute to a psychologically healthy workplace, most managers tend to look solely at recognition programs as the only solution. This chapter has emphasized that programs per se are not where a company needs to begin. In fact, to make a difference in the workplace, recognition programs are most likely one of the last things on which to focus. Looking carefully at what it is you want to achieve with employee recognition and how you want employees to feel is probably a far better starting point. The following recommendations can assist managers and consultants in creating a recognition game plan.

Start From Where You Are

To plan future recognition initiatives, first get a good handle on what is happening now with employee recognition. Assess all of the current recognition programs and collect all available data on the number of recognition touch points and outputs. For formal, informal, and day-to-day recognition, a manager or consultant needs to know what is happening in relation to recognition. In addition to the quantifiable measures, qualitative indicators can be obtained from employee surveys and focus groups to know how effective the recognition programs and practices really are. These metrics can be integrated and compared with HR measures (e.g., engagement scores, customer satisfaction, turnover, absenteeism) and analyzed for a more in-depth understanding. Taking an inventory of all your recognition programs can sometimes reveal how recognition has gotten off target despite potentially good intentions. Understanding deficits with current recognition programs and practices could be the starting point needed to form an excellent recognition strategy.

Lead With a Recognition Strategy

When managers speak of unsuccessful recognition programs, it is often a sign that there is either no recognition strategy in place or an existing strategy is not being followed. Making time to clearly define what recognition means and the corporate direction for why, where, and how recognition will be implemented will set the stage for making concrete and realistic plans and ensuring their successful implementation (Saunderson, 2011).

A recognition strategy enables everyone to be on the same page no matter where a manager or employee is within the company or even where he or she is in the world. Having a written recognition strategy provides an opportunity for greater consistency and effectiveness of employee recognition practices and programs. Objectives can easily be set after an audit of existing programs and practices because the gaps will be clearly known and the ideal future state will be more evident.

Enlist Senior Leader Involvement

A recognition strategy can rarely happen if senior leader endorsement and participation are not obtained first. Recognition programs and practices can be powerful tools for achieving business and people strategy initiatives because they can be designed to reinforce and reward achievement of business goals and the behaviors associated with them. Once senior leaders understand how recognition can catalyze measurable gains in employee engagement, productivity and performance, they will be more willing to study and support recognition initiatives. Senior leaders hold the purse strings and are naturally protective of a company's funds. When they are involved in establishing a recognition strategy and setting related business objectives, C-suite executives will be more willing to fight for the resources necessary to support these efforts.

Focus on Your People

Throughout this chapter, the terms *recognition practices* and *recognition programs* have been used intentionally. Unfortunately, because of a lack of strategic focus placed upon recognition, most companies tend to focus solely on recognition programs and neglect the need for recognition practices. When we look at the greater impact and higher frequency of occurrence with everyday recognition, we can see that by focusing on people for who they are and their contributions, far more can be recognized and acknowledged (Katcher, 2012). People are different, and they are determined to make a difference in their own way. Managers, leaders, and peers can all master the art of expressing thanks, appreciation, and congratulations verbally or in writing to acknowledge the daily actions and behaviors that generate the product and service outputs from all employees.

Focus On and Live by Principles

The culture of an organization—beliefs, values, and norms that drive behavior—helps to create an environment and a set of expectations that promote recognition. A strong organizational culture that values and promotes recognition will have a stronger effect on the actual recognition practices used than any program or policy will. Following and living by principles such as courtesy, respect, integrity, and caring will help to promote an attitude that treating people right is good common sense and good business practice, which is why creating a culture of recognition should be based on the mission, vision, and values of an organization to make recognition authentic and genuine. In turn, recognition can be given informally or formally to honor exemplary employees who are found to demonstrate the living of an organization's values.

Expect Good Recognition Practices

Recognition practices are the actions each person can take to show appreciation for the people we work with and associate with. This may mean making extra time and effort to stop and recognize a colleague, direct report, or manager for something that made a difference to you, a customer, or the company as a whole. These practices may also include using technology to cue yourself to give recognition and developing skills and confidence to give recognition more effectively in accordance with the preferences of individual employees.

Develop Programs to Assist Practices

With a recognition strategy in place and a concerted focus on people and principles first, managers and practitioners responsible for recognition can then look at programs as an effective tool. Too many times companies look to recognition programs and forget the limited impact they may have. Incentive or points-based recognition programs or even formal recognition awards can lose their meaning and effectiveness if done improperly or without sincerity.

Keep Recognition Accountable

Leaders and managers responsible for recognition programs and practices must be held accountable for achieving target goals as outlined in the recognition strategy. For recognition programs, this means mining the data for regular recognition outcomes and metrics to determine the people recognized, by whom, their business areas, and the performance objectives reached or behaviors they were recognized for. HR metrics, such as employee satisfaction and engagement scores, can supplement and allow comparisons among various business units and managers.

CONCLUSION

Employee recognition can be a powerful tool when used correctly. Like any tool, recognition must be kept in top condition, and the owner must learn how to use is properly to obtain the best results. As HR professionals have become more transformational and strategic in their focus, recognition efforts have similarly evolved. Employees benefit from recognition practices that are well-designed and implemented. Furthermore, the benefits of recognition in the workplace are more than just having productive people and reaching performance targets. Employees who feel valued for their contributions, receive positive feedback on a regular basis, and are honored for what they do have less stress and are healthier (American Psychological Association, 2012; Brun et al. 2003).

REFERENCES

Aberdeen Group. (2013). *The power of employee recognition.* Retrieved from http://aberdeen.com/research/8750/ai-employee-recognition-program/content.aspx

American Psychological Association. (2012). *APA survey finds feeling valued at work linked to well-being and performance* [Press release]. Retrieved from http://www.apa.org/news/press/releases/2012/03/well-being.aspx

American Psychological Association. (2014). *Employee recognition survey.* Retrieved from http://www.apaexcellence.org/assets/general/employee-recognition-survey-results.pdf

Bersin, J. (2012). *New research unlocks the secret of employee recognition.* Retrieved from http://www.forbes.com/sites/joshbersin/2012/06/13/new-research-unlocks-the-secret-of-employee-recognition/2/

Brun, J.-P., Biron, C., Martel, J., & Ivers, H. (2003). *Évaluation de la santé mentale au travail: Une analyse des pratiques de gestion des ressources humaines, Chaire en gestion de la santé et de la sécurité du travail dans les organisations* [Assessment of mental health at work: An analysis of human resources management, chair in occupational health and safety management]. Montreal, Quebec, Canada: Université Laval.

Cargill, Inc. (2012a). *At a glance.* Retrieved from http://www.cargill.com/company/glance/index.jsp

Cargill, Inc. (2012b). *Our company.* Retrieved from http://www.cargill.com/company/index.jsp

Incentive Marketing Association. (n.d.). *Glossary of incentive industry terms.* Retrieved from http://www.incentivemarketing.org/?278

Katcher, B. L. (2012). *Improving the workplace—Employees plead for praise.* Retrieved from http://www.discoverysurveys.com/articles/itw-039.html

Rath, T., & Clifton, D. (2004). *How full is your bucket: Positive strategies for work and life.* New York, NY: Gallup Press.

Recognition Professionals International. (n.d.). *Standard 1: Recognition strategy.* Retrieved from http://www.recognition.org/default.asp?page=best_practices

Recognition Professionals International. (2006). *Certified recognition professionals courses.* Retrieved from http://www.recognition.org/?page=crp_course_descript

Recognition Professionals International. (2008). *2008 RPI Best practice overall recipient: Cargill, Inc.* Retrieved from http://c.ymcdn.com/sites/recognition.site-ym.com/resource/resmgr/imported/Cargill-Whitepaper.pdf

Saunderson, R. (2004). Survey on the effectiveness of employee recognition in the public sector. *Public Personnel Management, 33,* 255–275.

Saunderson, R. (2011). How to get your recognition strategy right. *Workspan, 54*(5), 66–71.

Society for Human Resources Management. (2008). *Employee recognition training for supervisors* [PowerPoint presentation]. Retrieved from http://www.shrm.org/templatestools/samples/powerpoints/documents/09-ppt-new-hire%20orientation_final.ppt

Towers Watson. (2009). *Turbocharging employee engagement—The power of recognition from managers—Part 1: The engagement engine.* Retrieved from https://www.towerswatson.com/DownloadMedia.aspx?media=%7B22183FD3-E565-43C6-8C45-CA25A4C74799%7D

WorldatWork. (n.d.). *Glossary.* Retrieved from http://www.worldatwork.org/waw/Glossary

WorldatWork. (2013). *Trends in employee recognition: A survey of WorldatWork members, June 2013.* Retrieved from http://www.worldatwork.org/waw/adimLink?id=72689

9

HEALTH AND SAFETY: PREVENTION AND PROMOTION

LOIS E. TETRICK AND JOSÉ M. PEIRÓ

Work is an important activity to which a large proportion of the adult population devotes a significant amount of time, effort, and even identity. The work's context, conditions, and activities may produce hazards and accidents or an environment in which to thrive and flourish. Reductions in workplace hazards and strategies for developing and maintaining safe, healthy work environments have been the focus of considerable research (Tetrick & Peiró, 2012).

The World Health Organization at its conference at Alma-Ata in 1978 defined *health* from a positive perspective that does not just consider it as the absence of illness, but rather as an enduring positive state encompassing biological, psychological, and social components (Tetrick, Quick, & Quick, 2005). Thus, monitoring the health of workers requires establishing programs to prevent injuries and illness and to promote health. Although much of the focus has been on prevention, there is a growing recognition

http://dx.doi.org/10.1037/14731-010
The Psychologically Healthy Workplace: Building a Win–Win Environment for Organizations and Employees,
M. J. Grawitch and D. W. Ballard (Editors)

that safety assurance and health promotion are important goals. Thus, the biopsychosocial healthy workplace involves the prevention of injuries and illness and the promotion of a healthy and safe work environment.

The growth of the field of occupational health psychology has integrated safety, health promotion, and wellness programs to ensure the safety and health of both workers and organizations (Hofmann & Tetrick, 2003). As a result, a number of interventions have been developed and implemented to incorporate fitness, nutrition, recognition and rewards, and various health care benefits (for recent reviews, see Bennett & Tetrick, 2013; Tetrick & Haimann, 2014; Tetrick, Quick, & Gilmore, 2012). The successes of these interventions appear to depend on the specific organizational context and theoretical grounding of the design of the interventions. Therefore, in this chapter, we present a number of well-established psychological theories that have generated consistent empirical evidence about organizational safety climate and the role of leadership in promoting a psychologically healthy workplace. Moreover, we review the occupational stress research based on exchange theories and job demands-control misfit to understand the relationship between work stressors and worker health and well-being. These theories have inspired programs to promote safety climate in organizations and psychologically healthy workplaces. Both the negative, harmful effects of the work environment and the positive, beneficial effects of the work environment on employee health and well-being are considered. We also pay attention to the key variables that, according to these theories, play a role in facilitating or inhibiting program and intervention effectiveness.

We focus on climate for safety and health and leadership as working conditions. Climate for safety and health is important, as this is the intersection between the "objective" work environment and employees' experience of that environment. These constructs are essential for promoting safety and health in organizations, as safety climate influences safety behaviors (Zohar, 2011; Zohar & Hofmann, 2012) and health climate influences health behaviors (Mearns, Hope, Ford, & Tetrick, 2010). Similarly, leadership and management commitment to safety and health are known to be core aspects of safety and health climate; therefore, the literature on transformational leadership and leader–member exchange (LMX) theories are reviewed. Leadership's contributions to safety in organizations (e.g., Barling & Frone, 2004) and employee health and well-being are well documented (e.g., Peiró & Rodriguez, 2008), and those results have been useful to promote management awareness and behaviors for ensuring safety and promoting healthy work environments. After discussing leadership theories, social exchange theory, psychological contract theory, and the effort–reward imbalance (ERI) model of stress are reviewed relative to their contribution to understanding the development and maintenance of a psychologically healthy workplace. The last section of the chapter presents the rationale and evidence in support of the job demands–control–support model of stress and the vitamin model of stress and associated interventions. These two occupational stress theories emphasize the critical role of job redesign strategies in improving well-being and health and the importance of adequate fit with employee characteristics.

CLIMATE FOR SAFETY AND HEALTH

Organizational climate is a collective phenomenon consisting of the shared perceptions of an organization's members about some of its relevant features, such as rules, procedures, arrangements, and shared habits (Schneider, Ehrhart, & Macey, 2011; Zohar & Hofmann, 2012). Climate is an important component of the social environment that affects individual and collective behaviors. Therefore, influencing and shaping this climate may be an effective intervention to promote certain behaviors and outcomes in the organization.

Safety climate is recognized as a major contributor to the experience of safety in the workplace (Zohar, 2011). Drawing on the broader organizational climate literature, Zohar (1980) argued that a specific climate for safety arises through employees' shared perceptions about safety policies, procedures, and practices in an organization. These shared perceptions reflect the consistency to which safety procedures are adhered and are taken to reflect the priority that safety is given within the organization. Research has linked safety climate to both employee safety compliance and participation (Clarke, 2006), although it appears to be only weakly related to actual accidents and injuries. Christian, Bradley, Wallace, and Burke's (2009) meta-analysis found support for safety climate leading to safety knowledge and safety motivation that result in increased safety compliance and safety participation, ultimately reducing accidents and injuries.

Management commitment to safety is the most important dimension of safety climate (Flin, Mearns, O'Connor, & Bryden, 2000), signifying the importance of leadership in establishing and maintaining a climate for safety. Safety climate may also be promoted through the reward system, the rules and norms, and the environmental design and its behavioral constraints and enhancers. In fact, climate engineering attempts to influence members' shared perceptions in order to promote social realities (e.g., safety climate, culture) and their consequent outcomes (e.g., compliance with safety behaviors, and prevention of accidents).

Following on the theoretical development of safety climate, the notion of a climate for health has been advanced (Ribisl & Reischl, 1993). Interestingly, the emphasis in the climate for health literature is slightly different from the safety climate literature, in that the focus is expanded from a public health perspective on well-being to incorporate the influence of workplace factors beyond the control of workers (Ribisl & Reischl, 1993). Climate for health also takes a more positive perspective on health promotion rather than emphasizing prevention (Basen-Engquist, Hudmon, Tripp, & Chamberlain, 1998). Assessments of health climate reflect these differences but continue to emphasize the importance of policies, procedures, and practices relative to the promotion of health and well-being. The focus of health climate may differ from safety climate, but there is a common element of management commitment to a healthy work environment and the health of employees that parallels safety climate (Basen-Engquist et al., 1998; Bruns, Walrath, Glass-Siegel, & Weist, 2004; Ribisl & Reischl, 1993). It might be argued that safety climate and health climate are not distinct, though Basen-Engquist et al. (1998) and Mearns et al. (2010) have provided empirical support that they are unique, but correlated, constructs.

Therefore, theory and empirical evidence suggest that the development and maintenance of a positive safety climate in which there are shared perceptions of the priority of safety is important for the prevention of accidents and injuries and the promotion of safe behaviors. There is considerably less literature on health climate, although what research exists supports a similar effect of health climate on the promotion of healthy behaviors (Basen-Engquist et al., 1998; Bruns et al., 2004; Mearns et al., 2010).

LEADERSHIP

Management commitment and leadership have been identified as critically important in the development of a positive safety and health climate. Management plays several important roles in promoting safety and health. Managers set up the policies, strategies, and priorities of the company; they initiate and support safety and health promotion programs; they can effectively promote active participation in these programs; and they can evaluate programs' effects on individuals and the organization.

In this section, we review the evidence for the role of leadership in creating and sustaining a psychologically healthy workplace. Two leadership theories that have significantly contributed to the improvement of employee health and safety are transformational leadership theory and LMX theory (for a complete review, see Avolio, Walumbwa, & Weber, 2009; Peiró & Rodriguez, 2008). Recent research has shown out that these two approaches focus mainly on a relational (leader–follower) rather just on an individual (leader) approach (Day, 2000) and complement each other to better understand leadership processes and their effects (Henderson, Liden, Glibkowski, & Chaudhry, 2009).

Transformational Leadership Theory

According to Burns (1978) and Bass (1985), the essential feature of leadership is not the transactions between leader and followers but the capacity of the leader to augment these transactions by influencing others. This may be done through visionary and inspirational messages, individualized attention and intellectual stimulation of the followers, and/or the leaders' moral values. This approach has been characterized as *transformational leadership*, and it is composed of four types of behaviors: *idealized influence* or charisma based on the leader's moral commitment, *inspirational motivation* contributing to excellent performance of the followers, *intellectual stimulation* challenging employees for intellectual development, and *individualized consideration* or showing genuine interest for followers (Bass, 1998). At the beginning, transformational and transactional leadership were viewed as opposite ends of a single continuum, but Bass (1985) saw them as separate concepts that could both be present in the same leader. Later, Bass (1998) formulated the augmentation effect, pointing out that "transformational leadership styles build on the transactional base in contributing to the extra effort and performance of followers" (p. 5). Judge and Piccolo (2004) found support for the augmentation effect showing that transformational leadership contributes beyond the effects of transactional and laissez–faire leadership.

Followers of transformational leaders generally aspire to higher order values (e.g., altruism, sense of mission; Avolio, Walumbwa, & Weber, 2009) and are more satisfied (Belias & Koustelios, 2014), displaying more positive attitudes, trust, positive affect, and emotional responses (Dumdum, Lowe, & Avolio, 2002; Judge & Piccolo, 2004). These results suggest that transformational leadership may play an important role in follower well-being (Jacobs et al., 2013; Kuoppala, Lamminpää, Liira, & Vainio, 2008). In fact, transformational leadership has been found to be negatively associated with burnout (Corrigan, Diwan, Campion, & Rashid, 2002) and negative affect and threat appraisals (Lyons & Schneider, 2009) and positively related to social support perceptions and self-efficacy beliefs (Lyons & Schneider, 2009). In addition, transformational leadership can play an important role in improving health by promoting workplace safety climate and safety behaviors (Zohar, 2002). Kelloway, Mullen, and Francis (2006) found that safety-specific transformational leadership positively influenced safety consciousness and safety climate and reduced safety-related events and injuries. Moreover, Inness, Turner, Barling, and Stride (2010) found that transformational leadership is positively associated with job safety participation, a measure of contextual safety performance.

Research has focused on identifying mediating variables that help to better understand the way transformational leadership enhances well-being, health indicators, and safety. Several studies have found that transformational leaders influence employee well-being indirectly, through their influence on follower perceptions and beliefs about work, or about their appraisal of personal beliefs, such as self-efficacy. For example, Arnold, Turner, Barling, Kelloway, & McKee (2007) found that meaningful work mediated the influence of transformational leadership on burnout. This result emphasizes the role of transformational leaders in influencing beliefs and perceptions of their followers as a way of improving well-being. Similarly, research supports the role of transformational leadership in improving the perception of work characteristics, such as role clarity, meaningfulness and opportunities for development, thereby improving well-being of followers (K. Nielsen & Munir, 2009). Additional mediating mechanisms that have been proposed are self-efficacy, trust in management, meaningful work, regulation motivation, perceptions of organizational justice, empowerment and identity with the organization and occupation (Conchie, 2013; Kelloway, Turner, Barling, & Loughlin, 2012; Sirvanathan, Arnold, Turner, & Barling, 2004; Walsh, Dupré, & Arnold, 2014) and mentoring (Sosik & Godshalk, 2000). Finally, it is interesting to note that the influence of transformational leadership on follower health and well-being may be moderated by cultural variables. In fact, Walumbwa and Lawler (2003) found that in collective cultures, transformational leaders are more effective in influencing job satisfaction, organizational attitudes and turnover intentions. In a later study, Walumbwa, Lawler, and Avolio (2007) extended these results, showing that both individual values and cultural values of the society in which people live affect the impact of transformational leadership on followers' attitudes and outcomes. In fact, the authors found that transformational leadership had a more positive effect among allocentrics, who view themselves in terms of the in-groups to which they belong, than it did among idiocentrics, who view themselves as the basic social unit in a collectivistic culture.

The study of transformational leadership has also paid attention to the fact that in some cases there exist pseudo-transformational leaders (Bass & Steidlmeier, 1999). In this context, a new concept emerged that has recently attracted research interest (Avolio et al., 2009). Luthans and Avolio (2003) defined *authentic leadership* as "a process that draws from both positive psychological capacities and a highly developed organizational context, which results in both greater self-awareness and self-regulated positive behaviors on the part of leaders and associates, fostering positive self-development" (p. 243). Macik-Frey, Quick, and Cooper (2009) pointed out that authentic leadership may be considered a pathway for followers' positive health. They conceptualized *positive health* as purpose, positive relationships, self-mastery, and learning from misfortune. When leaders feel these experiences, they may become contagious and, in turn, promote health in their followers through the generation of these experiences. Moreover, M. B. Nielsen, Eid, Mearns, and Larsson (2013) found that authentic leadership is negatively associated with risk perceptions and positively related to perceptions of safety climate. Thus, promoting positive health and safety climate is a crucial role for leaders in the pursuit of healthy organizations and employees. However, more research is needed to identify the dynamics of these influences of authentic leadership on the facets of follower health.

LMX Theory

Vertical dyad linkages develop between the leader and each of his or her followers, who differ in terms of the quality of their exchange relationships. Differences in quality produce different effects on followers (Graen & Uhl-Bien, 1995). Some of the members have a high-quality exchange relationship, and they receive better work assignments and more autonomy and responsibility from their supervisor, which provide more opportunities for career development. The supervisor receives, in turn, more support and exerts more influence on these members than they do on those members with a lower quality exchange relationship. For those members of the work unit with lower quality exchange relationships, their roles are more circumscribed to what is expected on the basis of explicit rules. The opportunities provided to these employees are fewer, and the influence of the leader on their attitudes and behaviors is less than that of the members with higher quality LMX. Thus, higher quality LMX is related to several positive outcomes for employees and the organization (Bolino & Turnley, 2009; Graen & Uhl-Bien, 1995).

The quality of LMX has been found to relate to a broad array of outcomes, though mutual support, trust, liking, latitude, attention, and loyalty are considered to be the most relevant (Schriesheim, Castro, & Cogliser, 1999). Antecedents of high-quality LMX include goal congruence (Uhl-Bien, Graen, & Scandura, 2000), leader and member agreement about the psychological contract with each other (Tekleab & Taylor, 2003), and the use of impression management (Colella & Varma, 2001). Nahrgang, Morgeson, and Ilies (2009) found that personality characteristics (e.g., team-member extraversion, leader agreeableness) were significantly related to LMX quality at the outset, whereas leader and member performance influenced the development of these relationships over time. Therefore, a variety of mechanisms appear to be antecedents to LMX quality.

Meta-analyses examining the consequences of LMX quality have mainly focused on performance and organizational citizenship behavior, although they have also included job satisfaction, organizational commitment, role clarity, role conflict, and turnover intentions (Ilies et al. 2007). In addition, a number of studies have focused on well-being, health, and safety outcomes

(Hofmann & Morgeson, 1999), job satisfaction (Major, Kozlowski, Chao, & Gardner, 1995), well-being (Epitropaki & Martin, 1999), stress (Peiró, González Romá, Ramos, & Zornoza, 1996), burnout (Rose, 1998), energy and involvement in creative work (Atwater & Carmeli, 2009). Recently, some studies have analyzed the paths through which LMX has an effect on well-being variables. Several mediators have proved significant, such as role conflict and job involvement for the relationship between LMX and stress (Lawrence & Kacmar, 2012); the need for competence, autonomy, and relatedness for its relationship with autonomous motivation and its attitudinal outcomes (Graves & Luciano, 2013); and individualistic versus collectivistic culture for the relations of LMX and citizenship behavior, justice perceptions, job satisfaction and turnover intentions (Rockstuhl, Dulebohn, Ang, & Shore, 2012).

For the most part, these studies have supported positive effects of a high-quality LMX. However, high-quality LMX does not always produce positive outcomes. For example, Harris and Kacmar (2006) found support for nonlinear relationships between LMX and stress, showing negative consequences for followers that experience extremely high-quality LMX. The authors suggested that this may happen because individuals in high-quality LMX relationships may feel pressure or obligation to do extra work and fulfill stressful demands to profit from opportunities.

Negative effects frequently have been identified for followers who experience lower LMX quality. Leader behaviors in these LMX are less supportive and provide fewer opportunities for advancement. The differentiation in treatment is often noticed by these employees (Maslyn & Uhl-Bien, 2005), leading to negative outcomes, especially when the situation is seen as unfair and unjust (Scandura, 1999; Walumbwa, Cropanzano, & Hartnell, 2009). On the basis of this evidence, some authors have raised doubts about the usefulness of differentiation between followers as a strategy for leadership. Scandura (1999) suggested that differentiation processes must be seen as fair by members with both high-quality LMX and those with low-quality LMX. However, other authors have recommended that managers should aim to build high-quality LMX with all their followers (Graen, Hui, & Taylor, 2006). Recently, Bolino and Turnley (2009) found that followers with lower quality LMX (especially when they perceive this poor quality as an important deprivation) experienced more negative effects from differentiation, especially when they were frustrated because they did not anticipate that this situation was going to change in the future. In other studies, it has been found that employees perceiving low-quality and unfair relationships with their supervisors tended to reciprocate with negative, vengeful, or organizational retaliation behaviors (Townsend, Phillips, & Elkins, 2000). The empirical evidence indicates that low-quality LMX more often than not results in negative consequences for followers and possibly the work unit and organization as a whole, although the research on differentiation has been conducted almost exclusively at an individual follower level (Henderson et al., 2009).

LMX theory is seminal in pointing out important issues about leading people and the positive and negative implications these issues have for health and safety. Issues include differentiation of followers, perceptions of fairness and justice, and personal and situational conditions that may increase negative effects. Because differentiation may produce important negative effects, several authors have recommended training the leaders to develop high LMX with all their followers. Thus, a challenge is to properly manage differentiation in a way that it is not perceived as discriminatory and unfair. A climate of justice and fairness may be an important moderating factor between differentiation and outcomes at the individual, group, and organizational levels (Henderson et al., 2009).

Nevertheless, there are few intervention studies seeking to improve safety and health at work based on the LMX leadership theoretical model; in fact, there have been relatively few interventions for any outcomes based on LMX theory (Avolio et al., 2009). Taking into account the strategies of leaders and leadership development, especially those based in a relational approach (Day, 2000), LMX provides an important number of relevant theoretical and evidence inputs to inspire such strategies as 360-degree feedback, coaching, mentoring, networking, job assignments, and action learning. However, LMX has not explicitly been formulated nor evaluated in the studies focusing on leadership development. More intervention studies addressing the efficacy of LMX theoretical contributions to improving employee health and well-being are needed. Interventions promoting leadership skills and competencies that may enhance the quality of leader-members exchange may significantly contribute to health and well-being promotion at work. Theory and empirical evidence suggest that in this interaction leaders have to pay attention in the interaction and exchange both to individual and collective fairness and justice perceptions.

In sum, leadership theories provide important inputs for safety and health promotion interventions. Leadership may be a direct antecedent of health and well-being at work, or it may be just the opposite, depending on the quality of the leader–member interaction. Leadership behavior may also influence safety and well-being as a mediator between some contextual factors and members' behaviors and outcomes. Transformational and authentic leadership may, through inspiration and charisma, promote safety and health behaviors at work and may promote the participation of employees in programs and interventions aiming to ensure safety at work and promote healthy behaviors.

SOCIAL EXCHANGE THEORY

Social exchange theory is one of the major theoretical perspectives seeking to explain workplace behavior (Cropanzano & Mitchell, 2005), and it is the underlying theoretical framework for LMX discussed above. According to social exchange theory, individuals interact with each other, and as a result, obligations are established based on the norm of reciprocity such that one individual's behavior toward another sets up an expectation that the target individual will respond in a like manner (Coyle-Shapiro & Conway, 2004). Social exchange theory underlies many concepts in organizational behavior such as LMX (Liden, Bauer, & Erdogan, 2003), psychological contract theory (Rousseau, 1995), and the ERI theory of stress (Siegrist, 1996). The role of leadership has already been discussed relative to the psychologically healthy workplace. Therefore, in this section, we discuss psychological contract theory and ERI theory as theoretical perspectives in developing and maintaining a psychologically healthy workplace.

Psychological Contract Theory

According to psychological contract theory (Rousseau, 1995), employees form beliefs that there are mutual obligations between themselves and their employers. These beliefs constitute their psychological contracts. Employers are obligated to provide certain resources including socioemotional resources, and employees are obligated to contribute to the organization through their efforts and loyalty. In Rousseau's early conceptualizations of the psychological contract, a number of obligations were enumerated, including employers' obligations with respect to fair pay, recognition, job security, training, and development. In many of the investigations of the elements of the psychological contract, the specific obligations have been determined for the particular organization or group of employees (e.g., Guest, Isaksson, & De Witte, 2010; Ho, Rousseau, & Levesque, 2006). Considering this, it is perhaps more surprising that safety and health are rarely explicitly included as specific obligations of the employer to the employee (Schalk et al., 2010).

Perhaps because safety has not typically been considered as part of the psychological contract, the literature is silent on the effects of psychological contract breach—perceived failure of the organization to fulfill its obligations to the employee—on safety performance. However, psychological contract breach has been found to have negative effects on health and well-being (Robbins, Ford, & Tetrick, 2012). It may be that the negative effects of psychological contract breach are the result of a perceived sense of injustice (Lester, Kickul, & Bergman, 2007). Presumably, if an employee has been meeting his or her obligations to the employer and the employer reneges, an inequity in the exchange relationship occurs. According to social exchange theory, this may result in withdrawal from the situation, neglect of responsibilities or obligations, voicing of concern about the inequity, and reduction of commitment and loyalty to the organization (Tetrick, Shore, Bommer, & Wayne, 2001). Perhaps because psychological contract theory was first advanced as existing within the individual (i.e., the psychological contract is the belief of the individual employee; Rousseau, 1995), there has not, to our knowledge, been research examining interventions based on psychological contract theory. However, psychological contract theory may be useful in informing interventions to enhance employee well-being to include such factors as the sense of betrayal associated with psychological contract violation and an experience of unfairness and inequity arising from the failure of reciprocity. The sense of inequity that results from psychological contract breach results in stress and subsequent dissatisfaction, propensity to leave (Chambel & Peiró, 2003), and ill-health, as suggested by Siegrist's (2002) ERI theory of stress.

Effort–Reward Imbalance

The ERI model of stress (Siegrist, 1996) explicitly draws on social exchange theory and essentially posits that if an individual's efforts are not reciprocated by the employing organization through equivalent rewards, the resulting imbalance reflects a high-cost/low-gain situation and produces negative emotions such as fear, anger, and demoralization, resulting in sustained autonomic arousal and distress. Siegrist (1996) suggested three major types of rewards—money, esteem, and status control—all of which can raise or lower the gains afforded by one's work. Additionally, he recognized two factors influencing effort expended by an individual: (a) the demands and obligations of the job and (b) intrinsic characteristics of the individual (e.g., need for control, motivation, and coping styles).

Epidemiological and laboratory studies have generally found support for the model across different occupations and a range of outcome variables, such as cardiovascular events, heart rate, physiological indicators of arousal, self-reports of health, satisfaction, absence, and intention to stay on the job and among employees around the globe including Asia, North America, Australia, and Europe (Siegrist, 2002; Tsutsumi & Kawakami, 2004). In general, when efforts exceed gains there is a negative relation with health and well-being both in cross-sectional and prospective studies, though there is some evidence that the effects of imbalance are moderated by such factors as overcommitment to work (e.g., Kinman & Jones, 2008) and gender (e.g., Ertel, Pech, Ullsperger, Von Dem Knesbeck, & Siegrist, 2005).

There has been some inconsistency as to the support for the interactive effect of efforts and rewards (e.g., Kinman & Jones, 2008; Tsutsumi &

Kawakami, 2004). Part of this inconsistency may be the different operation-alizations of ERI. For example, Siegrist originally operationalized ERI as the ratio of E to R on the basis of his Effort Reward Imbalance Scale (Siegrist, 1996). In other instances, researchers have examined the individual components of E, R, and their interactions (e.g., Kinman & Jones, 2008). Generally, when the separate components have been analyzed, the interactions have not been consistently supported. Future research untangling these differences in operationalization of the ERI may also clarify which effects are moderated and which are not. For example, in Kinman and Jones (2008), a three-way interaction between E, R, and overcommitment was found in predicting job satisfaction and intention to leave, but not in predicting psychological distress and physical symptoms. This raises a question as to whether the underlying mechanism differs according to the outcome being examined.

The ERI model complements some of the major occupational stress theories. For example, Ostry, Kelly, Demers, Mustard, and Hertzman (2005) found that the ERI and job demands–control models (JDC; Karasek, 1979) independently predicted poor health status, but the ERI predicted the presence of a chronic disease among the participants, whereas the JDC did not. Further, adding task-level control to the ERI was found to be a better predictor of health status and presence of a chronic disease than either model alone. Similarly, Dai, Collins, Yu, and Fu (2008), in a study of burnout among a sample of employees in Shanghai, found that all factors from both the JDC and ERI predicted emotional exhaustion, depersonalization, and personal accomplishment. ERI factors were stronger predictors of emotional exhaustion and depersonalization than the JDC factors. Personal accomplishment was predicted by social support and not demands or control and also was predicted by effort and rewards but not overcommitment. These studies suggest that the ERI and JDC models of stress are complementary but not redundant, as suggested by Tsutsumi and Kawakami (2004). The question arises as to whether other stress theories are complementary, distinct, or redundant. The next section of this chapter reviews two of the major theories of occupational stress and their role in creating a healthy and safe workplace.

OCCUPATIONAL STRESS

The literature on occupational stress provides considerable guidance on injury and illness prevention, as well as safety and health promotion. Reviews of the literature indicate that occupational stress may have important effects on psychosomatic health and well-being, with negative effects on musculoskeletal disorders, immune system functioning, and cardiovascular health (Arnetz & Ventimiglia, 2013; Gilbert-Ouimet, Trudel, Brisson, Milot, & Vézina, 2014;

Quick, Wright, Adkins, Nelson, & Quick, 2013). In this section, we focus on the two main sources and mechanisms of occupational stress: (a) the design of work and (b) working conditions.

Stress at work has been researched from different theoretical models, with a focus on three different perspectives: (a) a focus on why an environmental feature becomes a stressor and may hamper people's well-being and health (e.g., job and work redesign; improvement of working conditions), (b) a focus on personal characteristics that may help to understand the differences among people making them more vulnerable or more resistant to stressors and the processes that may explain individual and group differences when they perceive stressors or develop strategies to cope with them (e.g., training and stress management programs focusing on personal development), and (c) a focus on the person–environment interaction (e.g., strategies based on increasing personal resources to cope with the stressful demands; cognitive restructuring strategies, such as transactional theories of stress). In this section, we review two important theories formulated from the environmental perspective. One is the job demands–control–support (JD-C-S) theory of stress, and the other is the vitamin model of work characteristics. In both cases, attention is paid to the conceptual model and main constructs, empirical evidence obtained from research, interventions designed and implemented following the theoretical guidelines, and evaluation of the interventions when empirical evidence is available.

JD-C-S Stress Theory

More than three decades ago, Karasek (1979) formulated one of the most researched and utilized theories of stress at work: the JD-C model. This model has become one of the most influential models of occupational stress among policymakers, especially in Europe. In its original formulation the model postulated that "psychological strain results not from a single aspect of the work environment, but from the joint effects of the demands of a work situation and the range of decision-making freedom (discretion) available to the worker facing those demands" (Karasek, 1979, p. 287). The combination of these two dimensions provides two axes describing either stressful jobs or active and challenging jobs. High demands and low control result in strain, which can be reduced by increasing control through job redesign without sacrificing productivity. If job demands and control (i.e., job decision latitude) are both high, an active job results, leading to the development of new behavior patterns, learning, and development. Thus, the model formulates that more or less job decision latitude can translate high job demands into either positive or negative effects on the experience of strain. Johnson and Hall (1988) extended the model, incorporating social support as a third dimension that has additive and interactive effects with the other two dimensions. According to this model, when a high-stress condition occurs in an isolated (low social support) environment, it produces greater stress than when there is high social support.

Reviews of the literature on the JDC model of stress provide evidence about the main effects of demands, control, and support on work outcomes. In a review of longitudinal studies of the JDC, de Lange, Taris, Kompier, Houtman, and Bongers (2003) found very limited and weak support for the interactive effects. Some studies using longitudinal designs have found some evidence for a reverse or even a reciprocal effect in which unhealthy experiences, or mental strain has a negative effect on job demands, or at least the perception of job demands (Dalgard et al., 2009; de Lange, Taris, Kompier, Houtman, & Bongers, 2004; Tucker et al., 2008), but only a few have shown such relationships for control (de Lange et al., 2004; Taris, 1999; Tucker et al., 2008).

Moreover, longitudinal studies may help clarify the lagged effects of stressors and strain and the time frame in which these effects occur. For example, Tucker et al. (2008) provided support for the suggestions of previous literature that stress outcomes are most likely to occur within 3 months from the onset of a stressor and that the effects of stressors did not last beyond 3 months. The reverse causal effects that have been identified suggest a negative spiral of occupational stress, but we know little about the time frame of this effect and its dynamics or the reliability of this negative spiral because results are not totally consistent with those obtained by other studies (de Lange et al., 2004). Also, further clarification is required about the changes produced in job characteristics: Are they basically perceptual changes because of the strain experiences, or are these experiences really worsening the characteristics of the job?

The literature is generally consistent with the propositions that job demands increase strain and control, whereas support decreases strain. However, the interactions among job demands, control, and support posited by the model receives weak support, if any at all (de Lange et al., 2003; Haüsser, Mojzisch, Niesel, & Schulz-Hardt, 2010; Taris, 2006). Beehr, Glaser, Canali, and Wallwey (2001) pointed out that the inconsistency in the results about the effects of the interaction between job demands and control may be partly due to the inconsistencies in the operationalization of the basic constructs considered in the theoretical model. But even when these authors used the operationalization formulated by Karasek (1979), they failed to find support for the interactive effects. Other possible explanations for this weakness may be the curvilinear relations between job characteristics and strain or the existence of confounding variables in the studies carried out at the occupational level (e.g., socioeconomic status). Moreover, some studies do not even test the interaction effects, assuming that the additive effects of demands, control and support already represent a confirmation of the basic tenet of the theory.

In our view, the interaction should be considered an essential part of this theoretical model because it establishes the specific relationship of the three antecedents with strain experiences. Whether the model is interactive or additive is not only theoretically important but also important for practice. The interaction clearly suggests different strategies for reducing negative effects of work stressors. It is the combination of high demands and low control that creates the highest levels of distress, and in this instance we can reduce the harmful effects of high job demands by increasing the control or discretion of employees. Moreover, a significant interaction with social support would point out that negative effects of a high demand–low control job still could be mitigated by improving social support (Jones & Fletcher, 1996).

The JD-C-S model has inspired a large number of interventions. Recently, two reviews focused on the analysis of interventions with reference to that model. Egan, Bambra, et al. (2007) looked at the effects of interventions aiming to increase employee participation and control through workplace reorganization on health and psychosocial well-being, whereas Bambra, Egan, Thomas, Petticrew, and Whitehead (2007) paid attention to the microspecific interventions referred to as workers' daily task structure. Egan, Bambra, et al.'s (2007) review showed that

> interventions that improved workplace control and/or support did tend to improve employee health. Health improvements did not occur when control or support worsened, except in one case, where limited health improvements occurred when colleagues' support improved but supervisor support worsened. Interventions that reduced demands also improved health (as hypothesized by the model). However sometimes health improved even when intervention appeared to increase demands. (p. 952)

Results were inconsistent concerning the interactions and in general did not support the hypotheses that low demands and high control and/or support interact to improve health.

In the review of microspecific interventions based on daily task structure that included task variety, teamworking, autonomous groups, and a combination of changes in tasks and teamworking, Bambra et al. (2007) concluded that

> some task-restructuring interventions failed to alter the psychosocial work environment significantly, and so could not be expected to have a measurable effect on health. Those that increased demand and decreased control tended to have an adverse effect on health, while those that decreased demand and increased control resulted in improved health, although some effects were minimal. Increases in workplace support did not appear to mediate this relationship. (p. 1028)

In a recent umbrella review, Bambra et al. (2009) summarized the overarching findings of seven reviews (the two that we have reported above were included) during the period 2000–2007, dealing with the health effects of organizational-level changes to the psychosocial work environment. Three reviews examined increased employee control (Aust & Ducki, 2004; Bambra et al., 2007; Egan, Bambra, et al., 2007), whereas the other four evaluated the effects of changes to the organization of work such as shift work, privatization, and health and safety legislation (Bambra, Whitehead, Sowden, Akers, & Petticrew, 2008a, 2008b; Egan, Petticrew, Ogilvie, Hamilton, & Drever, 2007; Rivara & Thompson, 2000). In addition to the conclusions that we have presented previously, Bambra et al. (2009) concluded that other changes are relevant and have to be taken into account beyond demands, control, and support. For example, restructuring in shift work had positive impacts on work-life balance, health and safety legislation in the construction industry decreased fall-related injuries, and privatization with increased job insecurity and unemployment adversely affected mental health.

In sum, the JD-C-S has been influential in policy development for health promotion and psychosocial risk prevention. Evidence from intervention research supports the policies and directives promoting participation at work to increase job control and autonomy of workers as effective strategies to prevent risks and promote health. However, the model has some limitations. First as discussed above, there is a lack of support for the interactive effects included in the model. In fact, Taris (2006) included the demand–control interaction as one of the "zombie theories" in occupational health psychology—it persists even though the empirical support is very thin despite the huge number of studies aiming to test it.

In addition to this internal weakness of the model, several authors have presented its external limitations and have claimed the need for extensions in several directions. For example, there has been a call to consider other organizational characteristics and work arrangements (Bambra et al., 2009)—such as extended working conditions like staffing resources, communication, social hindrance, training opportunities, job skills, and material resources (Akerboom & Maes, 2006)—and nonstandard employment arrangements, such as independent contractors, on-call workers, temporary help agency workers, workers provided by contract firms, virtual work, and telecommuters (Ashford, George, & Blatt, 2007). In addition, there is a recognition of the need to consider personal characteristics and behaviors such as the match between job control and control-related individual characteristics like locus of control or self-efficacy (Meier, Semmer, Elfering, & Jacobshagen, 2008) and coping styles and behaviors (Ippolito, Adler, Thomas, Litz, & Hölzl, 2005). From the broader perspective of organizations, organizational features such as organizational culture, strategy, infrastructure, structure, technology, work system, climate and communication, policies and practices of human resources management, management and human capital constitute relevant contextual factors that may have an impact on workers' health and well-being (Peiró, 2000; Peiró & Martínez-Tur, 2008), and we need more examination of these organizational characteristics. One stress theory that also takes a broader perspective on work and contextual factors is the vitamin model of work (Warr, 1987).

Vitamin Model Theory

As does the previous theory, the vitamin model of work formulated mainly by Warr (1987, 2007) considers key work characteristics from an environmental perspective. This perspective is useful to inspire primary interventions for psychosocial risks and also to promote health and well-being at work. The vitamin theory takes into consideration a broader array of work features than the three considered by the JD-C-S model. It also distinguishes two patterns of relationships between the work features and well-being and health at work: linear versus curvilinear. To explain these differences, Warr (1987, 2007) used the vitamin analogy. He stated that health and happiness are influenced by the features of the environment in a similar manner as vitamins influence physical conditions. Vitamin deficiency contributes to ill health, but once the threshold of the required levels has been reached, there is no benefit from additional quantities. However, for certain vitamins (e.g., A, D), a large quantity may also have a negative effect on health, whereas others do not present such negative effects (e.g., C, E). Warr (1987) described nine primary characteristics of the work environment and pointed out that the first six relate to health in a similar manner as do vitamins A and D. These features are the following: opportunity for personal control, opportunity for skill use, externally generated goals, variety, environmental clarity, and contact with others. The other three characteristics included in the model have a relationship to health similar to those of vitamins C and E. These are the following: availability of money, physical security, and valued social position. Moreover, in his recent book, *Work, Happiness, and Unhappiness*, Warr (2007) identified three additional features in job settings that can be considered in the settings of paid employment: supportive supervision, career outlook, and equity and fairness in employment relationships. All three are classified by the author as CE (i.e., *constant effect*; used to denote effects similar to those of vitamins like C and E) features of work.

The theory also distinguishes three levels in the outcomes. The broadest one is characterized as context-free psychological well-being, and it captures well-being of life in general. A more specific level is characterized as domain-specific, which refers to well-being from a life space segment (e.g., work, family life). A third, still more specific, level of well-being is facet-specific, which refers to one particular aspect (e.g., intrinsic job satisfaction) within a domain. In each of these three levels the emphasis can be cognitive or affective (Warr, 2007). According to these distinctions, six types of happiness are differentiated in the model. At the broadest level, there are two types: context-free with affective emphasis (e.g., global affect measures) and context-free with cognitive emphasis (e.g., life satisfaction). At the domain-specific level, feelings about one's job represent a measure with affective emphasis, whereas job satisfaction presents cognitive emphasis. Finally, at the facet-specific level, cognitive versus affective emphasis has been considered in the measurement (e.g., feelings about or satisfaction with work colleagues).

Empirical evidence supporting this theory has been systematically reviewed by Warr (1987, 2007). Warr's review (2007) found mixed results for the additional decrement effects of opportunity for personal control, opportunity for skill use, externally generated goals, variety, environmental clarity, and contact with others in that evidence for the nonlinear component was not consistently supported. He argued that this may be because existing research has not included the full range of these features. For example, variety is generally positively related with well-being. At low levels, usually resulting from repetition of the same activities on short cycles, variety may be expressed as boredom and well-being deteriorates. Very high variety may require frequent shifts of concentration and attention that may produce strain; however, according to Warr (2007),

> it is not yet possible to document an additional decrement at very high levels of job variety. Given the lack of research in that segment of the proposed curve, it is not surprising that the entire curve has not been investigated in a single study. (p. 187)

Warr (2007) also argued that the constant effects of availability of money, physical security, valued social position, supportive supervision, career outlook, and equity and fairness have not been well researched, although there is evidence to support positive effects of these characteristics on well-being. The issue is that the research in many instances has not examined the full range of these characteristics on well-being or the existing studies did not test for nonlinear effects. For example, the relationship between valued social position and well-being has been found to be related to subjective well-being (Xie & Johns, 1995), but only linear relationships were examined, and the possibility of nonlinear relationships at high and moderate levels of these characteristics has not been tested.

Equity and fairness may be the one constant effect characteristic which has received sufficient empirical evidence in support of the vitamin model. Warr (2007) considered organizational justice (distributive and procedural)

as a relevant construct and pointed out evidence showing significant relationships between both types of justice and overall job satisfaction and also with
context-free depression, although with somewhat lower values (Colquitt et al.,
2001; Wilson, DeJoy, Vandenberg, Richardson, & McGrath, 2004). Similar
relationships have been found at a unit level with burnout (Moliner, Martínez-
Tur, Peiró, Ramos, & Cropanzano, 2005). Additionally, Taris, Kalimo, and
Schaufeli (2002) analyzed differences between underbenefited, equally treated,
and overbenefited and found a constant-effect type of relationship between
equity or fairness and emotional exhaustion. The construct of psychological
contract may also be considered in this context. The set of promises made to
employees and expectations raised constitute the psychological contract that
can be fulfilled or not (and sometimes violated) afterwards. The degree of fulfillment is clearly related to indicators of well-being such as overall satisfaction
(Guest et al., 2010).

In contrast to the JD-C-S, the contributions of the vitamin model to
the design of interventions to make work and its context healthier focus on
environmental work characteristics. This is particularly useful in designing
relevant interventions from a primary prevention approach with the emphasis being on redesigning jobs in a way that makes them healthier. The model
considers a broad array of characteristics, providing alternative opportunities for work improvement. Other broad formulations of work features were
recently presented (Morgeson & Humphrey, 2006). This expansion of the
number of characteristics introduces a complex set of relationships between
them, and in some cases the constructs appear to overlap. To date, there is not
much empirical evidence on the effects of different interactions and possible
nonlinear relationships. In fact, Taris (2006) also posed the question "Could
the notion that work characteristics affect well-being nonlinearly perhaps be
an urban myth?" (p. 100).

The vitamin model, with its emphasis on introducing changes in multiple job characteristics instead of changing only control or social support, as
is the case with the JD-C-S, has inspired a number of interventions that have
incorporated at least some of the characteristics. Semmer (2006) reviewed the
interventions oriented toward improving the environmental characteristics
of work and generally found support for interventions that redesigned task
characteristics, work conditions, and social conditions. The effects of these
interventions differed depending on the specific environmental characteristic and the specific indicator of well-being. Semmer concluded that "despite
all of the problems cautiously positive conclusion is warranted. Work-related
interventions have shown that they have the potential to improve health and
well-being" (p. 518).

Recently, Holman, Axtell, Sprigg, Totterdell, and Wall (2010) suggested
that studies evaluating the effects of changes in work characteristics on health

and well-being should test the mediating effect of such characteristics between employees' participation in the program and well-being. In a study of the effects of implementing lean manufacturing, Parker (2003) found that this change increased workers' job-related depression through decreases in job control, skill utilization, and participation in decision making. Similarly, Holman et al., in a participative job redesign intervention, found that job control, participation in decision making, feedback, and skill utilization mediated the effects of job redesign on job-related well-being. In general, interventions show that work characteristics included in the vitamin model are relevant for job redesign aiming to improve well-being. However, the nonlinear relationships with well-being are neither explicitly taken into consideration in the job redesign nor tested in the intervention studies. There is limited evidence of the nonlinear association of work characteristics with psychological well-being in longitudinal studies. Rydstedt, Ferrie, and Head (2006) tested curvilinear relations of decision latitude, job demands, and social support with well-being over a 5-year period in the Whitehall II study sample. A minor J-shaped effect was found between decision latitude and job satisfaction, and the U-shaped relation obtained between social support and job satisfaction was contrary to the hypothesis. The authors suggested that a shorter time lag would be more suitable to identify curvilinear relationships. However, Mäkikangas, Feldt, and Kinnunen (2007), using a time lag period of 3 years, did not find lagged nonlinear associations of job control and supportive climate with affective well-being. In sum, the vitamin model provides an important framework for analyzing the main characteristics of work environment that are relevant for well-being and health and also pays attention to the role of variations in the amount or intensity of those characteristics for employees' well-being. However, this last aspect of the theory is not well validated.

CONCLUSION

In this chapter, we have reviewed several theoretical perspectives for creating a psychologically health workplace. Occupational stress has been a major underlying framework for understanding harmful aspects of the work environment. However, not all work environments are toxic. By expanding our consideration of positive aspects of the work environment to include the vitamin model, social exchange theory, and leadership theories, it is possible to understand ways to offset the negative consequences and enhance the positive aspects of the work environment. These positive aspects have the potential to generate a safe and healthy work climate and a psychological healthy workplace.

REFERENCES

Akerboom, S., & Maes, S. (2006). Beyond demand and control: The contribution of organizational risk factors in assessing the psychological well-being of health care employees. *Work & Stress, 20,* 21–36. http://dx.doi.org/10.1080/02678370600690915

Arnetz, B. B., & Ventimiglia, M. (2013). Measurement of immune system functioning. In R. R. Sinclair, M. Wang, & L. E. Tetrick (Eds.), *Research methods in occupational health psychology: Measurement, design, and data analysis* (pp. 3–18). New York, NY: Routledge/Taylor & Francis.

Arnold, K., Turner, N., Barling, J., Kelloway, E. K., & McKee, M. C. (2007). Transformational leadership and psychological well-being: The mediating role of meaningful work. *Journal of Occupational Health Psychology, 12,* 193–203.

Ashford, S. J., George, E., & Blatt, R. (2007). Old assumptions, new work: The opportunities and challenges of research on nonstandard employment. *The Academy of Management Annals, 1,* 65–117. http://dx.doi.org/10.1080/078559807

Atwater, L., & Carmeli, A. (2009). Leader-member exchange, feelings of energy, and involvement in creative work. *The Leadership Quarterly, 20,* 264–275. http://dx.doi.org/10.1016/j.leaqua.2007.07.009

Aust, B., & Ducki, A. (2004). Comprehensive health promotion interventions at the workplace: Experiences with health circles in Germany. *Journal of Occupational Health Psychology, 9,* 258–270. http://dx.doi.org/10.1037/1076-8998.9.3.258

Avolio, B. J., Walumbwa, F. O., & Weber, T. J. (2009). Leadership: Current theories, research, and future directions. *Annual Review of Psychology, 60,* 421–449. http://dx.doi.org/10.1146/annurev.psych.60.110707.163621

Bambra, C. L., Egan, M., Thomas, S., Petticrew, M., & Whitehead, M. M. (2007). The psychosocial and health effects of workplace reorganization: 2. A systematic review of task restructuring interventions. *Journal of Epidemiology and Community Health, 61,* 1028–1037. http://dx.doi.org/10.1136/jech.2006.054999

Bambra, C. L., Gibson, M., Sowden, A. J., Wright, K., Whitehead, M. M., & Petticrew, M. (2009). Working for health? Evidence from systematic reviews on the effects on health and health inequalities of organizational changes to the psychosocial work environment. *Preventive Medicine, 48,* 454–461. http://dx.doi.org/10.1016/j.ypmed.2008.12.018

Bambra, C. L., Whitehead, M. M., Sowden, A. J., Akers, J., & Petticrew, M. (2008a). "A hard day's night?" The effects of compressed working week interventions on the health and work–life balance of shift workers: A systematic review. *Journal of Epidemiology and Community Health, 62,* 764–777. http://dx.doi.org/10.1136/jech.2007.067249

Bambra, C. L., Whitehead, M. M., Sowden, A. J., Akers, J., & Petticrew, M. P. (2008b). Shifting schedules: The health effects of reorganizing shift work. *American Journal of Preventive Medicine, 34,* 427–434. http://dx.doi.org/10.1016/j.amepre.2007.12.023

Barling, J., & Frone, M. R. (Eds.). (2004). *The psychology of workplace safety*. http://dx.doi.org/10.1037/10662-000

Basen-Engquist, K., Hudmon, K. S., Tripp, M., & Chamberlain, R. (1998). Worksite health and safety climate: Scale development and effects of a health promotion intervention. *Preventive Medicine, 27*, 111–119. http://dx.doi.org/10.1006/pmed.1997.0253

Bass, B. M. (1985). *Leadership and performance beyond expectations*. New York, NY: Free Press.

Bass, B. M. (1998). *Transformational leadership: Industrial, military, and educational impact*. Mahwah, NJ: Erlbaum.

Bass, B. M., & Steidlmeier, P. (1999). Ethics, character, and authentic transformational leadership behavior. *The Leadership Quarterly, 10*, 181–217. http://dx.doi.org/10.1016/S1048-9843(99)00016-8

Beehr, T. A., Glaser, K. M., Canali, K. G., & Wallwey, D. A. (2001). Back to basics: Reexamination of demand-control theory of occupational stress. *Work & Stress, 15*, 115–130. http://dx.doi.org/10.1080/02678370110067002

Belias, D., & Koustelios, A. (2014). Transformational leadership and job satisfaction in the banking sector: A review. *International Review of Management and Marketing, 4*, 187–200.

Bennett, J. B., & Tetrick, L. E. (2013). The "we" in wellness: Workplace health promotion as a positive force for health in society. In J. B. Olson-Buchanan, L. Koppes Bryan, & L. F. Thompson (Eds.), *Using industrial-organizational psychology for the greater good: Helping those who help others* (pp. 205–237). New York, NY: Taylor & Francis/Routledge.

Bolino, M. C., & Turnley, W. H. (2009). Relative deprivation among employees in lower quality leader–member exchange relationships. *The Leadership Quarterly, 20*, 276–286. http://dx.doi.org/10.1016/j.leaqua.2009.03.001

Bruns, E. J., Walrath, C., Glass-Siegel, M., & Weist, M. D. (2004). School-based mental health services in Baltimore: Association with school climate and special education referrals. *Behavior Modification, 28*, 491–512. http://dx.doi.org/10.1177/0145445503259524

Burns, J. M. (1978). *Leadership*. New York, NY: Harper & Row.

Chambel, M. J., & Peiró, J. M. (2003). *Alteraciones en las prácticas de recursos humanos y violación del contrato psicológico: Implicaciones para las actitudes y la intención de abandonar la organización de los empleados* [Changes in HRM practices and psychological contract violation: Implications on employees' attitudes and propensity to leave the organization]. *Arxius, 8*, 105–201.

Christian, M. S., Bradley, J. C., Wallace, J. C., & Burke, M. J. (2009). Workplace safety: A meta-analysis of the roles of person and situation factors. *Journal of Applied Psychology, 94*, 1103–1127. http://dx.doi.org/10.1037/a0016172

Clarke, S. (2006). The relationship between safety climate and safety performance: A meta-analytic review. *Journal of Occupational Health Psychology, 11*, 315–327. http://dx.doi.org/10.1037/1076-8998.11.4.315

Colella, A., & Varma, A. (2001). The impact of subordinate disability on leader-member exchange relationships. *Academy of Management Journal, 44*, 304–315. http://dx.doi.org/10.2307/3069457

Colquitt, J. A., Conlon, D. E., Wesson, M. J., Porter, C. O. I. H., & Ng, K. Y. (2001). Justice at the millennium: A meta-analytic review of 25 years of organizational justice research. *Journal of Applied Psychology, 86*, 425–445. http://dx.doi.org/10.1037/0021-9010.86.3.425

Conchie, S. M. (2013). Transformational leadership, intrinsic motivation, and trust: A moderated-mediated model of workplace safety. *Journal of Occupational Health Psychology, 18*, 198–210. http://dx.doi.org/10.1037/a0031805

Corrigan, P. W., Diwan, S., Campion, J., & Rashid, F. (2002). Transformational leadership and the mental health team. *Administration and Policy in Mental Health, 30*, 97–108. http://dx.doi.org/10.1023/A:1022569617123

Coyle-Shapiro, J. A.-M., & Conway, N. (2004). The employment relationship through the lens of social exchange theory. In J. Coyle-Shapiro, L. M. Shore, M. S. Taylor, & L. E. Tetrick (Eds.), *The employment relationship: Examining psychological and contextual perspectives* (pp. 5–28). Oxford, England: Oxford University Press.

Cropanzano, R., & Mitchell, M. S. (2005). Social exchange theory: An interdisciplinary review. *Journal of Management, 31*, 874–900. http://dx.doi.org/10.1177/0149206305279602

Dai, J. M., Collins, S., Yu, H. Z., & Fu, H. (2008). Combining job stress models in predicting burnout by hierarchical multiple regressions: A cross-sectional investigation in Shanghai. *Journal of Occupational and Environmental Medicine, 50*, 785–790. http://dx.doi.org/10.1097/JOM.0b013e318167750a

Dalgard, O. S., Sørensen, T., Sandanger, I., Nygård, J. F., Svensson, E., & Reas, D. L. (2009). Job demands, job control, and mental health in an 11-year follow-up study: Normal and reversed relationships. *Work & Stress, 23*, 284–296. http://dx.doi.org/10.1080/02678370903250953

Day, D. V. (2000). Leadership development: A review in context. *The Leadership Quarterly, 11*, 581–613. http://dx.doi.org/10.1016/S1048-9843(00)00061-8

de Lange, A. H., Taris, T. W., Kompier, M. A. J., Houtman, I. L. D., & Bongers, P. M. (2003). "The very best of the millennium": Longitudinal research and the demand-control-(support) model. *Journal of Occupational Health Psychology, 8*, 282–305. http://dx.doi.org/10.1037/1076-8998.8.4.282

de Lange, A. H., Taris, T. W., Kompier, M. A. J., Houtman, I. L. D., & Bongers, P. M. (2004). The relationships between work characteristics and mental health: Examining normal, reversed and reciprocal relationships in a 4-wave study. *Work & Stress, 18*, 149–166. http://dx.doi.org/10.1080/02678370412331270860

Dumdum, U. R., Lowe, K. B., & Avolio, B. J. (2002). A meta-analysis of transformational and transactional leadership correlates of effectiveness and satisfaction: An update and extension. In B. J. Avolio & F. J. Yammarino (Eds.), *Transformational and charismatic leadership: The road ahead* (pp. 35–66). Amsterdam, the Netherlands: JAI Press.

Egan, M., Bambra, C. L., Thomas, S., Petticrew, M., Whitehead, M. M., & Thomson, H. (2007). The psychosocial and health effects of workplace reorganization. 1. A systematic review of organizational-level interventions that aim to increase employee control. *Journal of Epidemiology and Community Health, 61,* 945–954. http://dx.doi.org/10.1136/jech.2006.054965

Egan, M., Petticrew, M., Ogilvie, D., Hamilton, V., & Drever, F. (2007). "Profits before people"? A systematic review of the health and safety impacts of privatizing public utilities and industries in developed countries. *Journal of Epidemiology and Community Health, 61,* 862–870. http://dx.doi.org/10.1136/jech.2006.053231

Epitropaki, O., & Martin, R. (1999). Short research note: The impact of relational demography on the quality of leader–member exchanges and employees' work attitudes and well-being. *Journal of Occupational and Organizational Psychology, 72,* 237–240. http://dx.doi.org/10.1348/096317999166635

Ertel, M., Pech, E., Ullsperger, P., Von Dem Knesbeck, O., & Siegrist, J. (2005). Adverse psychosocial working conditions and subjective health in freelance media workers. *Work & Stress, 19,* 293–299. http://dx.doi.org/10.1080/02678370500307289

Flin, R., Mearns, K., O'Connor, R., & Bryden, R. (2000). Measuring safety climate: Identifying the common features. *Safety Science, 34,* 177–192. http://dx.doi.org/10.1016/S0925-7535(00)00012-6

Gilbert-Ouimet, M., Trudel, X., Brisson, C., Milot, A., & Vézina, M. (2014). Adverse effects of psychosocial work factors on blood pressure: Systematic review of studies on demand-control-support and effort-reward imbalance models. *Scandinavian Journal of Work, Environment & Health, 40,* 109–132. http://dx.doi.org/10.5271/sjweh.3390

Graen, G. B., Hui, C., & Taylor, E. A. (2006). Experience-based learning about LMX leadership and fairness in project teams: A dyadic directional approach. *Academy of Management Learning & Education, 5,* 448–460. http://dx.doi.org/10.5465/AMLE.2006.23473205

Graen, G. B., & Uhl-Bien, M. (1995). Relationship-based approach to leadership: development of leader-member exchange (LMX) theory of leadership over 25 years: Applying a multi-level, multi-domain perspective. *The Leadership Quarterly, 6,* 219–247. http://dx.doi.org/10.1016/1048-9843(95)90036-5

Graves, L. M., & Luciano, M. M. (2013). Self-determination at work: Understanding the role of leader-member exchange. *Motivation and Emotion, 37,* 518–536. http://dx.doi.org/10.1007/s11031-012-9336-z

Guest, D. E., Isaksson, K., & De Witte, H. (Eds.). (2010). *Employment contracts, psychological contracts and employee well-being: An international study.* Oxford, England: Oxford University Press. http://dx.doi.org/10.1093/acprof:oso/9780199542697.001.0001

Harris, K. J., & Kacmar, K. M. (2006). Too much of a good thing: The curvilinear effect of leader-member exchange on stress. *The Journal of Social Psychology, 146,* 65–84. http://dx.doi.org/10.3200/SOCP.146.1.65-84

Haüsser, J. A., Mojzisch, A., Niesel, M., & Schulz-Hardt, S. (2010). Ten years on: A review of recent research on the job demand-control (-support) model and psychological well-being. *Work & Stress, 24*, 1–35. http://dx.doi.org/10.1080/02678371003683747

Henderson, D. J., Liden, R. C., Glibkowski, B. C., & Chaudhry, A. (2009). LMX differentiation: A multilevel review and examination of its antecedents and outcomes. *The Leadership Quarterly, 20*, 517–534. http://dx.doi.org/10.1016/j.leaqua.2009.04.003

Ho, V., Rousseau, D. M., & Levesque, L. L. (2006). Social networks and the psychological contract: Structural holes, cohesive ties, and beliefs regarding employer obligations. *Human Relations, 59*, 459–481. http://dx.doi.org/10.1177/0018726706065370

Hofmann, D. A., & Morgeson, F. P. (1999). Safety-related behavior as a social exchange: The role of perceived organizational support and leader–member exchange. *Journal of Applied Psychology, 84*, 286–296. http://dx.doi.org/10.1037/0021-9010.84.2.286

Hofmann, D. A., & Tetrick, L. E. (Eds.). (2003). *Health and safety in organizations: A multilevel perspective.* Organizational Frontier Series, Society for Industrial and Organizational Psychology. San Francisco, CA: Jossey-Bass.

Holman, D. J., Axtell, C. M., Sprigg, C. A., Totterdell, P., & Wall, T. (2010). The mediating role of job characteristics in job redesign interventions: A serendipitous quasi-experiment. *Journal of Organizational Behavior, 31*, 84–105. http://dx.doi.org/10.1002/job.631

Ilies, R., Nahrgang, J. D., & Morgeson, F. P. (2007). Leader-member exchange and citizenship behaviors: A meta-analysis. *Journal of Applied Psychology, 92*, 269–277. http://dx.doi.org/10.1037/0021-9010.92.1.269

Inness, M., Turner, N., Barling, J., & Stride, C. B. (2010). Transformational leadership and employee safety performance: A within-person, between-jobs design. *Journal of Occupational Health Psychology, 15*, 279–290. http://dx.doi.org/10.1037/a0019380

Ippolito, J., Adler, A. B., Thomas, J. L., Litz, B. T., & Hölzl, R. (2005). Extending and applying the demand-control model: The role of soldier's coping on a peacekeeping deployment. *Journal of Occupational Health Psychology, 10*, 452–464. http://dx.doi.org/10.1037/1076-8998.10.4.452

Jacobs, C., Pfaff, H., Lehner, B., Driller, E., Nitzsche, A., Stieler-Lorenz, B., . . . Jung, J. (2013). The influence of transformational leadership on employee well-being: Results from a survey of companies in the information and communication technology sector in Germany. *Journal of Occupational and Environmental Medicine, 55*, 772–778. http://dx.doi.org/10.1097/JOM.0b013e3182972ee5

Johnson, J. V., & Hall, E. M. (1988). Job strain, work place social support, and cardiovascular disease: A cross-sectional study of a random sample of the Swedish working population. *American Journal of Public Health, 78*, 1336–1342. http://dx.doi.org/10.2105/AJPH.78.10.1336

Jones, F., & Fletcher, B. C. (1996). Job Control and health. In M. J. Schabraq, J. A. M. Winnubst, & C. L. Cooper (Eds.), *Handbook of work and health psychology* (pp. 121–142). Chichester, England: Wiley.

Judge, T. A., & Piccolo, R. F. (2004). Transformational and transactional leadership: A meta-analytic test of their relative validity. *Journal of Applied Psychology, 89,* 755–768. http://dx.doi.org/10.1037/0021-9010.89.5.755

Karasek, R. A. (1979). Job demands, job decision latitude, and mental strain: Implications for job redesign. *Administrative Science Quarterly, 24,* 285–308. http://dx.doi.org/10.2307/2392498

Kelloway, E. K., Mullen, J., & Francis, L. (2006). Divergent effects of transformational and passive leadership on employee safety. *Journal of Occupational Health Psychology, 11,* 76–86. http://dx.doi.org/10.1037/1076-8998.11.1.76

Kelloway, E. K., Turner, N., Barling, J., & Loughlin, C. (2012). Transformational leadership and employee psychological well-being: The mediating role of employee trust in leadership. *Work & Stress, 26,* 39–55.

Kinman, G., & Jones, F. (2008). Effort-reward imbalance and overcommitment: Predicting strain in academic employees in the United Kingdom. *International Journal of Stress Management, 15,* 381–395. http://dx.doi.org/10.1037/a0013213

Kuoppala, J., Lamminpää, A., Liira, J., & Vainio, H. (2008). Leadership, job well-being, and health effects—a systematic review and a meta-analysis. *Journal of Occupational and Environmental Medicine, 50,* 904–915. http://dx.doi.org/10.1097/JOM.0b013e31817e918d

Lawrence, E. R., & Kacmar, K. M. (2012). Leader-member exchange and stress: The mediating role of job involvement and role conflict. *Journal of Behavioral and Applied Management, 14,* 39–52.

Lester, S., Kickul, J. R., & Bergman, T. J. (2007). Managing employees' perceptions of the psychological contract over time: The role of social accounts and contract fulfillment. *Journal of Organizational Behavior, 28,* 191–208. http://dx.doi.org/10.1002/job.410

Liden, R. C., Bauer, T. N., & Erdogan, B. (2003). The role of leader-member exchange in the dynamic relationship between employer and employee: Implications for employee socialization, leaders, and organizations. In J. A-M. Coyle-Shapiro, L. M. Shore, M. S. Taylor, & L. E. Tetrick (Eds.), *The employment relationship: Examining psychological and contextual perspectives* (pp. 226–252). Oxford, England: Oxford University Press.

Luthans, F., & Avolio, B. J. (2003). Authentic leadership development. In K. S. Cameron, J. E. Dutton, & R. E. Quinn (Eds.), *Positive organizational scholarship* (pp. 241–258). San Francisco, CA: Berrett-Koehler.

Lyons, J. B., & Schneider, T. R. (2009). The effects of leadership style on stress outcomes. *The Leadership Quarterly, 20,* 737–748. http://dx.doi.org/10.1016/j.leaqua.2009.06.010

Macik-Frey, M., Quick, J. C., & Cooper, C. L. (2009). Authentic leadership as a pathway to positive health. *Journal of Organizational Behavior, 30*, 453–458. http://dx.doi.org/10.1002/job.561

Major, D. A., Kozlowski, S. W. J., Chao, G. T., & Gardner, P. D. (1995). A longitudinal investigation of newcomer expectations, early socialization outcomes, and the moderating effects of role development factors. *Journal of Applied Psychology, 80*, 418–431. http://dx.doi.org/10.1037/0021-9010.80.3.418

Mäkikangas, A., Feldt, T., & Kinnunen, U. (2007). Warr's scale of job-related affective wellbeing: A longitudinal examination of its structure and relationships with work characteristics. *Work & Stress, 21*, 197–219. http://dx.doi.org/10.1080/02678370701662151

Maslyn, J. M., & Uhl-Bien, M. (2005). LMX differentiation: Key concepts and related empirical findings. In G. Graen & J. A. Graen (Eds.), *Global organizing designs, LMX leadership: The series* (Vol. 3, pp. 73–98). Greenwich, CT: Information Age.

Mearns, K., Hope, L., Ford, M. T., & Tetrick, L. E. (2010). Investment in workforce health: Exploring the implications for workforce safety climate and commitment. *Accident Analysis and Prevention, 42*, 1445–1454. http://dx.doi.org/10.1016/j.aap.2009.08.009

Meier, L. L., Semmer, N. K., Elfering, A., & Jacobshagen, N. (2008). The double meaning of control: Three-way interactions between internal resources, job control, and stressors at work. *Journal of Occupational Health Psychology, 13*, 244–258. http://dx.doi.org/10.1037/1076-8998.13.3.244

Moliner, C., Martínez-Tur, V., Peiró, J. M., Ramos, J., & Cropanzano, R. (2005). Relationships between organizational justice and burnout at the work-unit level. *International Journal of Stress Management, 12*, 99–116. http://dx.doi.org/10.1037/1072-5245.12.2.99

Morgeson, F. P., & Humphrey, S. E. (2006). The Work Design Questionnaire (WDQ): Developing and validating a comprehensive measure for assessing job design and the nature of work. *Journal of Applied Psychology, 91*, 1321–1339. http://dx.doi.org/10.1037/0021-9010.91.6.1321

Nahrgang, J. D., Morgeson, F. P., & Ilies, R. (2009). The development of leader–member exchanges: Exploring how personality and performance influence leader and member relationships over time. *Organizational Behavior and Human Decision Processes, 108*, 256–266. http://dx.doi.org/10.1016/j.obhdp.2008.09.002

Nielsen, K., & Munir, F. (2009). How do transformational leaders influence followers' affective well-being? Exploring the mediating role of self-efficacy. *Work & Stress, 23*, 313–329. http://dx.doi.org/10.1080/02678370903385106

Nielsen, M. B., Eid, J., Mearns, K., & Larsson, G. (2013). Authentic leadership and its relationship with risk perception and safety climate. *Leadership & Organization Development Journal, 34*, 308–325. http://dx.doi.org/10.1108/LODJ-07-2011-0065

Ostry, A. S., Kelly, S., Demers, P. A., Mustard, C., & Hertzman, C. (2005). A comparison of the effort-reward imbalance and demand control models. In K. V. Oxington (Ed.), *Psychology of stress* (pp. 113–127). Hauppauge, NY: Nova Biomedical Books.

Parker, S. K. (2003). Longitudinal effects of lean production on employee outcomes and the mediating role of work characteristics. *Journal of Applied Psychology, 88,* 620–634. http://dx.doi.org/10.1037/0021-9010.88.4.620

Peiró, J. M. (2000). Assessment of psychosocial risks and prevention strategies: The AMIGO model as the basis of the prevenlab/psicosocial methodology. *Psychology in Spain, 4,* 139–166.

Peiró, J. M., González Romá, V., Ramos, J., & Zornoza, A. (1996). Relationships between leadership and professionals' job attitudes and perceptions: Comparison of two leadership models. *Work & Stress, 10,* 195–208. http://dx.doi.org/10.1080/02678379608256800

Peiró, J. M., & Martínez-Tur, V. (2008). Organizational development and change. In N. Chmiel (Ed.), *An introduction to work and organizational psychology* (2nd ed., pp. 351–376). London, England: Blackwell.

Peiró, J. M., & Rodriguez, I. (2008). Work stress, leadership, and organizational health. In V. Weber (Ed.). *Health is the greatest wealth: The key to future economic prosperity and business excellence in Europe.* Bielefeld, Germany: Bertelsmann Stiftung, BKK Bundesverband.

Quick, J. C., Wright, T. A., Adkins, J. A., Nelson, D. L., & Quick, J. D. (2013). *Preventive stress management in organizations* (2nd ed.). Washington, DC: American Psychological Association. http://dx.doi.org/10.1037/13942-000

Ribisl, K. M., & Reischl, T. M. (1993). Measuring the climate for health at organizations. Development of the worksite health climate scales. *Journal of Occupational Medicine, 35,* 812–824. http://dx.doi.org/10.1097/00043764-199308000-00019

Rivara, F. P., & Thompson, D. C. (2000). Prevention of falls in the construction industry: Evidence for program effectiveness. *American Journal of Preventive Medicine, 18*(Suppl.), 23–26. http://dx.doi.org/10.1016/S0749-3797(00)00137-9

Robbins, J. M., Ford, M. T., & Tetrick, L. E. (2012). Perceived unfairness and employee health: A meta-analytic integration. *Journal of Applied Psychology, 97,* 235–272. http://dx.doi.org/10.1037/a0025408

Rockstuhl, T., Dulebohn, J. H., Ang, S., & Shore, L. M. (2012). Leader-member exchange (LMX) and culture: A meta-analysis of correlates of LMX across 23 countries. *Journal of Applied Psychology, 97,* 1097–1130. http://dx.doi.org/10.1037/a0029978

Rose, M. R. (1998). An integrative investigation of job stress, situational moderators, and group-level patterns within the leader-member exchange model of leadership. *Dissertation Abstracts International: Section B, 58*(11-B).

Rousseau, D. M. (1995). *Psychological contracts in organizations: Understanding written and unwritten agreements.* Thousand Oaks, CA: Sage. http://dx.doi.org/10.4135/9781452231594

Rydstedt, L. W., Ferrie, J., & Head, J. (2006). Is there support for curvilinear relationships between psychosocial work characteristics and mental well-being? Cross-sectional and long-term data from the Whitehall II study. *Work & Stress, 20,* 6–20. http://dx.doi.org/10.1080/02678370600668119

Scandura, T. A. (1999). Rethinking leader-member exchange: An organizational justice perspective. *The Leadership Quarterly, 10,* 25–40. http://dx.doi.org/10.1016/S1048-9843(99)80007-1

Schalk, R., De Jong, J., Rigotti, T., Mohr, G., Peiró, J. M., & Cabeller, A. (2010). The psychological contracts of temporary and permanent workers. In D. E. Guest, K. Isaksson, & H. De Witte (Eds.), *Employment contracts, psychological contracts, and employee well-being: An international study* (pp. 89–120). Oxford, England: Oxford University Press. http://dx.doi.org/10.1093/acprof:oso/9780199542697.003.0005

Schneider, B., Ehrhart, M. G., & Macey, W. H. (2011). Perspectives on organizational climate and culture. In S. Zedeck (Ed.), *APA handbook of industrial and organizational psychology: Vol. 1. Building and developing the organization* (pp. 373–414). Washington, DC: American Psychological Association.

Schriesheim, C. A., Castro, S. L., & Cogliser, C. C. (1999). Leader-member exchange (LMX) research: A comprehensive review of theory, measurement, and data analytic practices. *The Leadership Quarterly, 10,* 63–82. http://dx.doi.org/10.1016/S1048-9843(99)80009-5

Semmer, N. K. (2006). Job stress interventions and the organization of work. *Scandinavian Journal of Work, Environment & Health, 32,* 515–527. http://dx.doi.org/10.5271/sjweh.1056

Siegrist, J. (1996). Adverse health effects of high-effort/low-reward conditions. *Journal of Occupational Health Psychology, 1,* 27–41. http://dx.doi.org/10.1037/1076-8998.1.1.27

Siegrist, J. (2002). Effort-reward imbalance at work and health. In P. Perrewé & D. Ganster (Eds.), *Research in occupational stress and well-being: Vol. 2. Historical and current perspectives on stress and health* (pp. 261–291). New York, NY: JAI Elsevier.

Sirvanathan, N., Arnold, K. A., Turner, N., & Barling, J. (2004). Leading well: Transformational leadership and well-being. In P. A. Linley & S. Joseph (Eds.), *Positive psychology in practice.* (pp. 241–255). Hoboken, NJ: Wiley.

Sosik, J. J., & Godshalk, V. M. (2000). Leadership styles, mentoring functions received, and job-related stress: A conceptual model and preliminary study. *Journal of Organizational Behavior, 21,* 365–390. http://dx.doi.org/10.1002/(SICI)1099-1379(200006)21:4<365::AID-JOB14>3.0.CO;2-H

Taris, T. W. (1999). The mutual effects between job resources and mental health: A prospective study among Dutch youth. *Genetic, Social, and General Psychology Monographs, 125,* 433–450.

Taris, T. W. (2006). Bricks without clay: On urban myths in occupational health psychology. *Work & Stress, 20,* 99–104. http://dx.doi.org/10.1080/02678370600893410

Taris, T., Kalimo, R., & Schaufeli, W. B. (2002). Inequity at work: Its measurement and association with worker health. *Work & Stress, 16,* 287–301. http://dx.doi.org/10.1080/0267837021000054500

Tekleab, A. G., & Taylor, M. S. (2003). Aren't there two parties in an employment relationship? Antecedents and consequences of organization–employee agreement on contract obligations and violations. *Journal of Organizational Behavior*, *24*, 585–608. http://dx.doi.org/10.1002/job.204

Tetrick, L. E., & Haimann, C. R. (2014). Employee recognition. In A. Day, E. K. Kelloway, & J. J. Hurrell, Jr. (Eds.), *Workplace well-being: Building positive and psychologically healthy workplaces* (pp. 161–174). Oxford, England: Wiley-Blackwell.

Tetrick, L. E., & Peiró, J. M. (2012). Occupational safety and health. In S. W. J. Kozlowski (Ed.), *The Oxford handbook of organizational psychology* (Vol. 2, pp. 1228–1244). New York, NY: Oxford University Press.

Tetrick, L. E., Quick, J. C., & Gilmore, P. L. (2012). Research in organizational interventions to improve well-being: Perspectives on organizational change and development. In C. Biron, M. Karanika-Murray, & C. L. Cooper (Eds.), *Improving organizational interventions for stress and well-being: Addressing process and context* (pp. 59–76). East Sussex, England: Routledge.

Tetrick, L. E., Quick, J. C., & Quick, J. D. (2005). Prevention perspectives in occupational health psychology. In A. G. Antoniou & C. L. Cooper (Eds.), *Research companion to organizational health psychology* (pp. 209–217). Cheltenham, England: Edward Elgar. http://dx.doi.org/10.4337/9781845423308.00022

Tetrick, L. E., Shore, L. M., Bommer, W. H., & Wayne, S. J. (2001, April). *Effects of perceptions of employers' failure to keep their promises: An application of ELVN-P*. Paper presented at the annual meeting of the Society for Industrial and Organizational Psychology, San Diego, CA.

Townsend, J., Phillips, J. S., & Elkins, T. J. (2000). Employee retaliation: The neglected consequence of poor leader-member exchange relations. *Journal of Occupational Health Psychology*, *5*, 457–463. http://dx.doi.org/10.1037/1076-8998.5.4.457

Tsutsumi, A., & Kawakami, N. (2004). A review of empirical studies on the model of effort-reward imbalance at work: Reducing occupational stress by implementing a new theory. *Social Science & Medicine*, *59*, 2335–2359. http://dx.doi.org/10.1016/j.socscimed.2004.03.030

Tucker, J. S., Sinclair, R. R., Mohr, C. D., Adler, A. B., Thomas, J. L., & Salvi, A. D. (2008). A temporal investigation of the direct, interactive, and reverse relations between demand and control and affective strain. *Work & Stress*, *22*, 81–95. http://dx.doi.org/10.1080/02678370802190383

Uhl-Bien, M., Graen, G. B., & Scandura, T. (2000). Implications of leader-member exchange (LMX) for strategic human resource management systems: Relationships as social capital for competitive advantage. In G. R. Ferris (Ed.), *Research in personnel and human resources management* (Vol. 18, pp. 137–185). Oxford, England: JAI Press/Elsevier Science.

Walsh, M., Dupré, K., & Arnold, K. A. (2014). Processes through which transformational leaders affect employee psychological health. *German Journal of Research in Human Resource Management*, *28*, 162–172.

Walumbwa, F. O., Cropanzano, R., & Hartnell, C. A. (2009). Organizational justice, voluntary learning behavior, and job performance: A test of the mediating effects of identification and leader-member exchange. *Journal of Organizational Behavior, 30,* 1103–1126. http://dx.doi.org/10.1002/job.611

Walumbwa, F. O., & Lawler, J. J. (2003). Building effective organizations: Transformational leadership, collectivist orientation, work-related attitudes and withdrawal behaviors in three emerging economies. *The International Journal of Human Resource Management, 14,* 1083–1101. http://dx.doi.org/10.1080/0958519032000114219

Walumbwa, F. O., Lawler, J. J., & Avolio, B. J. (2007). Leadership, individual differences, and work-related attitudes: A cross-culture investigation. *Applied Psychology, 56,* 212–230. http://dx.doi.org/10.1111/j.1464-0597.2006.00241.x

Warr, P. B. (1987). *Work, unemployment, and mental health.* Oxford, England: Oxford University Press.

Warr, P. B. (2007). *Work, happiness, and unhappiness.* Mahwah, NJ: Erlbaum.

Wilson, M. G., DeJoy, D. M., Vandenberg, R. J., Richardson, H. A., & McGrath, A. L. (2004). Work characteristics and employee health and well-being. Test of a model of healthy work organization. *Journal of Occupational and Organizational Psychology, 77,* 565–588. http://dx.doi.org/10.1348/0963179042596522

Xie, J. L., & Johns, G. (1995). Job scope and stress. Can job scope be too high? *Academy of Management Journal, 38,* 1288–1309. http://dx.doi.org/10.2307/256858

Zohar, D. M. (1980). Safety climate in industrial organizations: Theoretical and applied implications. *Journal of Applied Psychology, 65,* 96–102. http://dx.doi.org/10.1037/0021-9010.65.1.96

Zohar, D. M. (2002). The effects of leadership dimensions, safety climate, and assigned priorities on minor injuries in work groups. *Journal of Organizational Behavior, 23,* 75–92. http://dx.doi.org/10.1002/job.130

Zohar, D. M. (2011). Safety climate: Conceptual and measurement issues. In J. C. Quick & L. E. Tetrick (Eds.), *Handbook of occupational health psychology* (2nd ed., pp. 141–164). Washington, DC: American Psychological Association.

Zohar, D. M., & Hofmann, D. A. (2012). Organizational culture and climate. In S. W. J. Kozlowski (Ed.), *The Oxford handbook of organizational psychology* (Vol. 1, pp. 643–666). New York, NY: Oxford University Press.

10

HEALTH AND SAFETY: PERSPECTIVES FROM THE FIELD

REBECCA K. KELLY AND MELONDIE CARTER

This chapter provides a review of health and safety initiatives, including key components, tips for organizations and managers interested in designing health and safety programs, practical examples, and challenges related to the development, implementation, and evaluation of such programs.

Workplace health and safety programs are designed to improve the physical and mental health of employees and promote healthy lifestyle and behavior choices. By investing in the health and safety of their employees, organizations may benefit from greater productivity and reductions in health care costs, absenteeism, and accident/injury rates (Centers for Disease Control and Prevention [CDC], 2015). Practical efforts to address health and safety issues in the workplace include (a) training and safeguards that address workplace safety and security; (b) health improvement efforts to include programs related to stress management, weight control, and tobacco cessation; (c) adequate physical and mental health benefit coverage; (d) health screenings; (e) access to fitness

http://dx.doi.org/10.1037/14731-011
The Psychologically Healthy Workplace: Building a Win–Win Environment for Organizations and Employees,
M. J. Grawitch and D. W. Ballard (Editors)

and recreation opportunities; and (f) promotion and coordination of health-related resources addressing work–life issues to include employee assistance programs and referrals for mental health services (American Psychological Association [APA], Center for Organizational Excellence, 2015).

THE BUSINESS CASE FOR WORKSITE HEALTH AND SAFETY PROGRAMS

Employees are frequently spoken of as critical business assets, and yet many organizations treat workplace practices benefitting employees as costs of doing business rather than investments in the functioning and success of the company. The business case for and the value of safety programs have been more commonly understood in many corporate sectors. In addition to federal and state regulations related to safety practices, organizations can clearly measure the impact of an accident in terms of both cost and loss of productivity (Committee on the Review of NIOSH Research Programs & Institute of Medicine and National Research Council, 2009).

In contrast to safety programs, the business case for health and wellness programs has been more readily accepted only in recent years. In addition to an increase in health insurance premiums resulting from higher medical costs, employers are also facing the impact of poor health with increases in absenteeism, presenteeism, workers' compensation claims, disability claims, and life insurance premiums (Baicker, Cutler, & Song, 2010; Chapman, 2012; Kaspin, Gorman, & Miller, 2013; Loeppke et al., 2009; Pelletier, 2001). Workplace health promotion represents one of the most significant strategies for enhancing workers' health and productivity. According to a comprehensive review of the literature in health and safety programs, both an investment of money and a commitment of time are essential. Chapman (2012) updated his previous meta-analysis by analyzing 62 peer-reviewed journal articles and found that, in general, health promotion programs have been effective in improving employee health, with a positive economic return. The summary of evidence demonstrates reductions of approximately 25% in sick leave, health plan costs, workers' compensation, and disability insurance costs.

In addition, Baicker et al. (2010) conducted a meta-analysis of 32 original publications exploring both health care costs and savings associated with workplace wellness programs. Results indicated that for each dollar spent on wellness programs, medical costs dropped by $3.27 and costs related to absenteeism were reduced by $2.73. This suggests that greater adoption of workplace health programs can be beneficial for employers as both a cost-saving and productivity-enhancing strategy.

More recently, Goetzel et al. (2014) determined that a review of the past 3 decades of workplace employee health programs showed favorable health and financial outcomes for organizations. Programs must be not only well-designed and delivered but also grounded in evidence-based principles of health promotion.

APA's (2008) publication *By the Numbers: A Psychologically Healthy Workplace Fact Sheet* aggregates high-impact statistics about the trends in and effectiveness of healthy workplace practices and can be a useful resource for human resources professionals, consultants, and others who need to communicate the business case for health and safety programs to their organizations' leaders. The fact sheet provides reliable information about workplace issues and practices, including workplace stress, work demands, work–life balance and flexibility, employee health and health care costs, mental health, and employee and organizational outcomes.

Employee health and safety programs strive to promote a healthy and safe workplace for employees, promote a healthy lifestyle for individuals, and identify strategies to prevent or delay the onset of chronic health conditions. Such programs also work to maintain or improve health while reducing the risk of injury and illness.

KEY CHARACTERISTICS OF A SUCCESSFUL HEALTH AND SAFETY PROGRAM

Kaspin et al. (2013) noted that successful workplace health and safety programs use a connection between the program and corporate culture. Employees and their leadership are highly motivated to support health programs, and employees are supported by policies that promote wellness programs and create a healthy environment. Programs evolve on the basis of the continually changing needs and interests of the employees; and local community health organizations provide support, education, and treatment. Finally, successful programs use technology to facilitate health-risk assessments and wellness education.

These characteristics align with APA's systems-based approach to addressing employee well-being and organizational performance. Knowing an organization's culture and workplace characteristics can help an employer develop more effective messages and policies around employee health.

CAPTURING SENIOR-LEVEL MANAGEMENT SUPPORT

Critical to the success of any initiative at the workplace is the willingness of managers and senior-level leaders to set a strategic vision, establish goals, and move to achieve or exceed such goals. Identifying the business case for a health and safety program is necessary to initiate and maintain the support of senior-level management. This senior-level support will help build a culture of health and safety in the workplace and promote employee participation in programs that are developed.

To obtain and sustain the support of senior-level management, managers and consultants should keep abreast of industry best practices and the programs that are demonstrating cost savings and share these and other recent research developments with senior- and mid-level managers. They should describe the effects of the health promotion initiatives on workflow, productivity, and employee morale. Once programs have been put in place, managers should keep communication lines open and continually evaluate the programs and initiatives and provide senior-level administration updates on participation numbers, testimonials, health care costs, claims data, and absenteeism reports.

Senior-level administrators are often interested in staying updated on the progress of and insight from their peers. The Partnership for Prevention's series of publications titled *Leading by Example* provides practical examples of how CEOs and their organizations can align health and safety programs with their core business strategies (see http://www.prevent.org/Initiatives/Leading-by-Example.aspx). These publications provide an assessment of health management initiatives, CEO perspectives on employee health, and highlights from leading health and safety programs.

ASSESSING WORKPLACE HEALTH AND SAFETY PROGRAMS

It is important for organizations and managers to understand their current practices and review their previous efforts when building or expanding a workplace health and safety program. An organizational assessment can help determine the progress, limitations, and future goals for a program. During the assessment, multiple components should be addressed, including workplace culture, leadership support, facilities, communication methods, current wellness programming, employee health benefits and policies, and access to data to evaluate the program.

Comprehensive workplace health and safety assessments should be done prior to developing any new initiatives and then again at least every 2 years as follow-up assessments to identify program changes that may be needed. Key components of the workplace health and safety assessment include (a) key stakeholder interviews, (b) focus groups, (c) employee demographics and surveys, (d) environmental assessments, and (e) benchmarking analyses.

Key Stakeholder Interviews

The purpose of the key stakeholder interview is to better understand business needs and the link to employee health, safety, and productivity while identifying potential causes of poor health and loss of productivity. Key stakeholders usually include the CEO or president, chief financial officer, and one or more vice presidents. Interview results help to shape a program's overall mission, goals, and strategy. Exhibit 10.1 outlines sample interview questions that can be prepared when meeting with key organizational stakeholders. The interview usually begins with the identification of the goal of the health and safety program, for example, "To build an environment that fosters a wellness culture."

Focus Groups

Employee focus groups can help organizations elicit suggestions for ways in which health and safety programs may better meet the needs of employees and their family members (if appropriate). Focus groups can also serve as an opportunity to collect information on the health and safety issues about which employees are concerned and that are most pertinent to their health.

Focus groups can also explore which types of educational sessions employees prefer—individual coaching sessions, group classes, online courses, self-guided study programs, books, or brochures. This feedback will help organizations better design effective communication tools and educational opportunities. Key findings from any focus group should be summarized and reported to the stakeholders and used in strategic planning for the program (Table 10.1 provides an outline and sample focus group questions).

EXHIBIT 10.1
Sample Stakeholder Interview Questions

Describe the health issues of your employees.

In your opinion, describe the most valuable benefit you could attain from providing a health and safety program.

What types of health and safety programs do you feel are necessary to achieve this benefit?

As you think about the next 5 years, what is the most important health and safety issue that your organization faces? How does this issue affect individual performance and business success?

What are the greatest challenges of implementing a health and safety program within the organization?

Using four measures, how would you define a successful health and safety program?

What are the key financial goals for your organization (e.g., increase in revenue, improvement in margins, reduction in employee health care costs, higher return on assets)?

Are there specific employee performance and safety goals, and if so, what are they?

TABLE 10.1
Sample Focus Group Questions and Outline

Sample	Description
Representative population	8 to 10 employees with varying representatives from multiple departments, shifts, and levels within the organization.
Purpose	To discuss the employee's thoughts on worksite health programs for designing a well-constructed program that meets the needs of the employees.
Questions	• How do you define health? What does being healthy mean to you? • What areas of health would you be interested in learning more about? • As you think about the next 5 years, what are the most important issues you and your family face in order to achieve good physical health? • As you think about the next 2 years, what are the most important safety issues you and your coworkers face? • What type of educational programs would be beneficial for employees to learn how to deal with these health and safety concerns? • Rank-order your preferred learning methods (e.g., face-to-face: lectures, sharing ideas/knowledge with each other, discussions, sharing stories; communication vehicles: movies, reading, Internet research, experience, etc.). • On a scale of 1–5 (1 = *little*, 3 = *good*, 5 = *great*), how much control do you have over your health? • On a scale of 1–5 (1 = *little*, 3 = *good*, 5 = *great*), how much control do you have over your safety at work? • What challenges are in the way of being successful with any health changes? • What challenges are in the way of being successful with workplace safety? • What does a healthy and safe work environment look like to you? • What are your personal motivators (e.g., being a role model for my family members, feeling better, looking good, compliments, winning/competitions, peer pressure, saving money, avoiding injury or sickness, or other consequences)? • Please tell us what health activities you are currently involved in at home, in your community or at work?

Employee Demographics and Surveys

Even though health and safety programs are tailored to address the needs of a specific employee population, employee and family participation and adherence are vital to the effectiveness of these programs. To better understand the opportunities for enhancing participation levels, program managers must consider important employee and plan member demographics. Working with the organization's human resources, safety, and health departments allows an organization to capture data on employees' and dependents' gender, age, educational level, job role, absenteeism because of personal illness, health care costs, and worker's compensation costs for the previous 2 to 3 years, which will assist in the design of health and safety interventions.

Another aspect of program planning is to explore the health disparities that exist among people of varying race, ethnicity, gender, age, income level, and geographic location. In addition, health resources must be sensitive to health literacy and be time sensitive to attract all segments of the workforce. Because many employees elect family coverage, efforts must be made to target health improvement solutions not only for the employee but also for his or her spouse and family members.

Organizations may also want to gather health care cost data. By gathering these data, an organization can identify the most critical health issues for its particular workplace on the basis of disease and cost of medications. Information may include the last 2 to 3 years of the most costly major disease categories by number of claims and cost by category, the most costly therapeutic classes of drugs, and the most frequently prescribed and filled therapeutic classes of drugs.

Furthermore, by using health promotion cost calculators and worksheets, an estimate of potential financial savings can help make the case for health and safety programs to senior leaders. The CDC developed the Healthier Worksite Initiative (2010b) to include online cost calculators specific to depression, tobacco use, alcohol use, physical activity, and obesity. These calculators help organizations estimate the costs of lifestyle factors and preventable diseases. An alternative health care costs and return on investment (ROI) calculator is available online at the WellSteps website, which also provides a free tool with references linked to its use (see http://www.wellsteps.com/roi/resources_tools_roi_cal_health.php).

Environmental Assessment

Numerous tools are available to use to identify opportunities for improving the environment and culture of an organization in ways that support healthy behaviors at the individual level. An organization's health and safety environment and culture can be crucial to the success of a workplace wellness program. Environment and culture include the attitudes of employees, managers, and senior leaders toward healthy behaviors such as physical activity, proper nutrition, and being tobacco free. They also include manager and supervisor attitudes toward employees taking time to participate in initiatives such as stretch breaks, tobacco cessation programs, and diabetes education classes. It is important to explore the workplace environment to determine whether it supports or hinders the efforts to promote employee health. For example, does the on-site cafeteria have healthy food options?

Are healthy snacks available in vending machines? Do supervisors support employees who wish to work out an extra 15 minutes at lunch with a flexible work option? Sample audits are available online at the CDC (2010c) Healthier Worksite Initiative.

Surveys and Health and Safety Assessments

In the design and planning of a health and safety program, the organization and managers can benefit from benchmarking assessment tools. These tools provide valuable content to assist an organization in establishing a strategic plan, engaging leadership support, building organizational and staffing infrastructures, defining the program components, identifying the keys to employee engagement, and completing the methods for program measurement and evaluation. These tools are valuable for the early stages of program planning and for updating more advanced or mature programs. These assessment tools can help organizations identify the gaps and opportunities for improvement within their program and serve as instruments for recognition and awards. Individual health assessment tools and surveys are also valuable in helping to guide an organization's overall health and safety plan. These assessments are available through simple questionnaires or advanced online assessments with tailored messages and can be a part of the program's benchmarking for individual and organizational change. (Table 10.2 lists resources for health and safety evaluation and recognition tools.)

TABLE 10.2
Health and Safety Survey Assessment Tools

Resource	Website
CDC Worksite Health ScoreCard	http://www.cdc.gov/dhdsp/pubs/docs/HSC_Manual.pdf
Health Enhancement Resource Organization (HERO) Employee Health Management Best Practice Scorecard	http://hero-health.org/scorecard/
The Health Project's C. Everett Koop National Health Award criteria	http://www.thehealthproject.com/award-information/
Occupational Safety and Health Workforce Assessment Employer and Provider Survey Instruments	http://www.cdc.gov/niosh/oshworkforce/
Partnership for Prevention's Leading by Example Health Publications	http://www.prevent.org/Initiatives/Leading-by-Example.aspx
U.S. Department of Health and Human Services, Healthy People 2020 Program Planning Tools	http://www.healthypeople.gov/2020/tools-and-resources/program-planning

CONNECTING KEY ELEMENTS OF AN OPERATING PLAN WITH PRACTICAL EXAMPLES

Building on the assessment and business case for health and safety programs and taking the next step following the design of a health and safety program, a strategic operating plan is essential. This plan should align the program with the vision, goals, and objectives of the organization and include a marketing and communication plan, the infrastructure necessary to successfully deliver the program, implementation strategies, timeline, resources, budget details, and an evaluation plan.

Vision Statement

Guiding an organization and the health and safety program, a vision statement provides a direction for the future, whereas the goals provide concrete statements that define what the health and safety program is intended to achieve. An example of an organization whose vision and goals include an emphasis on health and safety programs is Lincoln Industries, the nation's leading supplier of products requiring high-performance metal finishing. Lincoln Industries has been recognized as a leader in creating a corporate culture of talent, health, and well-being. According to chair and CEO Marc LeBaron (2009), "creating a great culture has been the right strategy for many good reasons. The health and happiness of our people—and our company—top the list" (p. 10). By design, Lincoln Industries included the statement that "wellness and healthy lifestyles are important to our success" (p. 10) as one of the core beliefs and drivers for the organization. This approach has led Lincoln Industries to be recognized as a national leader in health, wellness and safety (Lincoln Industries, 2012). With its nationally recognized wellness program, Lincoln Industries strives to engage its workforce, believing that healthier employees are both happier and more productive.

Objectives

Writing good objectives is a challenging task that demands significant effort on the part of the organization. To be successful, objectives should be specific, measurable, attainable, realistic, and time bound (i.e., the SMART method; Doran, 1981). Objectives that are specific are clearly written and easily understood. Measurable objectives involve how the standard needs to be reached and includes a quantity metric. Objectives are attainable if they are appropriate for the organization or individual and realistic if the organization or individual can meet the expected outcome. Objectives should also be time bound to meet the overarching goal.

L. L. Bean Corporation is a three-time C. Everett Koop National Health Award Winner (Health Project, 2012). The goal of L. L. Bean's Employee Health, Safety and Wellness program is to provide programs and create an environment that encourages people to take individual responsibility for achieving their personal best in health and safety. L. L. Bean has identified safety and health improvement goals and objectives using the SMART method. The goal of L. L. Bean's Healthy Bean program is to provide programming and create an environment that encourages people to take individual responsibility for achieving their personal best in health and safety (Health Project, 2012). The company's annual objectives have included the following: (a) increase the overall health, fitness, and related quality of life of employees (e.g., improve employee health habits to be comparable with the 75th percentile of healthiest companies); (b) reduce injuries and illnesses; (c) reduce time lost from work; and (d) reduce health care, workers' compensation, disability, and absenteeism costs.

Each objective is further defined by the L. L. Bean program director and by their wellness team. Once defined, goals and objectives are measured with an intent for annual achievement. L. L. Bean provides its employees a variety of health education and physical activity classes, subsidizing the expenses in an effort to keep them affordable. The company also tailors its health improvement offerings for different areas within the company on the basis of aggregate data obtained from health-risk appraisals. Targeted health risks include weight control, physical activity, heart health, diabetes management, and mental health programming.

Implementation and Timeline

This section of the operating plan provides detailed information specific to program implementation and a timeline to include the dates, times, and locations of program services and events. Information concerning individual responsibilities and methods of accountability can also be contained in the operating plan. The implementation timeline can be very effective in helping to guide the overall direction and plan for the program.

Marketing and Communications Plan

Organizations can use a variety of marketing and communication vehicles to get their message out to employees. Brochures and newsletters, e-mail, Intranet, website, social media, videos, digital signage, promotions and training are all potential mechanisms for disseminating information. Focus groups can assist organizations with determining the best methods of communication and marketing to capture the highest level of engagement. One of the main challenges in the design of an effective program is to identify the optimal contexts, channels, content, and reasons that will motivate people to pay attention to and use health information. In such an environment, people do not always pay attention to all communications they receive, but they may selectively attend to and purposefully seek out information.

An effective communications plan should begin by identifying the health behavior you are trying to influence and considering the timing of when you want to promote it. Next, the target audience should be defined by age, gender, education level, and income level, to explore what motivates them and the best way to reach them. Finally, the unique qualities of the target audience—interests, preferred activities, values, life goals, concerns, work habits and biases—should be determined.

Many organizations can tap into their existing marketing, advertising, public relations, or communications departments to assist in implementing focus groups (consisting of individuals from the target audience), crafting messages, developing a communications plan, and measuring results. However, organizations do not need a lot of resources to accomplish this step. Informal techniques such as one-on-one conversations with coworkers, friends, and family can also help the organization better understand its audience.

After defining the target population and following the steps for designing an effective communication plan, crafting compelling or motivating messages to the target audience can be a challenge. As an example, the CDCynergy Program (CDC, 2010a) recommends testing concepts on your audience so that you can develop the most effective messages possible. Concept data can be collected from primary and secondary sources. Important questions to consider when designing a communication campaign include: What appeals to the target audience? What do employees want to hear and see? What motivates them? What are their information needs? And what strengths and resources do employees have that can be considered in designing concepts?

After concept testing the target population, organizations can develop a more accurate message that delivers upon the key characteristics of clarity, consistency, main points, correct tone, truthfulness, credibility, and audience relevance.

Infrastructure

For many organizations, building a health promotion infrastructure begins with identifying a coordinator of health and safety. Individuals responsible for carrying out these program goals may vary from organization to organization, from directors of safety to employee benefits specialist in the human resources department, or others. It is important to dedicate staff that have expertise in the areas of health and safety. Desirable characteristics include interest and experience in health and fitness or safety, solid communications skills, experience in health behavior change, environmental audits, and program design and implementation, as well as strong assessment and evaluation skills.

Organize Wellness Committees

To integrate a workplace health and safety program into an organization's culture, committees or teams should be organized with representation from all levels of the organization, from entry level to upper management. Obtaining upper management buy-in is essential to launching and maintaining an effective program. Employees must understand that management is supportive of the wellness initiative. A steering committee with representatives from upper management can guide the program at a high level by setting priorities and designating resources. Another committee can be created to oversee the actual design and delivery of the initiative. The size and enthusiasm of an organization will determine the number of committees necessary for the wellness initiatives.

At the University of Alabama, the organizational structure for promoting a healthy culture is guided by the director of the Office of Health Promotion and Wellness in collaboration with a variety of individuals and groups, including the provost; the Wellness Advisory Board; ambassadors of health, who serve as liaisons between their respective departments, colleges, or schools and the Office of Health Promotion and Wellness; the staff of the Office of Health Promotion and Wellness; and multiple departments, colleges, and schools. Each entity plays a pivotal role in creating a healthy workplace infrastructure.

The provost is a key leader who models top-down health behaviors to create an environment for an initiative's success. She or he serves to provide the overarching vision, support, and direction. This individual communicates support and, along with the president and other high-level executives, offers financial support, and participates in monthly updates and meetings with the director of the Office of Health Promotion and Wellness.

The director of the Office of Health Promotion and Wellness works closely with the advisory board to create the strategic vision, mission, goals, and objectives. The staff members also design the health promotion and wellness programs. This office is responsible for coordinating resources to oversee and evaluate the health promotion and wellness program, developing the communication and marketing strategy, and integrating resources for maximum efficiency.

The Wellness Advisory Board is a group of up to 15 members who provide guiding advice and support for the Office of Health Promotion and

Wellness and serve as champions for the faculty and staff wellness program. Board members identify opportunities, resources, and tools for the wellness program and provide resources (e.g., time, students, services).

Wellness coordinators serve as program spokespersons and help to deliver the message of health; recruit for program offerings; and share health-related resources, tools, and services with their respective departments, colleges, and schools.

Leveraging Resources

Where health and safety initiatives are not yet firmly established, there is a need to identify other individuals, support departments, or partners to assist in planning, implementation, and evaluation. Sometimes current employees do not have the health program planning or behavior change expertise needed for designing effective health promotion programs. Financial savings may be gained by purchasing a preexisting program that has the evaluation data behind it to support its effectiveness, and outside partners or staff can be recruited to implement or complete evaluations for the workplace, or even design, deliver, and evaluate an initiative.

Potential partners may include health plans, employee assistance programs, human resources departments, community health departments and health care organizations, and other local and community health groups. These partners may offer support for health and safety initiatives, health-risk assessments, staff to support initiatives, and data for analysis. Unions may also provide business representatives for the bargaining unit to support the health and safety programs. In addition, community partners can include health care facilities, nonprofit health related agencies, county health departments, universities and colleges, local recreation and fitness centers, and food service and grocery stores that make free or low-cost health and wellness resources available to employers.

Itemized Budget

Health promotion programs need not require enormous resources; but for them to be effective, an investment in the health and safety of employees is essential. This portion of the plan should provide comprehensive information concerning the amount of money it will take to achieve the desired outcomes. Determining the amount to budget for an effective, comprehensive health and safety program requires consideration by management as well as a review of the literature. Health care expert and researcher Ron Goetzel recommended an investment of $200 to $500 per employee per year for a health improvement program (Wellness Council of America, 2012). Goetzel further suggested that programs cover the costs for a comprehensive program design to allow for the best ROI. Budgets for safety programs vary greatly by industry setting. The investment for a safety program would depend on the nature of the industry.

A health and safety program budget may include salaries for staff or contract employees, fees for space, equipment, and supplies, educational and communication tools and materials, as well as incentives, legal expenses, and other health- and safety-related needs. (See http://www.cdc.gov/national healthyworksite/docs/Sample_Worksite_Health_Budget_508.pdf for a sample budget.)

Although the employer carries the primary cost of the program, the employee can often share expenses, such as paying a portion of the enrollment fee for a weight loss class or receiving reimbursement for a gym membership. Rewards and prizes can be used to increase the number of participants in a workplace wellness program. They can be as small as free fruit and pedometers or as large as exercise equipment, paid time off, and gift certificates. Incentives continue to be used extensively for engaging and sustaining employee participation in health and safety programs.

The Right Incentives to Reach and Engage the Members

A well-designed and well-implemented incentive strategy can generate interest, provide a tangible goal and catalyst for change, and support the organization's commitment to employee health. Employers are increasingly using incentives to encourage employee participation in wellness programs. Effective in 2014, the Affordable Care Act allows the total amount of wellness program rewards to increase to 30% of health benefit costs. Employers are also linking participation in wellness programs to the cost of health coverage for the employee (e.g., by decreasing the amount the employee must pay in deductibles for health care services; Health Affairs, 2012).

Incentives can increase simple behaviors such as completion of a health screening or a health-risk appraisal. Employers implementing incentives may want to consider additional types of monetary or nonmonetary incentive approaches designed to increase participation in wellness programs. According to a number of medical organizations, examples of participation-based incentives opportunities include: reimbursement of the partial or full cost for membership in a fitness center, diagnostic testing participation award, waiving a deductible to increase preventive care, reimbursement for smoking cessation programs, allowing company time for participation in wellness events, and recognizing achievements through token giveaways.

Some industry experts believe that incentive amounts ranging from $40 to $60 per month are enough to promote behavior change for many participants. Incentives of greater cash value my decrease the development of intrinsic motivation, which aids the employee in sustaining needed change. The Consensus Statement of the Health Enhancement Research Organization, American College of Occupational and Environmental Medicine, American Cancer Society and American Cancer Society Cancer Action Network, American Diabetes Association, and American Heart Association (2012) recommends considering the following questions when determining the incentive amount:

> (a) Does the incentive amount fit with your culture? (b) Will the incentive amount drive behavior change? (c) If penalties are used, will they have disproportionate financial impact across different levels or racial/ethnic groups? (d) Is the incentive so large that it results in significant cost shifting to nonparticipating or nonattaining employees, jeopardizing their ability to afford coverage? (p. 894)

In addition, it is important to remember that cash benefit incentives may have tax implications for the employee. Program managers are encouraged to work with benefits managers to consider any tax implications of the health and safety program, as taxes may diminish the value and power of the incentive. It is advised that employers seek legal consultation prior to administering an incentive to their employee population.

Removing Barriers so More Employees Can Participate

In some cases, identifying and eliminating the barriers that keep individuals from participating may be an effective approach in combination with, or in place of, offering incentives. To remove barriers, consider offering programs at convenient times, on company time, and with child care options. It is important to create a supportive environment, which includes getting management involved in programs, giving employees an opportunity to establish ownership in the program, and establishing a highly visible healthy organizational culture. Finally, try and remove financial burdens such as material or registration fees or other program costs.

O'Neal Industries, a family of closely related companies, all engaged in the metals service center business, utilizes a fitness and recreation reimbursement policy. Launched in 2011, O'Neal's signature health and wellness program (LiveSMART Go Platinum!) provides comprehensive health, wellness, and safety programs for their approximately 2,800 U.S. employees. As a benefit to participation, wellness participants can receive reimbursement of up to 50% or $400 per year for fitness, recreation, and health-related expenses, including memberships to fitness centers, personal training sessions, and enrollment in local and national fitness events (O'Neal Industries, 2012).

Evaluation Plan

The final section of the operating plan is the evaluation of the program. Information to guide evaluation can be garnered from the results of the key stakeholder interviews. There are two basic types of program evaluations: process and outcome evaluations (CDC, 2010c). Process evaluations are used to determine if the program design and delivery is working well. This type of evaluation explores aspects of the program activities, staffing, budget, immediate impact of the intervention, and if components were delivered as planned. Process evaluations are usually conducted during the time of the program delivery or thereafter and may include participation rates, program costs, and satisfaction.

Outcome evaluations explore the greater impact of the program and determine if the goals and objectives were met. This type of evaluation may include changes of participant attitudes, knowledge, and behaviors, as well as clinical health indicators and risk factors (e.g., body mass index, blood pressure, cholesterol value). Outcome evaluations may also explore the cost benefit and/or ROI of a program and includes measures of absenteeism, productivity, medical cost, and utilization, as well as baseline and follow-up measurements of participants' health status. To evaluate a health improvement program, we define value using the elements highlighted in Table 10.3.

Ongoing monitoring and annual evaluation of the health improvement program require an understanding of how to quantify the desired outcomes and what type of data to collect that will be valid and repeatable for demonstrating progress and effect. As noted earlier, sample program evaluation and ROI tools are available.

DELIVERING AN EFFECTIVE HEALTH AND SAFETY PROGRAM

There are many different ways to positively influence behavior change. A coordinated, systematic, and comprehensive wellness program will include a variety of offerings because no one approach is a "perfect" fit for everyone. The coordinated plan must include a comprehensive approach and inclusion of programs, policies, health benefits, and health care plan, as well as positive leadership and environmental support. Addressing both individuals and groups can be beneficial. According to the CDC's (2013) Workplace Health Model, a comprehensive approach looks to put interventions in place that address multiple risk factors and health conditions concurrently and recognizes that the interventions and strategies chosen influence multiple levels of the organization, including the individual employee and the organization as a whole.

TABLE 10.3
Key Metrics for Consideration With Health Improvement Programs

Program evaluation metrics	Goals
Participation: Based on practical experience, employee participation is critical for success in a health improvement program. It is recommended that up to 90% participation (over a 3-year period) be achieved. Participation levels will be recorded every 12 months and compared with the previous 12 months if applicable.	Goal: 80% of workforce participated in at least one signature health program within 12 months; 80% of the participating employees felt program was very or extremely valuable.
Health status: Based on related research and practical experience, up to 50% of individuals should modify their behavior relating to measurement of health risk. Behavior change should begin immediately with noted achievements completed during a 3-year period.	Goal: 30% of participants improved health status; percentage of participants that is categorized as low risk/healthy; annual increment of change of clinical health indicators of those participating.
Effect on business: Includes cost and performance that resulted from a healthy and safe prepared workforce. Improved health status correlates to job performance, which may include absenteeism, health care costs, disability and workers' compensation claims.	Goal: 30% of participants improved health status; percentage of participants that is categorized as low risk/healthy; annual increment of change of clinical health indicators of those participating.
Quality of life: Includes thriving workers and family members who take personal responsibility for their health, guide and participate in healthy behaviors at work, embrace workplace health and safety policies and environments, and encourage one another to be healthy and safe each day.	Goal: A culture of health and safety at work, at home, and into retirement.

Key Interventions

Core components of health and wellness programs include interventions that address physical health, nutrition and weight management, tobacco control, stress management, injury prevention, and ergonomics, as well as condition-specific health program such as diabetes prevention and management. Programs tailored to individuals can create motivation and change in employees by increasing knowledge, influencing attitudes, and changing beliefs, and vehicles can include one-on-one coaching, classes, interactive web-based approaches, and self-study courses. Useful emerging technologies include telemedicine, social networks, and mobile applications (Towers Watson/National Business Group on Health, 2013).

The body of literature surrounding health behavior is rich with theories, models, and frameworks that help to explain behavior as well as provide steps to planning program interventions. Many examples for practitioners can be found in a monograph publication describing the many theories of health-related behaviors, processing of modifying behaviors, and the effects of community and environmental factors on behavior (National Cancer Institute, 2005). One of the most popular health behavior models used is the stages of change (transtheoretical) model. Developed by Prochaska and DiClemente (1983), the basic premise of the stages of change model is that behavior change is a process, not an event. As individuals attempt to modify a behavior, they move through one of five stages: precontemplation, contemplation, preparation, action, and maintenance. Each stage is an opportunity to provide different educational information and interventions tailored to the needs of the individual. This is one of many behavior change models that have been cited most commonly in regards to employee health programs. Others models and frameworks address not only individuals but also organizational change processes (National Cancer Institute, 2005).

Health Screening

Biometric health screening continues to serve as a core element of the University of Alabama's health and wellness programs and follows the biometric health screening guidelines set forth for employers. Outsourced and collaborative models that combine health screening and follow-up health coaching have helped employees to better understand their health status (Carter, Kelly, Alexander, & Holmes, 2011; see also Health Enhancement Research Organization, American College of Occupational and Environmental Medicine, and Care Continuum Alliance, 2013). In an effort to advance the health and well-being of University of Alabama employees, the Office of Health Promotion and Wellness developed WellBAMA, a collaborative health promotion and wellness model. WellBAMA partners with the Capstone College of Nursing to provide health screening and health coaching services to faculty and staff through its outreach efforts. Baseline and annual follow-up measures include body mass index, blood pressure, blood work (i.e., glucose, lipids), tobacco status, exercise status, as well as a health-risk questionnaire.

Health and safety programs that include a group focus recognize that group support and social identity are important and therefore can enhance motivation, adherence, and self-efficacy. Examples include buddy systems, clubs, support groups, and team-based health challenges. A sample program is Strive for Five, a team-based health improvement program and one of the many signature health and wellness programs offered at The University of

Alabama. Strive for Five is a 2-month program that encourages faculty and staff to adopt healthier lifestyle behaviors, be more physically active, and maintain or lose weight. The program includes free information, activities, incentives, educational sessions, check-ins, and the support of health and wellness staff to help participants reach their goals. Individuals and teams of up to five people select two or more health improvement daily goals from the following list: eat five or more fruits and vegetables; drink 5 of more cups of water; think five positive messages; move 5 days and 30 minutes each week; and maintain or lose 5 pounds of weight during the 2 months. With approximately 30% of all faculty and staff participating each year, this health improvement program has been accepted as a part of the healthy environment and culture at the university.

Offering both health improvement and disease management programs is also important. Health improvement efforts focus on promoting healthy lifestyles such as physical activity, healthy eating, tobacco cessation, and stress management, in contrast with disease management programs, which provide support and resources to assist employees in managing diseases such as hypertension and diabetes. Disease management services may be provided by the organization through onsite clinics or educators, disease management vendors, health plans, or public health organizations.

Finally, the delivery of the program should include a focus on systems-level change to include supportive environment initiatives that increase access to healthy foods (e.g., in vending machines and cafeteria, at meetings or in break rooms) or to places for physical activity (e.g., walking paths, fitness centers, accessible stairwells). Organizational policies are also a valuable aspect of system-wide change. Workplace policies can serve to formalize and reinforce the goals of the wellness program.

Healthy eating policies not only provide an opportunity for employees to eat well but also make it easier to do so. Companies can benefit from policies regarding catered foods for meetings and retreats, food and drinks offered in vending machine. Similarly, implementing tobacco-free workplace policies or programs to assist employees in quitting their tobacco use leads not only to a healthier work environment but also to lower health care costs for employers.

Physical activity policies provide opportunities for employees to incorporate activity into their daily work routines. Policies that encourage stretch breaks during meetings or time allowed to participate in physical activity opportunities during the work day can lead to healthier, more productive, and satisfied employees. Policies and workplace environments are essential in supporting a culture of health to maximize employee visibility and success in maintaining healthy behaviors at the workplace (Aldana et al., 2012).

Explore Programming Options

Once the organization has decided on the preferred approaches to target and prevent risk behaviors, program options can be considered. Programs can take many forms, from group education, self-studies, and computer-based personal coaching to support groups. One of the most important strategies is to ensure that the program reaches all the individuals it is intended to serve. For example, a weight loss program may reach only individuals who are interested in losing weight, yet a nutrition program may engage more of the total population with the ultimate goal of healthy eating, which includes reducing caloric intake if overweight.

Table 10.4 lists several methods of delivery for health and safety programs. It is important to focus on the design and delivery of programs and services that can reach the entire population of employees. This approach will help to maintain the health of those individuals at low risk, identify individuals who have moderate risk and guide them to appropriate resources to reduce those risks, and monitor the health of the high-risk population while identifying the care they need.

TABLE 10.4
Methods of Delivery for Health and Safety Programs

Method of Delivery	Example
Point-of-decision prompts	Signs to increase stair use, early detection health screenings, hydration, hand washing, and fruit and vegetable consumption
Screenings or wellness assessments	Blood pressure, blood cholesterol, blood glucose, height, weight, body mass index, waist circumference, and hearing screenings
Community events	Community health walks, runs, and bicycle rides: Form a worksite team to encourage support and create energy around the event.
Sponsorship	Pay the entry fee for a 5K event. Reduce out-of-pocket costs through reduced gym membership dues or subsidize the cost of fresh fruits and vegetable in the employee cafeteria or vending machines.
Awareness-building initiatives	Posters, bulletin boards, newsletter articles, public health campaign, paycheck stuffers, brochures, and safety meetings
Individual behavior change programs	Online and telephonic counseling services, one-on-one counseling, self-study programs
Group-based/support programs	Walking clubs, safety classes, and one-time seminars
Incentive-based programs	Reimbursements for health club memberships, discounts on community education classes, financial incentives for health promotion participation, gift cards, gifts for no lost work days

Legal Issues

There are various federal regulatory provisions that apply to the design of wellness programs, especially those that include outcomes-based incentives. Therefore, wellness programs must be carefully crafted. Employers should have their legal counsel review any wellness program before it is presented to employees.

CHALLENGES TO HEALTH AND SAFETY PROGRAMS

All organizations have unique challenges related to their health and safety programs. Overall, large organizations may have issues in communicating the program and engaging their workplace in changing behaviors or policies, whereas small organizations may have limited funds to support the staff to deliver a health and safety program. The following section outlines several key issues that face organizations and offers suggestions for how to overcome these barriers.

Lack of Senior- and Mid-Level Leadership Support

One of the most common mistakes made by health promotion professionals is that they fail to take into account the organization's strategic priorities when setting up their programs. As a result, the workplace health promotion initiative is viewed as something extraneous to the "important" business activities. To avoid being on the outside looking in, health promotion practitioners should dedicate themselves to better understanding the organization's business operations. This includes having a complete working knowledge of the company's vision, mission, financial position, and short- and long-term strategic priorities.

Limited or Inappropriate Staffing

Many health promotion professionals make the mistake of overpromising and underdelivering. Outcomes such as cost containment, increased productivity, and improved health status are routinely mentioned. The unfortunate reality is that these outcomes are often difficult to measure. Many organizations are limited by the number of available employees they have with the knowledge to lead a health and safety program. Safety officers may have limited knowledge of employee health and wellness practices. The same is true of health care or human resources professionals who are not experts in occupational safety issues. Furthermore, some organizations hire a health or safety professional in the hope that a single person can lead entire program efforts with great success. The best approach will be to invest in both the health and safety of an organization and to identify the individuals best prepared to lead these efforts. Consultants are also available to provide guidance to organizations that are smaller in size and lack the internal resources to staff a program on their own.

Lack of Data

Good assessment practices are essential to the design, measurement, and management of health and safety programs. Organizations that do not have the resources to secure or analyze the data will be at a disadvantage when attempting to report program outcomes, such as changes in behavior, clinical parameters, health care costs, or absenteeism. It is essential for all health and safety programs to have a software system to maintain participant records and files that are secure, confidential, and compliant with the regulations that are required by federal and state guidelines.

Delivering Programs Without an Overall Strategic Operating Plan

One of the most critical elements of success is a 3- to 5-year strategic plan with key elements of program design, delivery, and evaluation. Without a blueprint, health programs can get lost among an organization's priorities. A results-oriented wellness program does not start with health promotion activities. It starts with a thoughtfully designed annual operating plan that lays a foundation for the program.

Lack of a Supportive Environment

In a supportive environment, employees feel that the organization they work for provides them with encouragement, opportunity, and rewards for healthy lifestyles. For example, flextime can allow employees to come in early or work late in order to incorporate physical activity into their day or lower their stress levels by avoiding rush-hour traffic.

CONCLUSION

The adoption of health promotion and safety programs by employers can have a positive impact on both cost savings and improved health of their employees. Employers should continue to lead these efforts and share their processes and outcomes. Since most working-age adults spend a significant portion of their time at work, the workplace offers an excellent setting for building awareness of health and safety issues, but providing the right programs and environment is critical. Supportive leadership, excellent communication, effective interventions, a positive work environment, and well-crafted policies all play a critical role in improving employee health.

REFERENCES

Aldana, S. G., Anderson, D. R., Adams, T. B., Whitmer, R. W., Merrill, R. M., George, V., & Noyce, J. (2012). A review of the knowledge base on healthy worksite culture. *Journal of Occupational and Environmental Medicine, 54*, 414–419. http://dx.doi.org/10.1097/JOM.0b013e31824be25f

American Psychological Association. (2008). *By the numbers: A Psychologically Healthy Workplace program fact sheet.* Retrieved from http://www.apaexcellence. org/resources/goodcompany/newsletter/article/44

American Psychological Association, Center for Organizational Excellence. (2015). *Resources for employers: Health and safety.* Retrieved from http://www.apaexcellence. org/resources/creatingahealthyworkplace/healthandsafety

Baicker, K., Cutler, D., & Song, Z. (2010). Workplace wellness programs can generate savings. *Health Affairs, 29*, 304–311. http://dx.doi.org/10.1377/hlthaff.2009.0626

Carter, M., Kelly, R., Alexander, C., & Holmes, L. (2011). A collaborative university model for employee health. *American Journal of College Health, 59*, 761–763. http://dx.doi.org/10.1080/07448481.2010.544347

Centers for Disease Control and Prevention. (2010a). *CDCynergy lite.* Retrieved from http://www.cdc.gov/healthcommunication/cdcynergylite.html

Centers for Disease Control and Prevention. (2010b). *Healthier Worksite Initiative cost calculators.* Retrieved from http://www.cdc.gov/nccdphp/dnpao/hwi/program design/costcalculators.htm

Centers for Disease Control and Prevention. (2010c). *Healthier Worksite Initiative environmental audits.* Retrieved from http://www.cdc.gov/nccdphp/dnpao/hwi/ programdesign/environmental_audits.htm

Centers for Disease Control and Prevention. (2013). *Workplace health model.* Retrieved from http://www.cdc.gov/workplacehealthpromotion/model/index.html/

Centers for Disease Control and Prevention. (2015). *Workplace safety and health topics.* Retrieved from http://www.cdc.gov/niosh/topics

Chapman, L. S. (2012). Meta-evaluation of worksite health promotion economic return studies: 2012 update. *American Journal of Health Promotion, 26*(4), TAHP1–TAHP12.

Committee on the Review of NIOSH Research Programs & the Institute of Medicine and National Research Council. (2009). *Evaluating occupational health and safety research programs: Framework and next steps.* Atlanta, GA: The National Academies Press.

Consensus Statement of the Health Enhancement Research Organization, American College of Occupational and Environmental Medicine, American Cancer Society and American Cancer Society Cancer Action Network, American Diabetes Association, and American Heart Association. (2012). Guidance for a reasonably designed, employer-sponsored wellness program using outcomes-based incentives. *Journal of Occupational and Environmental Medicine, 54,* 889–896. Retrieved from http://www.acoem.org/uploadedFiles/Public_Affairs/Policies_And_Position_Statements/JOEM%20Joint%20Consensus%20Statement.pdf

Doran, G. T. (1981). There's a S.M.A.R.T. way to write management's goals and objectives. *Management Review, 70*(11), 35–36.

Goetzel, R. Z., Henke, R. M., Tabrizi, M., Pelletier, K. R., Loeppke, R., Ballard, D. W., . . . Metz, R. D. (2014). Do workplace health promotion (wellness) programs work? *Journal of Occupational and Environmental Medicine, 56,* 927–934. http://dx.doi.org/10.1097/JOM.0000000000000276

Health Affairs. (2012). *Workplace wellness programs* [Health Policy Brief]. Retrieved from http://www.healthaffairs.org/healthpolicybriefs/brief.php?brief_id=69

Health Enhancement Research Organization, American College of Occupational and Environmental Medicine, and Care Continuum Alliance. (2013). Biometric screening of employees. *Journal of Occupational and Environmental Medicine, 55,* 1244–1251. Retrieved from http://www.acoem.org/uploadedFiles/Public_Affairs/Policies_And_Position_Statements/Guidelines/Position_Statements/Biometric%20Hlth%20Screening%20Statement.pdf

Health Project. (2012). *L. L. Bean, Inc.* Retrieved from http://thehealthproject.com/winner/l-l-bean-inc-healthy-bean/

Kaspin, L. C., Gorman, K. M., & Miller, R. M. (2013). Systematic review of employer-sponsored wellness strategies and their economic and health-related outcomes. *Population Health Management, 16,* 14–21. http://dx.doi.org/10.1089/pop.2012.0006

LeBaron, M. (2009). Out in front: Leading people, leading organizations: A great corporate culture pays off with a happier, healthier and more engaged workforce. *Inside Supply Management, 20*(9), 10.

Lincoln Industries. (2012). *Wellness.* Retrieved from http://lincolnindustries.com/home/who-we-are/wellness

Loeppke, R., Taitel, M., Haufle, V., Parry, T., Kessler, R. C., & Jinnett, K. (2009). Health and productivity as a business strategy: A multiemployer study. *Journal of Occupational and Environmental Medicine, 51,* 411–428. http://dx.doi.org/10.1097/JOM.0b013e3181a39180

National Cancer Institute. (2005). *Theory at a glance.* Retrieved from http://www.sneb.org/2014/Theory%20at%20a%20Glance.pdf

O'Neal Industries. (2012). *LIVESMART Fitness and recreational activities reimbursement policy.* Retrieved from http://www.livesmartoni.com/files/LIVESMART.OFRFitnessandReimbursementPolicy.Application1.2012.pdf

Pelletier, K. R. (2001). A review and analysis of the clinical- and cost-effectiveness studies of comprehensive health promotion and disease management programs at the worksite: 1998–2000 update. *American Journal of Health Promotion, 16,* 107–116. http://dx.doi.org/10.4278/0890-1171-16.2.107

Prochaska, J. O., & DiClemente, C. C. (1983). Stages and processes of self-change of smoking: Toward an integrative model of change. *Journal of Consulting and Clinical Psychology, 51,* 390–395. http://dx.doi.org/10.1037/0022-006X.51.3.390

Towers Watson/National Business Group on Health. (2013). *Towers Watson/NBGH Survey on purchasing value in health care.* Retrieved from http://www.towerswatson.com/en/Insights/IC-Types/Survey-Research-Results/2013/03/Towers-Watson-NBGH-Employer-Survey-on-Value-in-Purchasing-Health-Care

Wellness Council of America. (2012). *Demystifying ROI.* Retrieved from http://www.lrpph.org/images/contentPages/Workplace_Wellness_Programs.pdf

CONCLUDING REMARKS—
INTO THE FUTURE

DAVID W. BALLARD AND MATTHEW J. GRAWITCH

The business world is in the midst of a sea change—a fundamental shift from a philosophy that focuses on maximizing shareholder wealth to one that strives to optimize stakeholder value. This change is far from superficial, and it has profound implications. Achieving the best possible outcomes for all parties requires attention to the relationships among employee, organization, customer, and community. From a systems perspective, employers must build the capacity needed to create and sustain long-term success. To this end, forward-thinking organizations reevaluate their work practices, provide employees with resources that support health and productivity, and apply new technologies that provide flexibility in when and where work is performed, so it is more meaningful and creates more value. These employers create psychologically healthy workplaces that are diverse, productive, resilient, and successful.

http://dx.doi.org/10.1037/14731-012
The Psychologically Healthy Workplace: Building a Win–Win Environment for Organizations and Employees,
M. J. Grawitch and D. W. Ballard (Editors)

On the surface, the psychologically healthy workplace model focuses on implementation of the types of programs and policies described throughout this book (i.e., employee involvement, growth and development, health and safety, work–life balance, employee recognition), but the mere presence of these workplace practices does not guarantee that the organization will meet the goal of optimizing employee and organizational outcomes. Despite the ubiquity of workplace wellness efforts and general agreement about the importance of a healthy workforce, many efforts fall short when it comes to employee and organizational outcomes. So, what makes one employer's practices successful, whereas another's fail miserably? Efforts to identify key success factors in organizational health (e.g., Fitz-enz, 1993; Goetzel, Guindon, Turshen, & Ozminkowski, 2001; Goetzel, Shechter, et al., 2007; Grawitch, Ledford, Ballard, & Barber, 2009; O'Donnell, Bishop, & Kaplan, 1997) have highlighted some common characteristics, including alignment with the organization's mission and values; coordination of comprehensive efforts; custom tailoring to meet the unique needs of an organization and its employees; employee involvement through the design, implementation, and evaluation of the program; support from senior leaders; effective two-way communication; ongoing evaluation; and a philosophy of continuous improvement. Case examples from organizations that the American Psychological Association (APA) has recognized for their successful efforts are available online at http://www.apaexcellence.org.

To engage the workforce and remain competitive, it is no longer sufficient to focus solely on benefits. Even with a robust menu of offerings available to employees, their broader needs frequently go unmet. DeJoy and Wilson (2003) argued that employees' perceptions and experiences at work are at least as important as the objective reality within the organization and that attention to these psychological factors is important. Although employers focus on pay and benefits as retention tools, in an APA (2012a) survey of the U.S. workforce, the top reasons people cited for why they stay with their current employers were work–life fit and enjoying what they do. Additionally, more than one third of American workers experience chronic work stress, and many employees feel stuck, with only 39% citing sufficient opportunities for internal career advancement and just 51% saying they feel valued at work (APA, 2013).

Feeling valued at work is critical to employee well-being and performance, as workers who feel valued by their employer are more likely to be engaged in their work. Employees who feel valued are significantly more likely to report having high levels of energy, being strongly involved in their work, and feeling happily engrossed in what they do (APA, 2014). An earlier APA (2012b) survey found that employees who feel valued by their employers are also more likely to report better physical and mental health, higher levels of satisfaction and motivation, and lower turnover intent, compared with those who do not feel valued. A variety of factors were linked to feeling undervalued at work, including having fewer opportunities for involvement, being less satisfied with the potential for growth and advancement, having less access to flexible work arrangements, and feeling that both monetary compensation and nonmonetary rewards were inadequate.

Trust also plays an important role in the workplace. Nearly one in four American workers say they do not trust their employer, only about half believe their employer is open and up-front with them, and one in three report that their employer is not always honest and truthful with them, according to APA's *2014 Work and Well-Being Survey*. Workers report having more trust in their company when the organization recognizes employees for their contributions, provides opportunities for involvement, and communicates effectively. The complex nature of these relationships highlights the interplay between psychological factors and various workplace practices and the importance of taking a comprehensive approach to promoting and supporting employee well-being and organizational performance.

Hence, organizations have to move beyond the idea that simply offering a particular type of workplace practice will improve organizational health. Rather than starting with a particular workplace practice (e.g., a wellness program, flexible work arrangement, or training effort), organizations need to consider (a) what they are trying to achieve, (b) how best to achieve that outcome, and (c) how a particular tactic (i.e., workplace practice) will fit within the larger organizational system. For example, if a goal is to help employees improve their work–life fit, so they can function more effectively on and off the job, adding a telecommuting option will be more effective when employees are involved in crafting the relevant policies and when coupled with health and safety practices that promote ergonomically sound home office configurations and training efforts to ensure that employees and supervisors have the skills necessary to navigate remote working arrangements. Similarly, attempting to drive health behavior change by adding financial rewards and penalties to wellness efforts may not achieve the desired results if employees lack the necessary resources, feel unsupported, and view the program as coercive and motivated solely by the organization's financial interests.

In that respect, the psychologically healthy workplace philosophy should be considered through a functional lens. Different practices can serve different functions, and how those practices are integrated and combined can ultimately influence realized outcomes. Delery and Doty (1996) described a configurational approach as one where the total system of organizational practices collectively determine the outcomes achieved. This approach requires that the practices an organization puts in place be aligned with one another and are a good fit for the characteristics of the organization, including its culture, structure, and context.

IMPLICATIONS FOR SCHOLARS AND PRACTITIONERS

This book was designed to be a resource for scholars and practitioners (i.e., both consultants and organizational leaders) interested in the various aspects of a psychologically healthy workplace. The intent was to provide a solid research foundation for each of the practices included in the APA model and then offer relevant examples and cases to demonstrate how these practices take shape within organizations. To that end, we offer several key takeaways that we hope readers will find useful moving forward.

This book highlights numerous considerations for scholars interested in the psychologically healthy workplace, though we focus on three of them here. First, the various chapters provide a snapshot of the breadth of research related to the individual practices. However, most of these practices have been studied in isolation from the others; therefore, more integrative research is necessary to determine whether the incorporation of practices that span multiple areas can provide a multiplicative benefit for employees and organizations. Second, though research has been rather expansive within the areas of employee involvement, work–life balance, health and safety, and employee growth and development, much less attention has been paid to the issue of employee recognition. Much of how we conceptualize employee recognition is borrowed from theories of motivation, but very little scholarly research has evaluated how well those theories actually generalize to practical application in organizations. Finally, though we mention the importance of the organizational context (as do many of the chapter authors), very little research has been conducted to examine how various aspects of that organizational context (e.g., culture, climate, trust, justice perceptions) influence the effectiveness of the various types of workplace practices. From an intra-organizational perspective, future research should study how employee perceptions of various contextual factors influence their use of practices and the outcomes achieved as a result. From an interorganizational perspective, future research may test how similar organizations with different contextual characteristics (e.g., structure, culture) differ in terms of their utilization of various types of practices and how those contextual differences impact results.

This book also offers several considerations for practitioners. First, as evidenced by many of the examples offered herein and those found on the APA Center for Organizational Excellence website (http://www.apa excellence.org), a psychologically healthy workplace is not relevant only to large organizations. It is not a matter of offering a larger selection of cafeteria-style benefits that produces greater levels of organizational health. Instead, it is a matter of offering strategically selected programs and practices that fit within the organization's unique context. Second, and perhaps relatedly, there are many options available for improving an organization's health, but organizations should be practical and realistic in this endeavor. Spending sufficient time and resources (including the appropriate level of involvement) to find the best solutions to issues and problems would likely produce greater benefits than would spreading resources thin in an effort to develop a larger number of practices that are not well-tailored to an organization and its workforce. Finally, there are many ways in which practices can be customized. This further highlights the importance of evaluating a given practice in terms of its design, implementation, and outcomes.

In summary, the ways in which organizations are conceptualized, developed, and managed have evolved markedly over the past 100 years. Scholars have produced an extraordinary amount of quality research that has informed practice, and practitioners have developed innovative ways of advancing organizational development, especially as it concerns organizational health. Clearly, there is more work to be done and more advancements to be made. To achieve what is possible, scholars and practitioners will have to work together, leveraging their strengths and talents in ways that produce innovative solutions to meet the complex needs of organizations and their employees.

REFERENCES

American Psychological Association. (2012a). *Workforce retention survey*. Retrieved from http://www.apaexcellence.org/assets/general/2012-retention-survey-final.pdf

American Psychological Association. (2012b). *Workplace survey*. Retrieved from http://www.apa.org/news/press/releases/phwa/workplace-survey.pdf

American Psychological Association. (2013). *2013 Work and well-being survey*. Retrieved from http://www.apaexcellence.org/assets/general/2013-work-and-wellbeing-survey-results.pdf

American Psychological Association. (2014). *2014 Work and well-being survey*. Retrieved from http://www.apaexcellence.org/assets/general/2014-work-and-wellbeing-survey-results.pdf

DeJoy, D. M., & Wilson, M. G. (2003). Organizational health promotion: Broadening the horizon of workplace health promotion. *American Journal of Health Promotion, 17*, 337–341. http://dx.doi.org/10.4278/0890-1171-17.5.337

Delery, J. E., & Doty, D. H. (1996). Modes of theorizing in strategic human resource management: Tests of universalistic, contingency, and configurational performance predictions. *Academy of Management Journal, 39*, 802–835. http://dx.doi.org/10.2307/256713

Fitz-enz, J. (1993). The truth about "best practice." *Human Resource Planning, 16*, 19–26.

Goetzel, R. Z., Guindon, A. M., Turshen, I. J., & Ozminkowski, R. J. (2001). Health and productivity management: Establishing key performance measures, benchmarks, and best practices. *Journal of Occupational and Environmental Medicine, 43,* 10–17. http://dx.doi.org/10.1097/00043764-200101000-00003

Goetzel, R. Z., Shechter, D., Ozminkowski, R. J., Marmet, P. F., Tabrizi, M. J., & Roemer, E. C. (2007). Promising practices in employer health and productivity management efforts: Findings from a benchmarking study. *Journal of Occupational and Environmental Medicine, 49,* 111–130. http://dx.doi.org/10.1097/JOM.0b013e31802ec6a3

Grawitch, M. J., Ledford, G. E., Ballard, D. W., & Barber, L. K. (2009). Leading the healthy workforce: The integral role of employee involvement. *Consulting Psychology Journal: Practice and Research, 61,* 122–135. http://dx.doi.org/10.1037/a0015288

O'Donnell, M., Bishop, C., & Kaplan, K. (1997). Benchmarking best practices in workplace health promotion. *Art of Health Promotion, 1,* 1–8.

INDEX

Organizational performance, 16–19
Osterman, P., 20
Ostry, A. S., 210
Overcommitment, 210

Parker, S. K., 218
Participative work practices, 14. *See also* Employee involvement
Partnership for Prevention, 234
Paterson, Chris, 38, 50
Payne, S. C., 64
Perkins Coie, 174
Personality, 65, 67, 122–123, 171, 205
Person–environment fit theory, 120
Peterson, Brent, 103
Petticrew, M., 213, 214
Physical activity, 125, 249
Piccolo, R. F., 203
Pilot projects, 42
Plante Moran, 37, 50, 54–55
Point-of-view transformation, 64
Porter, L. W., 161, 164
Positive health, 204–205
Positive reinforcement, 158, 160–161, 165
Power (employee involvement), 15
Presenteeism, 232
Prochaska, J. O., 248
Psychological contract theory, 200, 208–209
Psychologically healthy workplaces, 3–8, 258–259. *See also specific headings*
Psychosocial risk prevention, 214

Quality circles, 40
Quick, J. C., 204

Ragins, B. R., 70
Raju, N. S., 123
Ramsay, H., 23
Readiness (work–life fit), 149
Reciprocal determinism, 163
Recognition Professionals International (RPI), 182, 183, 185
Reinforcement
    positive, 158, 160–161, 165
    theory behind, 159–161
    types of, 158–159
Reporting structure, 93–95

Resource drain (work–life balance), 115–117
Return-on-investment, 51
Reverse causality, 18
Rewards, employee
    defined, 159
    and employee involvement, 15
    employee recognition vs., 184–190. *See also* Employee recognition
Riggio, R. E., 74
Riney, Bob, 37, 45, 56
Ritz Carlton, 57
Role theory, 115
Roscigno, V., 16
Rousseau, D. M., 208
RPI (Recognition Professionals International), 182, 183, 185
Rydstedt, L., 218

Safety practices. *See* Health and safety
Salanova, M., 48
Salas, E., 64, 67–68
Sandia Preparatory School, 38, 55
Scandura, T. A., 206
Schaufeli, W. B., 48, 217
Schmidt, R. A., 66
Schneider, B., 48
Scholarios, D., 23
Segmentation–integration (work–life balance), 115–117
Self-determination theory, 113
Self-efficacy, 162–163
Self-regulation, 162
Self-selection bias, 18
Semmer, N. K., 217
Sheehan, M., 19
SHRM (Society for Human Resource Management), 184, 185
Siegrist, J., 209–210
Sims, D. E., 67–68
Skill and work structures, 17
Smith-Jentsch, K. A., 64
Social cognitive theory, 163
Social exchange theory, 69, 200, 208–210
Social learning theory, 160–163
Social recognition, 159
Social support, 211–213
Society for Human Resource Management (SHRM), 184, 185

Spillover (work–life balance), 115–117
Sprigg, C. A., 217
Stages of change model (behavioral modification), 248
Stajkovic, A. D., 158
Stakeholders, 54, 123, 124, 235
Steers, R. M., 161
Strategic operating plans, 239–247
Strategy (employee involvement), 17–18
Stress
    and employee involvement, 22–24
    job demands–control theory of, 210–215
    research on, 210–218
    and vitamin model of work, 215–218
    and work–life balance, 118
Stride, C. B., 203
Stubblefield, A., 49
Sunshine State Health Plan, 38, 50
Supervisors
    and employee growth and development, 77, 100–103, 107
    employee support from, 111, 122
    training for, 88–90
Surveys, health and safety, 236–238

Talent development
    accountability for, 99–102
    with employee involvement, 50
Tangible recognition, 159
Taris, T., 212, 214, 217
TeamSTEPPS, 72
Telecommuting, 112
Thomas, S., 213, 214
Tobacco use, employee, 249
Top-down communication, 44
Totterdell, P., 217
Training, 65–68, 88–92, 95–99, 183
Transfer-appropriate processing, 65–66
Transformational leadership theory, 203–205
Trares, S., 63
Trust, 43
Tsutsumi, A., 210
Tucker, J. S., 212
Tuition reimbursement, 75
Turner, N., 203, 204
Turnley, W. H., 206

Turnover, 118
Two-way dialogue, 45

University of Alabama, 242, 248–249

van Grinsven, Gerard, 38, 48, 57
Vision statements, 239
Vitamin model of work, 215–218
Volvo, 14
Vroom, V. H., 164

Wages, 18–20, 31
Wall, T., 217
Wallace, J. C., 201
Wallwey, D. A., 212
Walumbwa, F. O., 204
Warhurst, C., 112–113
Warr, P. B., 215, 216
Wellness committees, 242–243
Wellness programs, 200, 232–234, 237–240, 244–249, 251, 252
WellSteps, 237
WERS (Workplace Employment Relations Survey), 14
Westminster Savings Credit Union, 45, 55–56
Whitehead, M., 213
WHO (World Health Organization), 4–5, 199
Wiley, C., 161
Wilson, M. G., 258
Wood, S. J., 24
Work cycles, 76
Workers' compensation claims, 232
Work flexibility, 118–120
Work, Happiness, and Unhappiness (P. B. Warr), 215
Work–life balance, 111–126, 135–155
    alignment of existing systems with, 142–143
    assessment and development of, 120–121
    case example, 144–153
    as component of psychologically healthy workplace, 5
    definitions of, 112–115
    flexibility for, 139–141
    getting feedback on, 123–124
    implementation and utilization of programs for, 121–123

ABOUT THE EDITORS

Matthew J. Grawitch, PhD, is a professor in Saint Louis University's School for Professional Studies where he has held numerous positions, including chair of the Organizational Studies Program, director of the Leadership and Organizational Development master's program, associate dean of academic development, and interim dean. Dr. Grawitch currently serves as the associate dean of graduate and professional education and guides the direction of graduate education within the school, focusing specifically on the MA program in leadership and organizational development and the MS program in applied analytics while teaching courses in the areas of leadership, the healthy workplace, and evidence-based decision making. He also works with the Center for Workforce and Organizational Development at Saint Louis University to oversee assessment and consultation services for client organizations and leads research and analytic efforts at the school. Dr. Grawitch conducts most of his research in the areas of stress and the healthy workplace and currently serves as the primary research consultant to the American Psychological Association for its Psychologically Healthy Workplace Program. He is dedicated to bridging the gap between scientists and practitioners as it relates to developing, implementing, and evaluating programs related to workplace health and stress. Dr. Grawitch received his doctorate degree in organizational psychology from Saint Louis University.

David W. Ballard, PsyD, MBA, is assistant executive director for organizational excellence at the American Psychological Association (APA). He provides leadership, direction, evaluation, and management for all activities related to APA's Center for Organizational Excellence, which works to benefit society and improve people's lives through the application of psychology to workplace issues. The Center houses APA's Psychologically Healthy Workplace Program (PHWP), a public education initiative designed to engage the employer community, raise public awareness about the value psychology brings to the workplace, and promote programs and policies that enhance employee well-being and organizational performance. Dr. Ballard has provided research, consultation, and training services to government agencies, corporations, medical schools, and universities in the areas of workplace health and productivity, public health, prevention, and health care finance and has experience in management, marketing, and consumer research. He is currently on the board of directors of The Health Project/ C. Everett Koop National Health Awards. He previously served on the board of directors for the Health Enhancement Research Organization and the External Advisory Board for the Mayo Clinic Center for Social Media, as well as on workplace advisory bodies for the National Business Group on Health and Partnership for Prevention. Dr. Ballard received his doctorate in clinical psychology and his MBA in health and medical services administration from Widener University, where he completed concentrations in organizational and forensic psychology.